CW00815816

Lys Offensive

Lys Offensive

April 1918

Andrew Rawson

Pen & Sword
MILITARY

N IMPRINT OF PEN & SWORD BOOKS L
YORKSHIRE · PHILADELPHIA

First published in Great Britain in 2018 by
PEN & SWORD MILITARY
An imprint of
Pen & Sword Books Ltd
Yorkshire – Philadelphia

Copyright © Andrew Rawson 2018

ISBN 978 1 52672 336 9

The right of Andrew Rawson to be identified as Author of this work has
been asserted by him in accordance with the Copyright, Designs and
Patents Act 1988.

A CIP catalogue record for this book is
available from the British Library.

All rights reserved. No part of this book may be reproduced or
transmitted in any form or by any means, electronic or mechanical
including photocopying, recording or by any information storage and
retrieval system, without permission from the Publisher in writing.

Printed and bound in England by TJ International Ltd, Padstow, Cornwall

Pen & Sword Books Limited incorporates the imprints of Atlas,
Archaeology, Aviation, Discovery, Family History, Fiction, History,
Maritime, Military, Military Classics, Politics, Select, Transport, True
Crime, Air World, Frontline Publishing, Leo Cooper, Remember When,
Seaforth Publishing, The Praetorian Press, Wharncliffe Local History,
Wharncliffe Transport, Wharncliffe True Crime and White Owl.

For a complete list of Pen & Sword titles please contact

PEN & SWORD BOOKS LIMITED
47 Church Street, Barnsley, South Yorkshire, S70 2AS, England
E-mail: enquiries@pen-and-sword.co.uk
Website: www.pen-and-sword.co.uk

Or
PEN AND SWORD BOOKS
1950 Lawrence Rd, Havertown, PA 19083, USA
E-mail: Uspen-and-sword@casematepublishers.com
Website: www.penandswordbooks.com

Contents

Regiments

Regiments in Alphabetical Order	Abbreviations Used
Argyll & Sutherland Highlanders Regiment	Argylls
Bedfordshire Regiment	Bedfords
Black Watch Regiment	Black Watch
Border Regiment	Borders
Buffs (East Kent) Regiment	Buffs
Cambridgeshire Regiment	Cambridgeshire
Cameron Highlanders Regiment	Camerons
Cameronians (Scottish Rifles) Regiment	Scottish Rifles
Cheshire Regiment	Cheshires
Coldstream Guards	Coldstreamers
Connaught Rangers	Connaughts
Devonshire Regiment	Devons
Dorsetshire Regiment	Dorsets
Duke of Cornwall's Light Infantry	DCLI
Duke of Wellington's (West Riding) Regiment	Duke's
Durham Light Infantry	Durhams
East Lancashire Regiment	East Lancashires
East Surrey Regiment	East Surreys
East Yorkshire Regiment	East Yorkshires
Essex Regiment	Essex
Gloucestershire Regiment	Gloucesters
Gordon Highlanders	Gordons
Green Howards (Yorkshire) Regiment	Green Howards
Grenadier Guards	Grenadiers
Hampshire Regiment	Hampshires
Herefordshire Regiment	Herefords
Hertfordshire Regiment	Hertfords
Highland Light Infantry	HLI
Honourable Artillery Company	HAC
Irish Guards	Irish Guards
King's (Liverpool) Regiment	King's

King's Own (Royal Lancaster) Regiment	King's Own
King's Own Scottish Borderers	KOSBs
King's (Shropshire Light Infantry) Regiment	Shropshires
King's Own (Yorkshire Light Infantry) Regiment	KOYLIs
King's Royal Rifle Corps	KRRC
Lancashire Fusiliers	Lancashire Fusiliers
Leicestershire Regiment	Leicesters
Leinster Regiment	Leinsters
Lincolnshire Regiment	Lincolns
London Regiment	Londoners
Loyal North Lancashire Regiment	Loyals
Manchester Regiment	Manchesters
Middlesex Regiment	Middlesex
Monmouthshire Regiment	Monmouths
Norfolk Regiment	Norfolks
Northamptonshire Regiment	Northants
North Staffordshire Regiment	North Staffords
Northumberland Fusiliers	Northumberland Fusiliers
Oxford and Buckinghamshire Light Infantry	Ox and Bucks
Queen's (Royal West Surrey) Regiment	Queen's
Queen's Own (Royal West Kent) Regiment	Queen's Own
Rifle Brigade	Rifle Brigade
Royal Berkshire Regiment	Berkshires
Royal Dublin Fusiliers	Dublin Fusiliers
Royal Fusiliers	Royal Fusiliers
Royal Inniskilling Fusiliers	Inniskilling Fusiliers
Royal Irish Fusiliers	Irish Fusiliers
Royal Irish Regiment	Irish Regiment
Royal Irish Rifles	Irish Rifles
Royal Munster Fusiliers	Munsters
Royal Scots Fusiliers	Scots Fusiliers
Royal Scots Regiment	Royal Scots
Royal Sussex Regiment	Sussex
Royal Warwickshire Regiment	Warwicks
Royal Welsh Fusiliers	Welsh Fusiliers
Scots Guards	Scots Guards
Seaforth Highlanders	Seaforths
Sherwood Foresters (Notts and Derbyshire)	Sherwoods
Somerset Light Infantry	Somersets
South Lancashire Regiment	South Lancashires
South Staffordshire Regiment	South Staffords

South Wales Borderers	SWBs or Borderers
Suffolk Regiment	Suffolks
Welsh Guards	Welsh Guards
Welsh Regiment	Welsh
West Yorkshire Regiment	West Yorkshires
Wiltshire Regiment	Wiltshires
Worcestershire Regiment	Worcesters
York and Lancaster Regiment	York and Lancasters

Introduction

This book focuses on the British Army's harrowing experiences during the second and third of the German offensives in the spring of 1918. Many sources have been used to create this account of the fighting between 9 and 26 April in Flanders and between 27 May and 1 June on the Aisne. The backbone of the story comes from the two relevant volumes of the Official History of the Great War. Brigadier General James Edmonds discovered that record-keeping was often incomplete during these two battles, making it difficult to compile an accurate account. Many officers were contacted for information, to complete the account, but the end result is a bland account of a very difficult and dangerous time for the British Army.

A lot of details were sourced from the divisional and regimental histories published in the years after the Great War. The quality of information these books offer varies, and while some are almost copies of the unit war diaries, others give the minimum of information. But they all give more information than the Official History. They always justify their successes and they sometimes blame others for their failures. But they all describe the daring actions of the brave members of their division or regiment.

Many of the divisional and regimental histories can be accessed for a small fee at the militaryarchive.co.uk. You are also able to look at medal rolls, army orders and army lists to get help with locating biographical information, awards and photographs of individuals. Joining the archive has given me annual access to these resources for the same cost as a day in the London archives.

Some of the information comes from the war diaries held by the National Archives at Kew, London. They are the original source material of a unit's battle experiences; however, information about the offensives is often sketchy because the diarists were fully occupied fighting. Many battalion records were destroyed so they would not be captured, while material was sometimes removed after the war, making this an inconsistent source of information. The war diaries can be accessed through ancestry. co.uk and similar websites, again for a reasonable fee.

I had to judge at what depth of detail to pitch the story. The reader learns very little if it is too shallow but the text can become overpowering if there is too much information. So this is not an exhaustive account of the German attacks on the Lys and on the Aisne but it is a comprehensive view of the British Expeditionary Force's (BEF) experiences in April and May 1918.

A detailed account of all aspects of the two battles would be twice the length and an exhaustive account would be even larger. The emphasis of the story has been, like with all the books in this series, on the experiences of the British and Empire soldiers. There is the minimum of information on the liaison between the War Cabinet, the Chief of the Imperial General Staff, the BEF's General Headquarters and the French *Grand Quartier Général* (GQG). The same applies to the Supreme War Council conferences. The meetings between British and French politicians and generals are referred to in brief and there is information on the preparations for the offensive, as well as British defensive preparations. There is also some discussion on the German tactics used but the detail of German units rarely goes below army level.

Few details of casualties are discussed unless they were exceptionally high or unusual. Many times battalions were reduced to a few dozen weary men who escaped the onslaught. Records during defensive battles are often incomplete while numbers changed as men returned to their units or were reported as prisoners. Casualties were always high and both sides suffered. I do not use personal diaries, which usually follow a depressing theme of mud and blood. Instead the chosen quotes reflect the men's pride in their spirit and their achievements during these difficult days for the BEF. Sometimes their dark humour illustrates a situation perfectly.

So what will you find in the book? Germany's strategic planning behind the attacks is covered, as well as the state of the BEF, during what was its low point of the war. The day by day attacks against each corps are considered, and the reasons behind the successes and failures. Often the men who led the defence or who staged the counter-attacks are mentioned; so are all the men who were awarded the Victoria Cross.

The British and Australian soldiers faced many tactical problems during the defensive battles in the open. A large number were in their first battle, having been sent to the front to replace the casualties suffered on the Somme. But time and again the men fought until their ammunition ran low and then, if necessary, withdrew to fight another day. Casualties were high but their morale rarely wavered, and while the line was often penetrated or driven back, it was never broken.

The saying is 'a picture is worth a thousand words' and I believe the same applies to maps. Many military books rely on a few small-scale maps which do little to complement the narrative. I believe this is wrong, so over sixty tactical maps are included to help the reader understand the campaign. Typically there is one for each corps on each day it was engaged. Plenty of detailed maps has been a feature of the all the books in this ten-part series on the Western Front.

My inspiration for this series was Noah Trudeau's *A Testing of Courage*, a book about the 1863 battle of Gettysburg during the American Civil War. Several books on this three-day engagement had left me confused but Trudeau's book used large-scale maps every few pages, preparing me for a visit to Gettysburg. I wanted to do the same for the battles of the Western Front.

The Official History maps are sometimes cited as good examples. The level of detail is too high on the large April and May 1918 maps, confusing the key information to the point of distraction. Where possible, this book uses various trench map extracts for the Lys battle for the topographical background. Different styles are involved to suit the scale or according to what is available. The usual grid system is 1,000 yards (914 metres) for each large square and 100 yards (91 metres) for each minor graduation. The terrain in Flanders has changed little – contours, roads, rivers, woods and villages have rarely altered. It means these maps can be used to help locate places on the battlefield.

The short time IX Corps was on the Aisne has meant I have illustrated the battle with skeleton maps detailing the main units, the rivers and main villages.

The symbols indicating movements have been kept the same on all the maps. The front lines at the beginning of the day are marked by solid lines, while any ground captured or abandoned is marked by a line of dots. Rivers are marked by dashed lines and army and corps boundaries are marked by a line of dashes and dots.

Each division, brigade or composite force is marked with its number. Battalions moved so often that it would be impossible to chart their progress without obscuring the topographical information. But it is quite easy to estimate a battalion's movements by checking the text and the maps together. Arrows are sometimes used to clarify the direction of an advance or a retreat.

I have also bucked the army convention of describing events from right to left. We read text and look at maps from left to right, so I have written the narrative the same way. This usually means that it follows the action from the north to south – the BEF's left to its right; occasionally the sequence of events dictates that it is best to describe events another way.

This is the eighth book in a ten-book series on the British Expeditionary Forces' campaigns on the Western Front in the Great War. I first visited the Lys area in detail in the early 1990s while planning to write something about a battle in which few were interested at the time. Fate meant I started writing about other conflicts but the research I carried out over twenty years ago was still relevant. So was my friendship with Professor John Bourne, who has guided me through my writing career over a similar length of time. Yet again he has given me advice and information while his extensive knowledge of the generals of the BEF has been particularly useful.

I have enjoyed writing about the battle which resulted in Field Marshal Sir Douglas Haig's infamous 'Backs to the Wall' order. It has again increased my understanding about how the British, Irish and Australian soldiers fought on under the most difficult of circumstances. I hope you enjoy reading about their deeds as well.

I stayed at the Hotel Regina in Ypres while looking at the Lys and my room overlooked the famous Cloth Hall, now home to the 'In Flanders Fields museum'. I also stayed at No 56 Bed and Breakfast in La Boisselle while covering the Aisne battle because I was studying the retreat across the Somme in March 1918 at the same time. David and Julie Thomson have looked after me many times at their 'Oasis on the Somme' during my battlefield research trips.

Andrew Rawson 2017

Chapter 1

There is No Question that the Men are Tired

Military Policy and Background

Never Enough Troops

The German Supreme Army Command, or *Oberste Heeresleitung* (OHL) had been considering an attack around Armentières, to break the deadlock on the Western Front, since 1915. General Erich von Falkenhayn, Chief of Staff at the time, had said they should strike at two points. One attack near Arras could drive a wedge between the British and French Armies while another in Flanders would push the British back to the Channel ports. Falkenhayn's plans would eventually evolve into Operation Michael on the Somme and Operation Georgette across the Lys.

Colonel Hans von Seeckt, Chief of Staff of the Eleventh Army, also wanted to attack between Arras and the Somme. The left wing would hold the French back while the right wing drove the British towards the coast and his plan would form the basis for Operation Michael.

The problem was OHL never had enough divisions because the Germans were fighting a two-front war. They were unable to attack in the West while they had to defend in the East, as the Verdun offensive in the spring and summer of 1916 proved. At the same time, German generals saw the British and French attack time and again with too few resources on the Somme in the summer and autumn of the same year.

OHL then decided to build a defensive position out of reach of the Allied guns, and the withdrawal to the Hindenburg Line in March 1917 took the Allies by surprise. It also shortened the Western Front by 30 miles, allowing both sides to increase the size of their reserve. The British could not breakthrough at Arras in April while the French offensive failed on the Aisne; so badly in fact that the army mutinied.

The British kept up the pressure in Flanders, capturing the Messines Ridge in June. But the attack east of Ypres failed to go far enough to warrant a landing on the Flanders coast. As the campaign ended due to bad weather and poor ground, German divisions helped the Italian armies break through at Caporetto on 24 October. The Flanders campaign was then closed down as Allied divisions rushed to Italy to help. The Russian armies were in a state of mutiny by the autumn of 1917 and the Bolshevik revolution overthrew the Provisional Government.

The signature of the Decree of Peace on 26 October meant Germany could move ten divisions a month to the Western Front, increasing the number to 195 by the end of March. That was nearly 250,000 extra rifles; a large number of artillery pieces would also be moved. Quartermaster General, General Erich Ludendorff, could at last consider putting what OHL's Operations Section recommended into practice; 'the decision lies in the Western theatre'.

Field Marshal Sir Douglas Haig knew that both the BEF and the French would be unable to attack in the spring and the Americans would not be ready to join any offensive. Meanwhile, the Supreme War Council was waiting for the military representatives to complete their study before they decided on a strategy for the spring. Meanwhile, spies were reporting on the trains filled with troops heading east to west. So all Haig could do as 1917 came to an end was to tell his army commanders to prepare their defences for the spring.

Where to Attack First?
Ludendorff asked the Chiefs of Staff of Crown Prince Rupprecht of Bavaria and Crown Prince Wilhelm for ideas on 11 November 1917. General Hermann von Kuhl wanted to attack the British in Flanders while Colonel Friedrich von der Schulenburg wanted to attack the French at Verdun. Ludendorff overruled them both with a plan to attack between the Scarpe and the Oise Rivers. He thought it would lead to an advance 'in a north-westerly direction, with the left flank resting on the Somme, and lead to the rolling up of the-British front'.

A month later, the head of OHL's Operations Section, Lieutenant Colonel Georg Wetzell, suggested several attacks, one after another, would have a better chance than one huge attack. He believed the British were worried the capture of Hazebrouck would cut off the Ypres Salient while the French feared an attack around Verdun the most. He suggested an initial attack on the Somme, to draw the BEF's reserves south, before striking in Flanders.

Ludendorff discussed many plans with his chiefs of staff on 27 December. They talked about Operation Saint George in Flanders and Operations Saint George II, Wood Feast and Hare Drive against the

Ypres Salient. They also considered Operation Mars around Arras, and Operation Michael on the Somme. On 24 January 1918 Ludendorff's first operation order stated that Michael would be launched in March. Saint George needed dry weather, so they could cross the Flanders plain, and it could not be guaranteed, so it would follow Michael when the opportunity presented itself.

The chiefs of staff had also looked at Operation Archangel south of the Oise, Operations Hector, Achilles and Roland east of Reims and Operations Castor and Pollux around Verdun. They were all shelved after Ludendorff issued his second operation order on 8 February, telling everyone to start planning Michael. Mars and Archangel could expand Michael if it stalled while Saint George and Roland could be added at a later date. OHL wanted

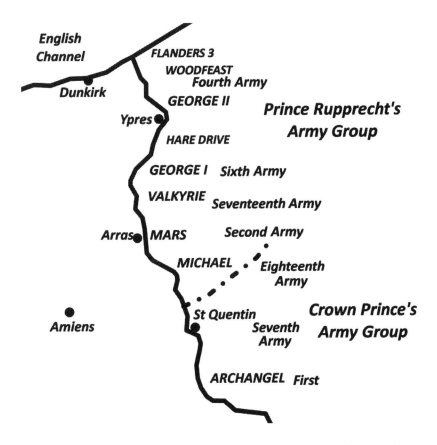

The many operations considered by OHL over the winter of 1917–18.

to make the Allies think the attack was aimed at the French not the British, so they started rumours and put out false intelligence. Battle preparations and artillery registrations were made across the Lys and Oise areas for three days to draw attention away from the real threat.

OHL's final operation order for Michael was issued on 10 March and it set Z-Day for 21 March and Z-Hour for 9.40 am. The late hour meant the artillery observers would be able to observe the final stages of the bombardment, weather permitting. Seventeenth Army and Second Army would cut off the Cambrai salient with a pincer attack, while Eighteenth Army dealt with the French on the south flank. OHL issued detailed attack instructions a few days later.

The British Problems

The French had asked the British to take over more of the front line when the battle of Cambrai ended, early in December 1917. Haig refused because the BEF had just taken over the line north of the Ypres Salient and it had sent divisions to the Italian Front. The BEF was also short of men after the fighting in the Ypres Salient and at Cambrai.

The War Office told Haig that the new French Prime Minister, Georges Clemenceau, would resign if the issue was not resolved, so the BEF had to take over another 25 miles. British soldiers deployed as far south as the Oise and while the French were confident the river marshes were impassable, a dry winter meant the Germans were able to cross. Ludendorff even believed St Quentin was the weakest part of the line 'because the ground offered no difficulties and it was passable in all seasons'.

Fifth Army's generals and soldiers were unhappy with the state of the Forward Zone, leaving little time to work on the Battle Zone. The Rear Zone was rarely more than knee-deep trenches protected by inadequate entanglements. The manpower shortage meant General Hubert Gough did not have enough labour to complete all the defensive measures before the spring.

The lack of manpower over the winter of 1917-18 also meant that the BEF's British divisions had to be reduced from twelve down to nine battalions (the Empire divisions remained at full strength). The Regular Army battalions were safe but many Territorial battalions were merged while a large number of New Army battalions were disbanded. The 'heart breaking business' of reorganisation took place in February as the war service of one hundred and fifteen battalions came to an end. Another thirty-eight battalions were merged while seven infantry battalions were converted into pioneer battalions.

The Portuguese Expeditionary Corps

Portugal had declared its neutrality when war broke out in August 1914 and it had remained so, despite skirmishes with German colonial troops in Africa. Its neutrality was tested when several German ships anchored in Lisbon harbour in March 1916. They were seized, Germany declared war, and Portugal joined the Allies. Over the next twelve months, 55,000 men were recruited and trained for General Fernando Tamagnini's Portuguese Expeditionary Corps (*Corpo Expedicionário Português* or CEP) and it joined the BEF on the Western Front early in 1917. Artillerymen were also formed into the Independent Heavy Artillery Corps (*Corpo de Artilharia Pesada Independente* or CAPI) and they would operate heavy railway guns for the French Army.

The Corps was organised into a reinforced infantry division, which was much larger than a British division. It was given responsibility for the Neuve Chapelle sector, a traditionally quiet area in French Flanders. The BEF took little notice of the Portuguese Corps throughout 1917, as it focused on the campaigns at Arras, Ypres and Cambrai. But the Portuguese soldiers suffered over the winter and General Henry Horne doubted they could resist an attack. The Government was not sending enough reinforcements making soldiers critical over the lack of leave; one battalion had even mutinied.

Lieutenant General Richard Haking was worried that 'the Portuguese troops in the line was a bait to the German troops.' He was right because one group invited the Germans to cross no man's land on January 30 to tell them they were weary of the war. The news soon reached Crown Prince Rupprecht and Ludendorff and they were both anxious to attack before the Portuguese were relieved. After the battle, prisoners told their interrogators that they 'were conscious of no particular grievance against Germany and why they should fight against her was incomprehensible'.

The Portuguese Corps' front was shortened at the end of December while First Army made arrangements to form a second line if it was attacked. The plan was 'each British corps would at once, on first sign of attack, throw back and man a defensive flank to the Rivers Lawe and Lys, and the line of these rivers would also be defended by British troops… Providing the British troops held up the enemy's advance on both flanks and in rear of the Portuguese, the situation would tactically and strategically remain sound.'

General Jan Smuts visited the Western Front at the end of January 1918, to check on the state of the BEF. The report to the War Cabinet contained both good and bad news: 'I am satisfied that the morale of the Army is good… There is no question that the men are tired. This applies more especially to the infantry…' But he also confirmed the Portuguese were a liability, so General Sir Henry Wilson, the Chief of the Imperial General Staff (CIGS), was instructed to look into the situation.

The Battlefield

The River Lys had been canalised by 1780 and it still meanders through the towns of St Venant, Merville, Estaires. It crossed the British front line at Armentières. The area is associated with the BEF's spring 1915 offensives at Neuve Chapelle and Festubert. The only other attack in the area was the disastrous attack at Fromelles on 19 July 1916.

The surrounding area is rich arable land divided into fields by hedgerows, and while they made excellent defensive lines, they also limited fields of fire. The spring crop of wheat also blocked the view and observers built lookout posts in trees and on top of buildings.

Many ditches drained water into the streams, so wheeled traffic was restricted to the roads. The infantry often had to trudge across the fields, with heavy clay clinging to their boots, and had to wade across the muddy watercourses.

The high water table meant any hole dug over a metre deep filled with water, so the engineers worked to drain the front line area. The soldiers spent a lot of their time building and living behind thick sandbag walls. The engineers also built a network of strongpoints, protected by thick belts of barbed wire, behind the lines.

GHQ believed the Lys area would be too wet and muddy to cross until the beginning of May but two factors conspired to dry it out sooner. The British engineers had drained the ground, so deeper trenches could be dug (they inadvertently lowered the water table as well). There was also less rain during early months of 1918, so the ground dried out earlier than usual.

Second Army held the Messines Ridge, north of the Lys, and a range of hills stretched west from it, rising over 130 metres (400 feet) above the plain. From west to east they are Mont de Cats, Mont Noir, Mont Rouge, the Scherpenberg and Kemmelberg. The lower Ravelsberg Ridge ran west to east between Bailleul and Neuve Église.

The La Bassée canal cut across the south side of the battlefield. It was opened in the 1820s to connect the Pas-de-Calais coal field to the emerging industrial cities of northern France. The single hill in the area was Mount Bernanchon which rose only 20 metres and Givenchy was on a lower rise; both were next to the canal.

The BEF had the Nieppe Forest around 9 miles behind its front and it measured some 8 miles across and over 2 miles deep. Formed troops could only march through the forest via one of the roads or rides but a neglected defensive line dating from 1915 ran through the centre. It was imperative that German troops did not enter it because Hazebrouck, and its important rail junction, was only 3 miles to the north.

Chapter 2

Keep Close Behind the Barrage

The Final Planning

Operation Michael and Operation Mars

Operation Michael was launched on 21 March, across a 45-mile front between Arras and St Quentin. Third Army initially held its ground southeast of Arras but Fifth Army had to fall back rapidly to the Somme and Crozat canals. It resulted in the French troops sent to help being caught up in the fighting before they could deploy. Third Army withdrew across the wasteland created by the 1916 battle and Fifth Army conformed but their situation had stabilised by 26 March.

An extension of the Somme attack was planned for 28 March, with Seventeenth Army launching Operation Mars towards Arras. Sixth Army could then launch Operation Valkyrie west of Lens, followed by Operation George II (as it was now known) towards Hazebrouck. However, Operation Mars was a complete failure and OHL had to revise its plans.

There was one last attack to be made on the Somme before the attack in Flanders was made. Crown Prince Wilhelm hoped his Army Group could gain ground on 4 April, so his heavy guns could get in range of Amiens. A second attack the following day would take advantage of the confusion caused by the bombardment of the city. That too failed, so the heavy guns and divisions earmarked for the attack headed for Flanders. Aerial observers soon spotted unusual activity behind the German front between Ypres and Béthune while spies reported movements on the rail lines between Lille and Lens. GHQ was sure that German Fourth and Sixth Armies were preparing to attack and it had issued a warning to First Army and Second Army on 2 April.

Third Army and Fifth Army had been able to fall back large distances across the Somme to escape the enemy. Time and again troops were able to fight in the day and withdraw during the night, meaning the enemy had to first locate and then shell the new line before they could attack. Second Army and First Army were unable to do the same because they were too

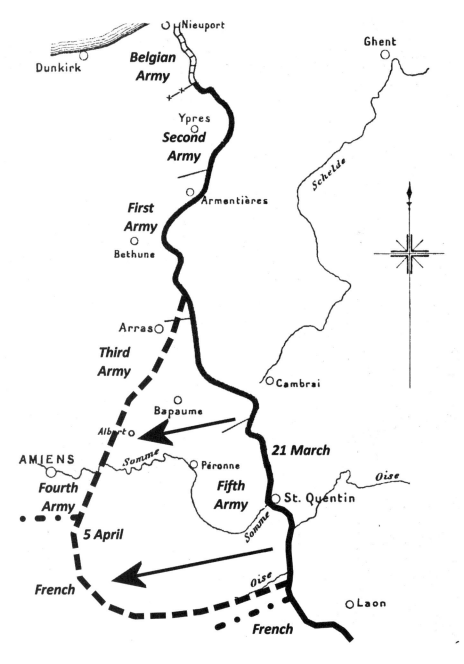

The Western Front before and after Operation Michael, between 21 March and 5 April.

close to the coast. Second Army could not withdraw because the German heavy artillery would be in range of the huge military camps around the ports of Calais and Boulogne. First Army could not withdraw because they had the Béthune coalfields, producing large amounts of coal for the French war machine, behind their front. Third Army could not afford to retire either, because the loss of Vimy Ridge or Arras would split the BEF in two.

The Evolution of Operation Georgette
Ludendorff had made it clear that Operation Michael would be the main offensive on 10 February. Four other attacks would follow in Flanders, beginning with Operation Saint George II. Sixth Army's attack would begin on 9 April, across a 12-mile front between Armentières and Givenchy. They would break through the Portuguese line, driving the left and centre of General Sir Henry Horne's First Army back across the River Lys and the Lawe canal, some 3 miles away. They would then head for Hazebrouck, another 10 miles to the north-west.

Second Army would be moving its reserve to help, just as the German Fourth Army attacked across an 8-mile front between Ypres and Armentières. Operation Wood Feast would hit the north side of the Ypres Salient while Operation Hare Drive crossed the Messines Ridge. Operation Flanders 3 would attack the Belgians if they wavered. The attack had been scaled down from the original plan and while Sixth Army would only have twenty-two divisions, Fourth Army would only have fifteen.

Fourth Army and Sixth Army would join forces to capture the Flanders hills around Kemmel. The seizure of Hazebrouck would force the BEF to abandon Ypres and fall back towards the Channel ports. Sixth Army could then send two divisions towards the ports of Gravelines and Dunkirk.

Ludendorff and Crown Prince Rupprecht kept changing their minds about the Lys offensive while the fighting raged across the Somme. Both Fourth and Sixth Armies continued their preparations, although Operations George I and II had now morphed into what would be called Operation Georgette. The attack had also been scaled down so General Ferdinand von Quast only had fourteen divisions to cross the Lys and Lawe while General Friedrich Sixt von Armin had just five to capture Messines Ridge.

Rupprecht was planning to launch Operation Mars, to extend the break in Third Army's line and threaten Arras. Operation Valkyrie would take place north of the city a day later and it was hoped it would disrupt the BEF's line to such an extent that there would be no need to carry out Operation Georgette.

As we have seen, Third Army's front had stabilised south-west of Arras by 26 March and Lieutenant Colonel Wetzell was urging Ludendorff to

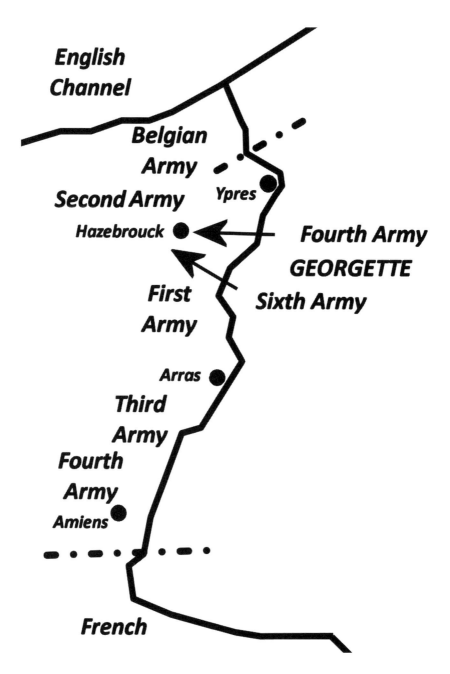

Operation Georgette involved the German Sixth and Fourth Armies making a pincer movement towards Hazebrouck.

carry out Georgette instead of Mars. He refused because it would take two weeks to move the heavy artillery and ammunition north for the attack. Mars was launched on 28 March but it failed so spectacularly that Valkyrie was cancelled and Ludendorff finally agreed to launch Georgette.

General von Quast's Sixth Army had four divisions ready to break the Portuguese Corps and advance north-west to the Lawe canal and River Lys. Two divisions would roll up 55th Division on the left, using the La Bassée canal to cover their south flank. Another two divisions would roll up 40th Division and cross the Lys to the west of Armentières. Fourth Army would follow up with Operation Flanders 3 but General Armin only had two divisions to drive IX Corps off the Messines Ridge.

Where Would the Germans Attack Next?
On 6 April Brigadier General Cox warned GHQ that the Germans were still considering capturing Vimy but he also believed they could attack the Portuguese, north of the La Bassée canal. Haig was worried so he asked Marshal Ferdinand Foch for help in three ways.

1.   An attack to divert German reserves away from the BEF.
2.   A reserve of French divisions around Arras, behind the BEF's centre.
3.   French divisions to relieve Fourth Army in front of Amiens.

Haig and Foch met the following day to learn that he thought the Germans would try to get closer to Amiens first. They would attack in Flanders once their artillery had cut the railway lines. So Foch wanted to attack east of Amiens instead, to keep the German reserves on the Somme. He refused to relieve Fourth Army and would only place a reserve around Amiens, behind the BEF's right flank.

General Sir Henry Wilson had also written to Foch, asking for help, stating that 'no success by the French arms south of the present Somme line can compensate for a disaster to the British arms north of it.' A frustrated Haig asked Wilson to travel to France, to speak to the *Généralissime* in person. He arrived on the morning of 9 April as the German Sixth Army was driving a huge hole in First Army's line. Only time would tell if the BEF could hold its line long enough for reinforcements to arrive.

Royal Air Force observers spotted definite signs of an imminent attack against First Army on 6 April. Photographs were circulated to the artillery and bombardments resulted in many explosions amongst the camouflaged ammunition dumps. They had seen wagons and carrying parties ferrying supplies to the front line while the roads and railway lines behind the front were also busy.

The German artillery started a forty-eight-hour barrage of First Army's batteries on 6 April, using mustard gas to make the battery positions uninhabitable. But GHQ's Intelligence Section had fallen for the fake preparations north of Arras and on 7 April it suggested the main attack would be against Vimy Ridge. The attack against the Portuguese, north of the La Bassée canal, would only be a subsidiary attack.

Haig visited General Horne on 8 April to hear about the increase of artillery batteries, the mustard gas bombardments and the registering of targets on First Army's front. He also heard about the massing of infantry divisions reported by prisoners and that the Germans had stopped all raids, so that no more prisoners were taken. As it grew dark, the troops could hear plenty of noise from across no man's land as the German troops made their final preparations. All the signs were there for an attack between Armentières and Béthune.

Haig was concerned enough to ask Foch again to send divisions north to Flanders. He wanted them to take over the Ypres Salient from Second Army so he could assemble a reserve of six British divisions. Foch again refused because he still believed the Germans were intent on renewing their attack on the Somme.

The British Dispositions
General Sir Herbert Plumer's Second Army had four corps holding a 20-mile-long sector. The Ypres Salient stretched in a large arc across the Passchendaele and Broodseinde ridges. Both II Corps and VIII Corps had muddy crater fields behind their lines, the result of the campaign the previous summer and autumn. It was a similar situation, if somewhat drier, where XXII Corps held the east slopes of the Messines Ridge. On the right, IX Corps held the quiet sector around Ploegsteert and its wood.

General Sir Henry Horne's First Army had five corps holding a 40-mile-long sector. In the north, XV Corps covered Armentières while XI Corps held the line either side of Neuve Chapelle. On the right, I Corps held the sector between the La Bassée canal and Lens. The Canadian Corps was still holding the Vimy area while XVII Corps, which was protecting Arras, would join it on 6 April. Despite holding such a long length of front, First Army only had one division in reserve.

What to do about the Portuguese?
Haig was sure an attack would drive the Portuguese back but he was happy with First Army's plans to form flanks along the Lawe and Lys if they did. He also thought the Lys plain was still too wet and muddy to advance across.

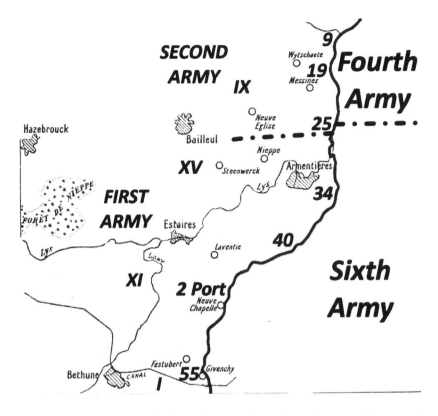

The British Second and First Army's dispositions between Ypres and Béthune before Operation Georgette.

The shortage of reinforcements from Portugal over the winter had left the CEP short of men, so it had been reorganised into two divisions. The changes were completed just before the attack and they left 2nd Division with three brigades in the front line and one in reserve. Meanwhile, 1st Division was left with two understrength brigades which would replace casualties in 2nd Division. But the situation was far from ideal because 2nd Portuguese Division was still 6,000 men short.

Generals Horne and Plumer met Lieutenant Generals John DuCane and Richard Haking on 8 April to discuss the relief of the Portuguese. They agreed that 50th Division and 55th Division would take over the line around Neuve Chapelle the following night. All the arrangements were in place but they had been made too late because the bombardment started early the following morning.

The British Defensive System

Both First Army and Second Army had adopted the three zone system of defence recommended by GHQ. The Forward Zone was well developed and wire entanglements would funnel troops into the killing zones of the machine-gun posts and strongpoints. Switch trenches had been prepared, so troops could form defensive flanks and enfilade the enemy. Plenty of work had also been done on the Battle Zone, 2 to 3 miles behind the Forward Zone. The corps reserves would deploy to the zone and rally retreating units before counter-attacking. Less work had been done on the Army Line (or Green Line) another 2 miles to the rear and in places the trenches had only been marked out.

The River Lys and Lawe canal were behind XV Corps. Platoons were detailed to man the bridgeheads, while troops crossed and the engineers prepared the crossing for demolition. All the permanent bridges had been wired up with explosives while the temporary bridges would either be burnt or pulled back to the friendly bank.

The field batteries behind XV Corps' line had always found it difficult to make good defensive positions. The fields were flat and the water table was high so the guns were usually hidden behind buildings or hedges, positioned to fire obliquely at targets. A small number were hidden in camouflaged emplacements close to the front line, ready to give direct support the infantry.

Sixth Amy's Final Preparations

The Royal Air Force had noted new airfields behind the German front but the *Deutsche Luftstreitkräfte* did not move new squadrons to the area until just before the attack was launched. It left the German pilots little time to familiarise themselves with the Lys area. They then had to spend much of their flying time checking the camouflage hiding the waiting assault troops and batteries.

Some fighter squadrons aimed to drive the Royal Air Force from the skies above the battlefield while others divided their time between protecting reconnaissance planes and carrying out ground attacks. Experience on the Somme had shown that strafing kept the enemy under cover while other planes monitored the progress of the infantry. Some flights were dedicated to locating targets for the artillery and the bombing squadrons, taking photographs so the damage could be assessed.

First Army and Second Army were aware an attack was imminent but Sixth Army carefully deployed its men and guns to keep Z-Day a secret. Around fifteen divisions carried out their *Aufmarsch*, or deployment march, over several nights. Around 250,000 men marched forward during the hours of darkness, resting during the day, until they were all in position.

The German Infantry Tactics

Scouts followed the creeping barrage as close as they dared when the attack began, because they had been told to 'keep close behind the barrage regardless of shell splinters. A single enemy machine gun which survives the bombardment does more harm than any number of our own shell splinters.' Platoons of shock troops, or *Stosstruppen,* armed with light machine guns, grenades and flame throwers, followed and 'make headway wherever resistance was weakening'. Their instructions were to 'push on, keep inside the divisional areas, do not trouble about what happens right or left'. They were to exploit gaps and avoid defensive positions, reporting their progress by firing green flares at 200 metre intervals. The ground or aerial observers could then report to the artillery, to coordinate the barrage with the advance. The flame thrower teams would also squirt burning fuel if necessary, to signal their progress to aerial observers.

Flares would be used to guide the support troops to the gaps in the enemy line. They could then outflank strongpoints and silence them with the help of bombers, flamethrowers, trench mortars and field guns. At least that was the plan, but April mornings were usually misty, hiding the flares and grounding planes. Experience on the Somme had shown that assault teams could either advance deep into enemy territory unseen or become disorientated in the mist.

Four detachments of tanks had been assembled using captured British tanks and the new German model which had first been deployed on 21 March. The A7V, or *Sturmpanzerwagen,* was 7.3 metres long, 3.1 metres wide, 3.3 metres high and weighed 33 tons. Fourteen men manned the 5.7 cm Maxim-Nordfelt cannon mounted in the front and the six MG08 machine guns. Another four dealt with the operating of the tank. It had a top speed of 9 miles an hour on roads which was reduced to 3 miles an hour across country. While it was faster than the British tank, it ran on twenty-four wheels and was unable to cross trenches, large shell holes or muddy ground. They were supposed to follow the attack and help silence the strongpoints, but when their time came they would either break down or become stuck in the mud, blocking the roads.

The Bombardment and Zero Hour

Oberst Georg Bruchmüller, the veteran artilleryman of the Eastern and Western Fronts, had again been chosen to plan the bombardment. It started with a forty-eight hour mustard gas barrage of First Army's batteries on 6 April. Then on the night of 7/8 April around 35,000 gas shells were fired at Armentières (nearly fifty shells a minute), resulting in 34th Division evacuating over 900 gas casualties to the rear. The following day a thick mist blinded the artillery observers, so the guns stayed silent. They were so quiet that Lieutenant General Haking told his artillery commander, Brigadier General Metcalfe, it looked like the Germans were about to attack. He just hoped they would wait until the Portuguese had been relieved but his wish was not granted because the bombardment began only a few hours later.

Sixth Army had 195 field batteries and 230 heavy and super-heavy batteries and each corps divided their guns into three groups. The Counter Artillery Groups (*Artilleriebekämpfungsartillerie* or *Aka*) would use their rapid firing field guns to neutralise the Allied batteries with gas shells. The heavy guns of the Deep Battle Artillery Groups (*Fernkampfartillerie* or *Feka*) would hit roads, headquarters and signalling centres to disrupt First Army's lines of communications. The Infantry Artillery Groups (*Infantriebekämpfungs-Artillerie* or *Ika*) were split into four sub-groups: (a) howitzers (b) heavy howitzers, (c) half the field guns, (d) the other half of the field guns. They would hit the Forward Zone before zero hour before firing the creeping barrage ahead of the advance.

The German guns opened fire at 4.15 am, smothering First Army's batteries with a mixture of 4½:1 gas to high explosive shells. Tear gas encouraged the gunners to remove their masks while mustard gas incapacitated anyone who did. The Forward Zone was targeted by trench mortars firing a similar mix of gas and high explosive shells, only they used phosgene gas because it dispersed quicker than mustard gas.

The heavy artillery hit the battery lines, communication centres and billets for one hundred minutes but the trench mortars stopped shelling the front line after only twenty. A second short but intense bombardment of the Forward Zone with high explosive was followed by another brief pause. Gas shells were simultaneously fired at the Battle Zone, to disrupt the deployment of reserves.

The Counter Artillery and Deep Battle Groups continued to hit their usual targets while the Infantry Artillery Groups checked their ranges before firing another short, intense bombardment at the Forward Zone and Battle Zone, starting at 7.10 am. The howitzers hit strongpoints while the field guns used tear gas and high explosive shells to further disrupt the reserves. Another short, intense bombardment was made at 8.20 am while a crescendo of shelling by all the guns at 8.40 am warned the storm troops to deploy in no man's land. Five minutes later the barrage crept forward and the storm troops followed; the attack had begun.

First Army's front line had been smashed to pieces. Parapets had been levelled, trenches filled in, fortifications demolished and machine-gun posts knocked out. Mist covered the battlefield and all communications had been cut, so the first the support companies knew of the attack was when they spotted the storm troops moving towards them. Or were they? The green Portuguese uniforms looked similar to the German Army's field grey and some soldiers held their fire until they were absolutely sure.

Chapter 3

Units Were to Fight it out Where They Stood

Sixth Army's Attack: 9 April

XV Corps

34th Division, Armentières

Major General Lothian Nicholson's command had only been holding the line around Armentières for a few days and he was still waiting for his artillery to arrive. The town was again hit by a gas bombardment before zero hour but there was no attack against 103 Brigade. Instead the storm troops moved past Brigadier General Chaplin's flank, heading for Erquinghem on the River Lys.

Lieutenant General DuCane ordered Nicholson to give 101 Brigade to 40th Division to help it protect the Lys. The 11th Suffolks and 16th Royal Scots were supposed to man the Green Line, south of Bac St Maur, but Lieutenant Colonels Tuck and Stephenson learnt that the enemy were already there. So the battalions were returned and Brigadier General Gore sent the 11th Suffolks to defend Erquinghem; they were soon joined by Captain Newton's company of the 10th Lincolns.

The Germans renewed their advance through Fleurbaix during the afternoon, finding the 12th Suffolks barring their way. Lieutenant Colonel Lloyd's men 'retired slowly, disputing every yard of the ground', but they lost many and only a few dozen men reached Erquinghem.

Lieutenant Colonel Stephenson was supposed to deploy south of Bac St Maur but Major Warr reported the Germans were already attacking the village. Instead two companies each of the 15th and 16th Royal Scots deployed around Fort Rompu, north-east of the village. Stephenson's men stopped the Germans reaching Erquinghem but they came under fire from across the river. They contained the east side of the Bac St Maur bridgehead with help from 121 Field Brigade's guns. The gunners then hooked up and cantered away.

40th Division, Fleurbaix and Bac St Maur

Major General John Ponsonby's division had been seriously mauled during the Somme offensive and the survivors were transported north to the Lys where they were joined by many replacements. The line south of Armentières was traditionally a quiet area but the move had placed Ponsonby's men in line for the next German offensive.

Raids had been planned for the night of 8 April and parties left their trenches and moved silently through the mist covering no man's land. Two groups from 119 Brigade entered Necklace and Nephew Trenches after midnight, only to find them empty. They would have found hundreds of assault troops waiting to attack if they had gone any further. They had withdrawn to the support trench to avoid casualties from the inevitable retaliation barrage. Two companies of the 20th Middlesex crossed no man's land at 3 am, only to be caught when the German bombardment began. None returned and it was some time before Lieutenant Colonel Vignoles realised they were missing. Initially it was thought the bombardment was being fired in revenge for the Middlesex raid but it was soon clear something more serious was happening and XV Corps' headquarters issued the code word 'Bustle'. It was time for everyone to man their battle stations.

The barrage intensified and one observer later recalled, 'such a hurricane bombardment as I never wish to experience again; many gas shells were intermixed with high explosive and common shell, entailing the wearing of our gas helmets for two hours on end.' The attack hit 121 Brigade's right flank, overrunning the remaining two companies of the 20th Middlesex. The survivors fell back through Bois Grenier onto Lieutenant Colonel Misken's 13th Green Howards and the Germans followed. Lieutenant Colonel Lloyd had deployed the 12th Suffolks around Fleurbaix but Brigadier General Campbell's line was in danger of being split in two. 'We had hardly a gun left in action and the line had been forced back by 2,500 yards, the Portuguese Division had collapsed and the Germans were now well around our flank.'

The 13th East Surrey stopped the attack against 119 Brigade's trenches, on the east bank of the Layes stream. Lieutenant Colonel Metcalfe was able to report that the Germans 'were mown down by Lewis Gun and rifle fire; reports from men and officers mentioning piles of dead in front of the detached posts.'

Most of the storm troops pushing past Brigadier Crozier's flank headed for Laventie but some turned against 119 Brigade. A frontal attack had also penetrated the 18th Welch's line but Lieutenant Colonel Brown's request for help was denied: 'he was told there was none for him, and that he must use his nearest posts if they could be moved without risk to the

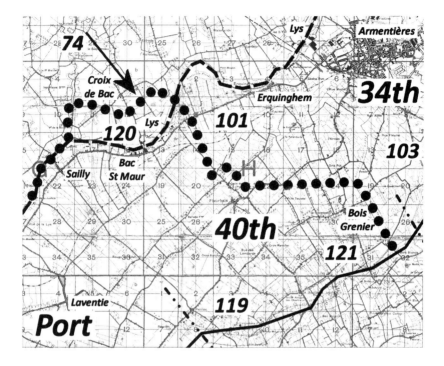

XV Corps' flank was pushed back over the Lys at Bac St Maur but the line held around Fleurbaix and Bois Grenier on 9 April.

situation.' The 18th Welsh were also firing on men moving past his flank and one company commander reported they had 'killed hundreds' around the Layes stream; the question was who were they because it was difficult to distinguish between friend and foe in the mist.

Crozier had sent the 21st Middlesex to Rouge de Bout, so they could form a defensive flank facing the Portuguese sector, when the bombardment began. They also opened fire on large bodies of men moving past them but the dark green Portuguese uniforms looked similar to German field grey ones in the mist and they were shooting at their allies. A warning was soon put out and the Welsh and Middlesex then held their fire longer than necessary, allowing many Germans to slip by.

The situation on Crozier's front was critical by the time the mist cleared. Lieutenant Colonel Brown reported the 18th Welsh's left company had been outflanked while his right company had been cut off. The reserve company was overrun and only sixteen wounded men were taken prisoner.

The Germans attacked Brown's headquarters next and 'they were engaged by the signallers, remnants of the headquarters company, the signals officer and OC battalion. The enemy were at times under 25 yards away and we had the pleasure of shooting at them and knowing that we could not miss.' Only Brown and six of the Welsh escaped to the 21st Middlesex headquarters in Winter's Night Post.

Some of the storm troops headed for Fleurbaix but others turned on the 13th Surreys and Lieutenant Colonel Metcalfe's last message reported they were behind his support trenches. Major General Ponsonby knew little of what was happening on his front but he issued a desperate order at 9 am: 'as the troops were not thoroughly familiar with the defences of the sector, there was to be no retrograde movement, units were to fight it out where they stood.' Ponsonby was anxious to give the corps' reserves time to deploy along the Lys.

Around one hundred men, who had just finished a training course, joined the Middlesex, but Lieutenant Colonel Richards' message illustrates how desperate the situation had become:

> *A very excited and wounded company sergeant major of the East Surreys rushed into my headquarters and informed me that their support line had gone and the enemy were advancing on my headquarters. My adjutant and second in command immediately took all the orderlies to Gunners' Walk. I then went in that direction and saw a large body of Germans advancing in extended order and in a north-easterly direction. My adjutant and second in command were surrounded by overwhelming numbers before we reached Gunners' Walk.*

Only a few men of 119 Brigade reached Bac St Maur on the River Lys where the engineers were preparing to demolish the bridges. The main bridge was a challenge because it 'was built on the remains of the permanent bridge wrecked in the earlier months of the war. It consisted of heavy timber trestles, bedded on to the old stone foundation piers, carrying a substantial roadway capable of taking all ordinary traffic.'

Nearly a ton of explosives had been stacked around the centre trestles and the engineers of 224th Field Company were busy checking their equipment:

> *Lieutenant Carr had received instructions to defer the destruction of the bridge until the last possible moment, to allow the maximum amount of transport to cross the river. The terminal box in the dug-out was unfastened and the leads tested for continuity at hourly intervals. As the morning advanced*

*and the fog cleared, it became evident to those stationed at
Bac St Maur that the enemy must be advancing fairly rapidly
if the volume of traffic westward over the bridge could be
taken as an index. For hours a mixed multitude, consisting of
civilian refugees, Portuguese soldiers and transport of every
description streamed steadily across the Lys.*

Bac St Maur was repeatedly shelled and the queue of traffic halted when
a shell burst hit a team of horses on the bridge. It was some time before it
was cleared and a new team hauled the howitzer off clear. The last man to
cross was 34th Division's GSO, Major Tower, early in the afternoon. Then
the 'enemy machine gunners obtained a footing in the houses on the east
side of the Lys and commenced machine-gun fire on the bridge. A few
minutes later, enterprising Germans opened fire with trench mortars from
the windows of the houses overlooking the bridge.'

Lieutenant Carr detonated the charges as German soldiers ran onto the
bridge but some of the leads had been damaged and only part of the bridge
collapsed in the explosion. Lieutenant Carr would be killed as his sappers
joined the fighting withdrawal towards Croix du Bac.

Brigadier General Crozier had instructed two companies of the 2nd
Scots Fusiliers to line the river bank around Bac St Maur. But they had
a problem because the ground was higher on the south bank 'which was
lined with houses. The slope, covered with still more houses, formed
terraces from which tiers of fire could be directed on the northern bank.'

They were soon joined by stragglers, engineers, pioneers and staff by the
bridges. The 18th Welch had ceased to exist but Lieutenant Colonel Brown
had led one hundred replacements towards Bac St Maur. They could see
the Germans advancing 'in lines of platoons two deep, with machine guns
on sledges. Colonel Brown's party succeeded in cutting the mooring ropes
of two of the temporary bridges and setting them adrift but the third bridge
was swept by heavy machine gun fire and the attempt had to be dropped.'

Lieutenant Lee's machine gun teams of 34th Division had helped the
Scots Fusiliers keep the enemy at bay all afternoon. They rushed the bridges
as soon as it was dark and 'it says much for the enterprise and forethought
of the enemy that they were able to fix their temporary bridge, which they
brought up from the rear on lorries, before midnight.'

The defence offered by a few Portuguese 'caused hardly a moment's
pause in the German advance until it came to the village line'. Major
General Ponsonby had instructed 120 Brigade to cross the River Lys
and man the Battle Zone. But the Germans reached Laventie first, so
Brigadier General Hobkirk had to deploy his men in the Green Line,

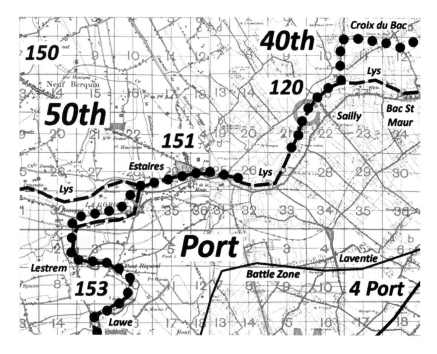

The Portuguese retreated quickly across the Lys on 9 April, leaving 40th Division's flank exposed and 50th Division to cover the bridges between Sailly and Estaires.

finding nothing more than shallow ditches to fight from. The 10/11th Highland Light Infantry, the 14th Highland Light Infantry and the 14th Argylls were soon engaged in the mist and only 400 men survived the running battle back to Sailly-sur-Lys. There they found Lieutenant Colonel Utterson-Kelso and the rest of the 2nd Scots Fusiliers guarding the bridges.

XI Corps

The 2nd Portuguese Division, Neuve Chapelle and Richebourg l'Avoué
General Gomes da Costa's men were holding a 5½-mile sector along the Layes stream. One of the first shells fired demolished Costa's conference room, throwing his staff into confusion at a critical time. Lieutenant Colonel Glover, the British liaison officer at the Portuguese headquarters, was shocked by the chaotic scenes, so he made emergency calls to both XV Corps and XI Corps. His advice was to deploy British troops to the Battle Zone behind the Portuguese line at once.

The bombardment cut communications with the three brigades, so Costa sent a mounted officer with orders for his reserve brigade to deploy in the Battle Zone. It took him an hour to find the brigadier in the pre-dawn mist and no one took any notice of the instructions. Many of the Portuguese soldiers had left their trenches, hoping to escape the shelling, and while most headed to the rear, others risked crossing no man's land to surrender. Nothing would be heard from the front line because those who stayed were either killed or captured by the first wave of storm troops.

When news did start to come in, it was bad. The division was disintegrating and General da Costa was the only one who remained unaffected by the depressing reports from the front. Major General Ponsonby had sent Captain Graham to find out what the Portuguese were doing on 40th Division's right flank. He spent half the morning on roads filled with escaping Portuguese soldiers, only to find Costa's headquarters in 'a rapid state of demolition'. The staff had left, but a couple of British officers took Graham to see the general. He described da Costa as 'an

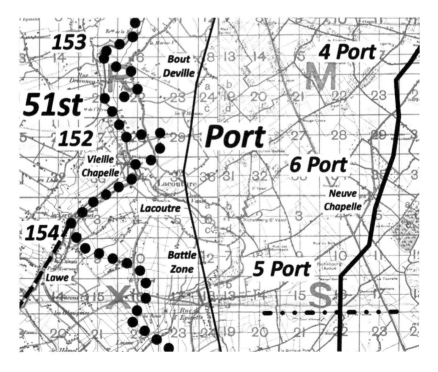

The Portuguese fell back across the Lawe, leaving 51st Division to support XI Corps' troops on 9 April.

exceptionally tall and melancholy man, sitting by himself in the attitude of a captain refusing to leave his sinking ship'. Graham learnt nothing useful and returned to Ponsonby none the wiser.

The Portuguese were in full retreat, leaving a huge gap in First Army's line. The men of the reserve brigade joined in when stragglers started passing through their lines spreading rumours of a disaster. Costa had wanted 3 Portuguese Brigade to man the Battle Zone but stragglers from the Forward Zone convinced them the battle was lost and virtually every man joined the exodus from the battlefield.

The only men going forwards were the XI Corps' cyclist battalion and the King Edward's Horse, the corps' mounted troops. Lieutenant General Haking had instructed them to cross the Lawe canal and man the Battle Zone on hearing about the Portuguese disaster. Major Davies led the 11th Cyclist Battalion to the Lacouture area but fleeing Portuguese soldiers stole their bicycles as they manned the trenches.

Lieutenant Colonel Lionel James's men were colonials who were residing in Great Britain or Britons who had lived in the colonies. The 1st King Edward's Horse, or King's Overseas Dominions Regiment, moved to the area south of Bout Deville. They were heading into the unknown but the hundreds of stragglers and refugees on the roads made it clear a disaster had befallen the Portuguese Division. The corps' mounted troops were supported by a few engineers and staff details who had gathered at the bridges over the Lawe canal. There they formed bridgeheads and the unarmed men took rifles and ammunition from the fleeing Portuguese.

The main problem for the Germans was getting forward across the muddy fields. Hedges and ditches delayed the infantry, while the gun limbers and supply wagons had to queue up to cross the bridges and culverts. A few Portuguese had stayed behind, including a couple of posts around Neuve Chapelle, while a small group joined the cyclists in the Battle Zone. Another group tried to fight the Germans off around Richebourg l'Avoué but only one soldier is mentioned: Aníbal Milhais.

Milhais continued to fire his Lewis gun long after his comrades had fled. The Germans had soon bypassed his position and he hid behind enemy line for three days. He discovered a wounded Scottish officer when he finally decided to move and carried him to safety. Milhais became known as *Soldado Milhões* (Soldier Millions) and he was awarded the highest Portuguese medal for bravery, the Military Order of the Tower and of the Sword, of Valour, Loyalty and Merit. His was the only success story in 2nd Portuguese Division's disaster. It is estimated that over 6,000 Portuguese were taken prisoner while another 13,650 men who had fled eventually assembled behind First Army's lines.

55th Division, Givenchy

General Quast had assembled three divisions opposite the West Lancashire's position around Givenchy. Captured documents noted that the division had been listed as being 'only fit for holding a quiet sector of the line'. The assessment was probably because its line had been broken during the German counter-attack near Cambrai on 30 November 1917. However, Major General Hugh Jeudwine had spent the past three months making sure his position was as strong as possible. The codename 'Bustle' put units on alert when the bombardment started but the storm troops were through the wire before they were seen.

To begin with, the Lancashire men did not know if the men moving past their flank through the mist were Portuguese or German, so they held their fire. They soon realised they were wearing the British style helmet, but one British officer, 'who had been sent to see what was happening, tried to rally them until they threatened to bayonet him'. Major General Jeudwine

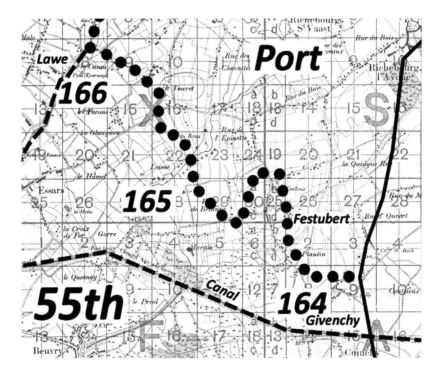

A staunch defence by 55th Division ensured that Festubert and Givenchy were held on 9 April, while a flank was thrown back to the Lawe Canal.

soon 'appreciated that the Portuguese had been overwhelmed and could no longer be considered as a fighting force'.

Brigadier General Boyd-Moss's outposts around Festubert sector were soon overrun but the storm troops faced three belts of wire and several water-filled ditches as they fought their way past 165 Brigade's machine-gun posts. The rest of the King's were manning the Village Line, a 'series of well-concealed breastworks, loop-holed walls and buildings. Cross fire from the various posts covered the ground in front and excellent enfilade machine-gun fire was possible from concrete emplacements.'

Lieutenant Colonel Buckley heard that the two companies of the 1/5th King's holding the Forward Zone had been overrun but 'the outposts at Festubert East and those in the Village Line remained intact.' The enemy pushed past the flanks of Lieutenant Colonel Potter's 1/7th King's but they failed to drive Lieutenant Colonel McKaig's 6th King's from the Village Line. A short trench mortar bombardment heralded a midday attack and while the Germans shouted 'cease fire' as they cut through the wire, 'their cries only spurred on the gallant garrisons who, increasing their volume of fire, shot down the enemy in bunches.'

One large shell hit the platoon detailed to occupy Route A Keep, killing and wounding many. The survivors then mounted their machine guns on the parapet, ready to shoot indirect fire rather than take them inside the bunkers, unaware the Germans were so close. An hour later they saw the storm troops jogging through the smoke towards them, so they opened fire. The machine guns were soon knocked out and bombers overran the strongpoint.

Brigadier General Kentish's 166 Brigade was sent forward from reserve around Locon and Essars as the Germans pushed past 55th Division's flank. A company of the 1/6th King's helped Potter and the 1/7th King's staff recapture Le Plantin South strongpoint. Major Munro's 1/10th King's then extended the left flank back to Loisne Central, reaching the strongpoint just before the Germans did.

Brigadier General Kentish ordered the 1/5th King's Own and 1/5th South Lancashires to deploy past Le Touret and threw a flank as far back as the Lawe canal. The 1/4th South Lancashires would join them, stopping the enemy crossing the Lawe canal at Locon. Finally, Major General Jeudwine sent his engineers, tunnellers and pioneers to the same area, where they were joined by the 4th Seaforths (from 51st Division) and a couple of hundred Portuguese soldiers who were still willing to fight.

Brigadier General Stockwell's 164 Brigade held the area around Givenchy on the north bank of the La Bassée canal with the 1/4th Loyals and the 4th King's Own. The creeping barrage moving forward at 8.45

am followed by the storm troops. Some penetrated between 165 and 164 Brigades, surrounding Moat Farm and occupying houses at Windy Corner, while others reached the church in the centre of Givenchy. More reached Pont Fixe, the bridge which crossed the canal, west of Cuinchy.

Elsewhere, Brigadier General Stockwell's men stopped the attack until the counter-attack platoons were ready: 'Owing to the thick fog and a large amount of wire, the fighting consisted of isolated combats carried on all over the area by small parties of officers and men.' The Lancashire men persisted and they were soon driving the Germans back to the front line.

Lieutenant Colonel Brighten had sent Captain Bodington's company of the 2/5th Lancashire Fusiliers to recapture Windy Corner. Captain Wilkinson was killed leading his company forward from the Tuning Fork but his men captured the Germans trying to escape Bodington's attack. Second Lieutenant John Schofield's group of nine men killed dozens, and captured twenty men before counter-attacking through Givenchy. Schofield climbed on the parapet under fire to encourage another 123 to surrender only to be killed a few minutes later; he was posthumously awarded the Victoria Cross.

Second Lieutenant Joseph Collin fought on next to the canal until only five men of his platoon of the 1/4th King's Own were still standing. They were falling back when Collin silenced one machine-gun team before turning a Lewis gun on a second. He was mortally wounded keeping the enemy at bay and would also be posthumously awarded the Victoria Cross.

Jeudwine's men could see hundreds of dead and wounded Germans laid around their trenches when the mist cleared. There were also Germans hiding in craters, so Captains Cook and Leach made sure the 1/7th Kings and 2/5th Lancashire Fusiliers rounded up 500 prisoners, including two battalion commanders. They also found a regimental band who were expecting to lead a triumphal march into Béthune; instead they found themselves marching into captivity. The Lancashire men also collected over one hundred light machine guns and automatic rifles.

1st Division, South of the La Bassée Canal
Major General Peter Strickland's men held the sector south of the La Bassée canal with 2 Brigade. He moved the 1st Gloucesters to Cuinchy, to stop the enemy crossing the canal bank. A few batteries pulled their guns out of their emplacements so they could shoot at targets around Givenchy, in 55th Division's sector.

The Corps' Reserves Shore Up the Line, 9 April
General Horne's plan was to use the Corps reserves to form a new line if the Portuguese Division fell back. However, they left the battlefield much

faster than expected and the storm troops reached the Battle Zone. It meant XV Corps had to deploy its reserves to the River Lys while XI Corps' reserves manned a line along the Lawe canal.

25th Division, Counter-Attack on Bac St Maur

Lieutenant General DuCane asked Lieutenant General Alexander Hamilton-Gordon for reinforcements during the afternoon to help with 'puttying up the gaps'. He particularly wanted to recapture Bac St Maur and Brigadier General Craigie-Halkett was told to assemble 74 Brigade of 25th Division. Men had to be recalled from the baths and the firing range but they were soon marching towards Steenwerck. The battalion commanders were briefed in front of the church but Craigie-Halkett soon learnt that the enemy could be in Croix du Bac. Lieutenant Colonel Wienholt rode into the village to discover it was true, and had to escape on foot after his horse was shot from under him.

It was dusk before 74 Brigade advanced and while the 3rd Worcesters reached the river near Fort Rompu, on the left, the 11th Lancashire Fusiliers and the 9th Loyals were pinned down in front of Croix du Bac. Lieutenant Colonel Wienholt was wounded but Major Nares made sure the Loyals had cleared the village before dawn.

50th Division, Manning the Lys Bridges

Around midday, Major General Henry Jackson instructed Brigadier General Rees to move his 150 Brigade to the Lys bridges. The 4th Green Howards marched to Sailly-sur-la-Lys and the 4th East Yorkshires to Le Nouveau Monde, where they found the engineers preparing the bridges for demolition. They also came under machine-gun fire from the far bank.

The Green Howards stopped several attempts to cross at Sailly while the engineers tried in vain to demolish the bridge. Meanwhile, the East Yorkshires used 'excellent fire control, a very praiseworthy thing considering that officers and men were practically new to each other'. The engineers eventually blew up Le Nouveau Monde bridge at dusk.

The last of the Portuguese had passed through 151 Brigade's position around Estaires by midday; 'they had left all their guns, from 9.2's down, in the hands of the enemy.' Soon afterwards patrols spotted the Germans advancing towards Brigadier General Martin's line from the direction of Laventie. The 6th Durhams' outposts had put up 'a gallant fight' around Cockshy House, Le Drumez Post and Carter's Post before 'they were practically wiped out'.

The Germans then split into two, with one column heading for Estaires. The 5th Durhams had orders to hold Pont Levis and Pont de la Meuse in Estaires, and the bridge at La Gorgue 'at all costs'. By nightfall, 'the enemy had brought up field guns and were systematically smashing up the bridgehead garrisons at point blank range.' Lieutenant Colonel Spence got permission to withdraw everyone to the north bank and blow the bridges up. Pont de la Meuse and the La Gorgue bridge were demolished but two attempts to bring down Pont Levis failed.

The second column overran the 6th Durhams in Riez Bailleul and Clifton Post and only sixty-four escaped across the Lawe, north of Lestrem. The Germans then attacked the 8th Durhams holding the Lawe canal between Lestrem and Fosse, driving them back across the canal at Lock de la Rault. The bridgeheads at Lestrem and Pont Riquel on the north side of the loop held, and arrival of the 7th Gordons secured the south side. The Scots would take over the whole Lestrem loop during the night.

While fighting raged along the river, Brigadier General Riddell marched his three battalions towards Estaires. The 4th Northumberland Fusiliers covered the damaged Pont Levis while the 5th and 6th Northumberland Fusiliers deployed north of the village. There was concern when the 4th Green Howards reported that the 21st Middlesex had been driven out of Bac St Maur during the evening. Large numbers were crossing the Lys and moving behind 50th Division's left flank, so Major General Jackson moved the 6th Northumberland Fusiliers to cover the threatened area.

All along the Lys men were digging in ready for the renewal of the attack in the morning. Many were inexperienced teenagers but everyone was impressed with the way 'the beardless youths from home, conquering inexperience and the first fright of battle, vied with our veterans in tenacity, resolution and faithfulness'.

51st Division, Along the Lawe canal

Lieutenant General Haking had instructed Major General George Carter-Campbell to deploy his 51st Division along the Lawe canal as soon as possible. However, Brigadier General Beckwith had to wait until evening before he could move 153 Brigade forward from Pacaut because 'the roads were so congested with Portuguese troops and refugees moving westwards.' Beckwith soon learnt that the Germans had already reached the Battle Zone and he was to head for the Lestrem loop and contact 50th Division. The 6th Black Watch deployed around Lestrem and Pont Riquel while the 7th Gordons covered the south side of the loop.

The men of 151 Brigade were marching towards the sounds of battle when they heard that the King Edward's Horse were engaged in a desperate battle for the Battle Zone north of Lacouture. So Brigadier General Dick-Cunyngham decided to deploy along the Lawe canal and the 5th Seaforths formed a bridgehead around Fosse. The farmers had only just fled with their families, taking what they could carry with them. Lieutenant Colonel Scott's men found 'cattle, pigs and fowls wandering around ownerless, while the fields, lately drilled and sown, were being torn up by shells or dug up in the making of trenches.' They even found a few elderly people 'who refused to budge, preferring to encounter the dangers of shot and shell than leave the old home.'

Captain Christie's company of the 6th Gordons joined Lieutenant Stein's squadron of the King Edward's Horse in Vielle Chapelle while the rest of the battalion dug a support line. The 6th Seaforths lined out along the canal, south of the hamlet, while the engineers tried in vain to blow up Boundary Bridge.

Brigadier General Buchanan moved 154 Brigade behind 55th Division's left flank. The 7th Argylls extended the line along the Lawe, east of Locon, while the 4th Gordons deployed west of the village. The 4th Seaforths reinforced the 1/4th South Lancashires (Pioneers) around Le Touret, closing the gap on 55th Division's left flank. The Lawe canal was safe by late afternoon, so the cyclists and the King Edward's Horse fell back to the Fosse and Vieille Chapelle bridgeheads under 'heavy enfilade machine-gun fire and bombing'.

The British Summary

By nightfall, German Sixth Army had driven a 10-mile-wide hole in the British First Army's line. West of Armentières, the Germans had been pushed back by XV Corps 4 miles to the Lys, crossing it at Bac St Maur. Meanwhile, XI Corps had been driven back 5 miles to the Lawe canal. The only successes of the day had been the stout defences on the flanks. While 40th Division had stopped the Germans cutting off Armentières, 55th Division had held onto Festubert and Givenchy.

Lieutenant Generals DuCane and Haking had deployed all their reserves to cover the gap where the Portuguese had been and reinforcements were some distance away. Artillery losses had been low on XV Corps' front because most of the howitzers had been north of the Lys, but fourteen heavy guns had been abandoned in 40th Division's sector. Many of the division's field guns had escaped over the Lys but some gunners had left it too late and twenty-five had to be disabled and abandoned. It was a different story in XI Corps' sector where all but three of the twenty-four heavy howitzers deployed behind the Portuguese Division had been lost. It left Haking short of heavy artillery and GHQ had to send him ten heavy batteries from its reserve.

The roads across First Army's area jammed with refugees, stragglers, artillery limbers and supply wagons, all looking to escape. There were bottlenecks at the river bridges while artillery fire was turning the towns of Merville, Estaires and Armentières into burning, gas-filled ruins. The casualty clearing stations had been sent back first because there had been problems evacuating them during the Somme retreat. Their wagons needed to get away first, so the staff would be ready to treat casualties as soon as possible.

Reinforcements were on their way but they were having to squeeze past the crowds on the roads. Often the only way to get forward was to take to the fields and move across country. Officers often did not know what lay ahead and their battalions moved in open order with scouts up ahead.

The German Summary

The Portuguese Corps had given little resistance but the British troops on the flanks put up a good fight. The morning fog had hidden the storm troops from the Lewis gunners while the British artillery had been unable to see the flares calling for SOS barrages. But it had also slowed some attacking parties down and disorientated others so they could not keep up with the creeping barrage.

A few aerial observers flew across battlefields when the mist cleared and the early reports were promising. So promising that Crown Prince Rupprecht instructed General Quast to push across the Lys during the night. However, the afternoon reports were less optimistic and the British spotter planes noted that the advance was slowing down because the Germans were victims of their own success. They could not move the guns, ammunition and supplies forward as fast as the infantry. A breakdown in logistics was stalling the advance rather than the British reserves.

The Allied Reaction to the Attack

Field Marshal Haig had received the first vague reports about the attack around midday. By the time Foch arrived at GHQ, he knew that the Portuguese had fallen back and both the Forward and Battle Zones had been lost, as had part of the Army Line. The corps reserves had deployed and so far they were holding on along the River Lys and the Lawe canal.

Haig again asked if the French could take over part of the BEF's front so he could form a reserve in Flanders. Foch again refused because he thought the attack was a feint to draw reserves away from the Somme. Instead he proposed moving four French divisions towards Amiens, but Haig objected because they would cause logistics problems behind Fourth Army. It meant Haig would have to find his own reserves. General Plumer agreed to withdraw from the Ypres Salient so Second Army could release 29th and 49th Divisions.

Chapter 4

Truly a Precarious Situation

Fourth Army Joins the Battle, 10 April

The plan was for Sixth Army to keep pushing across the River Lys on XV Corps' front and the Lawe in XI Corps' sector. Fourth Army was poised to attack Second Army's right flank, on the Messines Ridge. The two converging attacks would force First Army to evacuate Armentières, widening the bridgehead across the Lys. The light rain ended before first light and the mist cleared for a time around midday but low cloud returned to limit air activity.

Second Army
IX Corps

Ludendorff originally planned to wait until Sixth Army had crossed the River Lys before Fourth Army attacked north of Armentières. But he eventually decided the second attack would begin twenty-four hours after the first. It gave General Armin a definite date to work to but he only had five divisions to attack IX Corps between the Comines canal and Frélinghien. Ludendorff's first objective was to cut off Armentières but his main objective was the line of hills, stretching between Kemmelberg and Cassel, 10 miles north-west of the town. Their loss would force Second Army to evacuate the Ypres Salient and put the Channel Ports under threat.

Lieutenant General Alexander Hamilton-Gordon had the 9th, 19th and 25th Divisions in line. They were all still suffering from their trials in the recent Somme battle and many of the replacements they had received were inexperienced men. The ground east of the Messines Ridge was dry but it had been impossible to dig continuous trenches in the crater field, so IX Corps' Forward Zone was a line of outposts backed up by strongpoints. Some battalion commanders had wanted to withdraw from their exposed positions but they were not allowed to create a new one further back. Each division had a reserve position on the west side of the ridge and the reserves could count on plenty of old trenches to use if the Germans drove them off the summit.

Fourth Army had done little to conceal its preparations and the lack of secrecy had led some to thinking it was a demonstration to stop the movement of reserves to First Army. Everything was quiet on 9 April, while the battle raged to the south-west, but British patrols in no man's land reported a lot of noise later that night while flares and machine-gun fire stopped them entering the German trenches.

The German guns opened fire at 5.15 am and again gas shelling of batteries was a major feature of the bombardment. Next came the targeting of headquarters, crossroads, and observing stations with high-explosive, to disrupt communications. The barrage switched to the IX Corps' Forward Zone at 7.30 am and the infantry advanced fifteen minutes later.

Again mist and rain meant the British artillery could only shell pre-registered targets while the machine gun teams fired on pre-determined lines. This time though, the British observers could direct the heavy artillery onto targets because they had use of the deep signal cables which dated back to the Messines offensive.

9th Division, Ypres-Comines Canal
Major General Hugh Tudor was holding a narrow sector either side of the Ypres-Comines canal with 27 Brigade. The 'enemy's rush surprised the outposts, all of which were overwhelmed before they had time to offer resistance.' Major Innes Brown was killed as the 6th KOSBs lost ground north of the canal, but Lieutenant McGregor held on until the 11th Royal Scots manned the strongpoint covering the White Chateau. Brigadier General Croft then sent two companies of the 12th Royal Scots forward to drive the Germans back.

19th Division, East of Wytschaete and Messines
Major General George Jeffreys' men were waiting in the mist on the eastern slope of the Messines Ridge when the Germans attacked. Some outposts were overrun but others were bypassed as the storm troops headed for Wytschaete and Messines. The support waves dealt with any resistance, with the help of bombing teams, flamethrowers, machine guns and field guns. The speed of the attack again took the British battalion commanders by surprise and the first they knew of the disaster was when their headquarters came under attack.

The attack against 58 Brigade's line east of Oosttaverne started when the mist returned in the afternoon. The Germans overran 9th Welsh Fusiliers' outposts and drove Lieutenant Colonel Smeatham's men back towards Ravine Wood. The 6th Wiltshires were left isolated as 57 Brigade across the Wambeke stream fell back.

The fighting along IX Corps line was developing into two battles, so Lieutenant General Hamilton-Gordon divided it so. He gave 58 Brigade to 9th Division, so Major General Tudor could control the north end of the ridge. Meanwhile, Major General Jeffreys could focus on the disaster unfolding south of Messines.

Major General Tudor moved the 9th Seaforths (Pioneers) to Damm Strasse, to cover 58 Brigade's left flank, while the 9th Welsh were ordered to defend Wytschaete. He instructed Brigadier General Glasgow to withdraw his front line battalions to the support line, but it was too late. Some of the

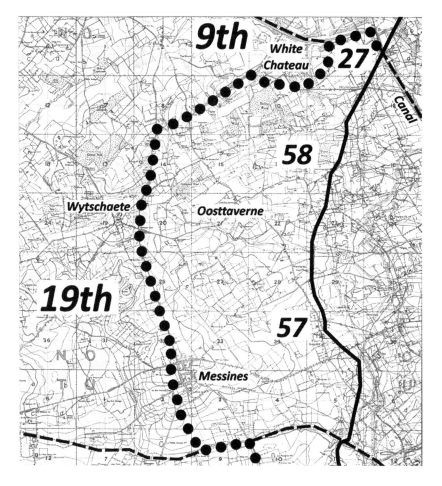

General Sixt von Armin's Fourth Army drove 19th Division back to the summit of the Messines Ridge on 10 April.

Welsh Fusiliers were falling back towards Damm Strasse while the rest had been cut off. Lieutenant Colonel Monreal never got the order to pull back and he was killed after the 6th Wiltshires were cut off. One Wiltshire post would hold on for 48 hours before escaping through the morning fog. Most of the 9th Welsh were overrun but enough held on to stop the Germans entering Wytschaete for a time.

Tudor handed over the 5th Camerons to help the shattered 58 Brigade hold the Battle Zone around Grand Bois. Brigadier General Kennedy sent a fighting patrol forward to check Wytschaete when it was dark and they discovered that the ruins were deserted. The few dozen Scots then kept the Germans at bay until reinforcements arrived.

Brigadier General Gater was instructed to secure Wytschaete and close the gap between 27 and 57 Brigades. Lieutenant Colonel Bastard was told that 9th Division's flank was 'in the air' and the 2nd Lincolns and 12/13th Northumberland Fusiliers found that the 'night was black, the ground was unknown and the road was difficult to keep to.' But Captain Pritchard was a 'very brave and resolute leader' and Brigadier General Gater later referred to the clearing of Wytschaete as 'the most difficult that I recollect being called to carry out'.

The attack between the Wambeke and Douve streams had cut off everyone in 57 Brigade's Forward Zone. So Major Eric Dougall got his crews to manhandle 88th Battery's guns to the summit of the Messines Ridge where they poured shrapnel into the advancing Germans. He rallied many stragglers, telling them that 'so long as you stick to your trenches I will keep my guns here.' The 10th Warwicks were eventually driven beyond Wytschaete while the 10th Worcesters and 8th Gloucesters retired from the Messines area. Only then would Dougall withdraw but his gunners had to haul their guns across half a mile of shell-cratered slopes to get to their new positions. He was killed four days later but would be awarded the Victoria Cross.

Brigadier General Cubitt deployed what engineers and pioneers he could find along the Corps Line, at the foot of the west slope. Lieutenant Hodgson's machine guns made sure the Germans could not leave Messines but two companies of the 8th North Staffords were unable to recapture the ruins.

The South Africans had marched up to Neuve Église during the afternoon and Brigadier General Tanner recorded the distressing scene his men encountered as they approached the battlefield:

> *...the shelling of the back areas had greatly increased, both in density and length of range. As a result, a large belt of country previously unmolested became subjected to a terrifying storm of long-range projectiles, and the inhabitants, who up to then*

had been conducting peacefully their farming operations, were compelled to flee for shelter beyond the reach of the enemy guns. As we approached Neuve Église the road presented a constant stream of fugitives, old men, women, and children, laden with what household goods they could remove in carts, wheelbarrows, and perambulators. The most pitiable sights were those of infirm old people being removed in barrows, pushed or pulled by women and children.

Lieutenant General Hamilton-Gordon wanted to recapture Messines Ridge but Major General Tudor protested because the South African Brigade had only just been rebuilt. It had been wiped out making a heroic last stand during the March retreat on the Somme. Virtually every one of the 1,300 officers and men had never been in the front line, never mind carried out a counter-attack against a strong position. But Tudor's protest was dismissed and Tanner supervised the deployment of his brigade east of Wulverghem late in the afternoon.

The artillery barrage failed to silence the Germans and the South Africans came under machine-gun fire from Messines as they climbed the slope. Captain Jacobs had to pull 2nd Regiment's left back behind the crest, where the Germans held onto Pick House, while Lieutenants Pope-Hennessy and Jenner were hit as the Regiment's right crossed the crest. The 1st South African Regiment was soon through the rubble that was once Messines but there was fierce fighting around Bethlehem Farm to the east. Both Captains Ward and Burgess had been hit by the time Lieutenant Colonel Young instructed 1st Regiment to fall back through the village.

25th Division, Hill 63 and Ploegsteert
Major General Guy Bainbridge had been warned that 34th Division was due to withdraw during the afternoon of 10 April. So he had deployed the 6th SWBs (Pioneers) and engineers to his south flank were two companies of the 2nd South Lancashires were digging in, north of the town.

German engineers had built footways across the Lys, where it was some distance from the British line, but the duckboards were just below the surface of the water so they could not be seen. Elsewhere pontoons had been dragged up to the river bank and they were pushed into the water while it was still dark. The storm troops ran across the bridges opposite 7 Brigade at zero hour, bypassing the outposts of the 4th South Staffords and 1st Wiltshires in the mist. The company of the 1st Wiltshire holding La Basse Ville was overrun but the rest of the two battalions held on while the Germans opened fire into their backs.

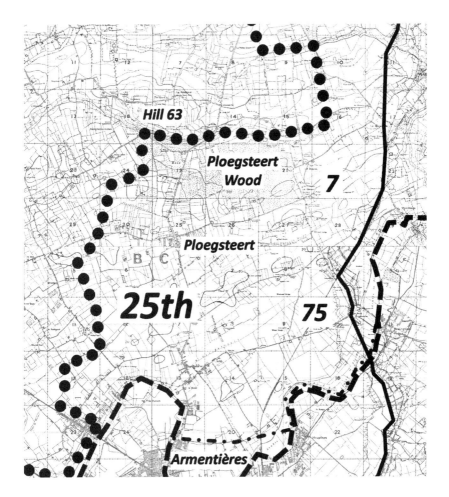

While 25th Division's left held on around Hill 63 on 10 April, the right was driven out of Ploegsteert and its wood.

The main attack came several hours later and Brigadier General Griffin ordered a withdrawal after 75 Brigade's line caved in to the south. Casualties were heavy as his men fell back to a small salient between the Douve stream and Ploegsteert Wood. One company of the South Staffords were cut off near Warneton and Captain Carr had to wait until it was dark before his men could escape.

The attack between Deûlémont and Frélinghien overran the 11th Cheshires' and 8th Borders' outposts and then 75 Brigade's main line collapsed. Lieutenant Colonel Darwell was wounded as the Cheshires were driven out of Ploegsteert Wood and they were so disorganised they could not retake Ploegsteert Wood. Only twenty-two men of the 8th Border Regiment escaped. Brigadier General Griffin deployed the 1/4th Shropshires (attached from 56 Brigade) to defend Hill 63 and Captain Wace's counter-attack stopped the Germans taking the summit. Brigadier General Hannay had too few troops to retake Ploegsteert Wood, so he formed a new line with two companies of 2nd South Lancashires and all the engineers and pioneers he could muster. They held on until Lieutenant Colonel Fulton's 9th Cheshires (attached from 56 Brigade) and the Army engineers reached them.

Major General Bainbridge had wanted to hold onto the west half of Ploegsteert Wood and the village but they were already in German hands. Brigadier General Hannay was arranging a counter-attack when another forty-three men of the 8th Border Regiment turned up. They reported that the village was full of Germans who were resting so Hannay decided to attack at once. The 10th Cheshires' left company entered Ploegsteert Wood but the right did not get the order to advance in time, so everyone had to withdraw. The day ended with 75 Brigade's left west of Ploegsteert and its right holding the Nieppe Switch, in contact with 34th Division, west of Armentières.

IX Corps Summary
Fourth Army had driven IX Corps back across an 8½-mile front, pushing 19th Division back one mile onto the summit of the Messines Ridge. But the big problem was on IX Corp's right, where 25th Division had fallen back over 2 miles around Ploegsteert.

First Army
XV Corps
Lieutenant General John DuCane was facing a difficult situation early on 10 April. Sixth Army had pushed past the south side of Armentières and the second attack by Fourth Army meant the town had to be evacuated. The rest of his front ran along the Lys but it had been compromised because the Germans had crossed at Bac St Maur. There were plans to eliminate the bridgehead but the troops holding Sailly, Estaires and Lestrem were also under attack.

34th Division, The Evacuation of Armentières
Major General Lothian Nicholson's men had just taken over the Armentières sector but they had not had time to settle down. After suffering hundreds of casualties during the recent Somme battle, the veterans were having to

organise and train over 2,700 replacements. Nicholson had been relying on 38th (Welsh) Division's artillery, and his own artillery was just arriving as the attack started. It meant the 'gunners were in the uncomfortable position being neither in nor out', so the Welshmen had to remain in their battery positions.

Armentières had been shelled with mustard gas several times, leaving 'the poisonous stuff hanging around in the houses for days'. Civilians had left many months before but soldiers were still living amongst the ruins and the gas seeped into the cellars and dugouts. The clean-up teams found 'it was impossible to clear the gas as the whole atmosphere of the town was permeated by it.' Gusts of wind blew the gas around and nauseous men took off their masks so they could vomit. The division had eventually suffered 900 gas casualties, including two entire companies of the 25th Northumberland Fusiliers.

Major General Nicholson had been concerned during 9 April but the threat to Armentières increased as Fourth Army's attack developed north of the town on 10 April. The Germans were executing a pincer movement creating 'truly a precarious situation'. Lieutenant General DuCane issued the evacuation order at 10 am and Nicholson's battalions had to establish rearguards ready for the front line troops to withdraw at 3 pm. Over 15,000 men and fifty artillery pieces had to get across the Lys before midnight and the engineers then had to demolish the bridges before the enemy crossed.

There were a handful of permanent bridges over the River Lys but the engineers had added many temporary pontoon bridges. They were 'moored along the bank, all ready to be swung into position when needed and carefully camouflaged'. All across 34th Division's back areas, preparations for a withdrawal were being made. Pioneers joined the men of 34th Machine Gun Battalion at the bridges and 'there was no cessation in the din as the hours passed, so we all realised that yet another day had arrived and all units and parties were stood to.'

The order reached Brigadier General Thomson, east of the town, before midday. The Germans did not trouble the 22nd, 23rd and 25th Northumberland Fusiliers as they withdrew through the north side of the ruins to Pont de Pierre and the adjacent temporary bridges. Then 102 Brigade deployed north of Pont de Nieppe.

The rest of 34th Division, and 121 Brigade's troops, had far more trouble escaping from the area south of Armentières. Brigadier General Chaplin told his messengers to 'run as hard as God would let them' to 103 Brigade's battalions after hearing the order at 101 Brigade headquarters. One reached the 1st East Lancashires, astride the Lille road, before 3 pm and the battalion escaped through the town. The 10th Lincolns, 13th Yorkshires and 9th

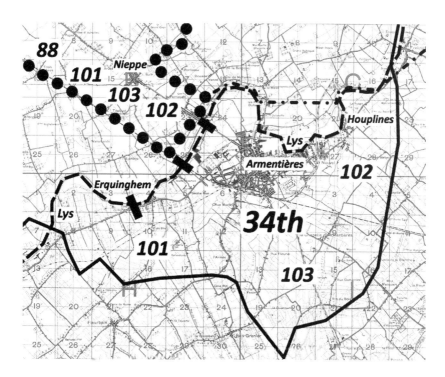

Most of 34th Division used the three main bridges to evacuate Armentières on 10 April; Pont de Nieppe, the railway bridge and Erquinghem bridge.

Northumberland Fusiliers, holding the apex, received the order to withdraw much later. The three battalion commanders had decided to delay their withdrawal, to allow the rearguards to organise, and Lieutenant Colonel Tuck was urged to hold on around La Rolanderie Farm, to stop the Germans reaching Erquinghem on the Lys. Major Wright coordinated the defence as the 11th Suffolks 'beat off attack after attack' and Captains Rodwell and Canning drove the Germans back each time they broke through.

The plan had been to start withdrawing at 4.30 pm but some men began leaving earlier, encouraging the Germans to advance from Bois Grenier. They tried to push past the 9th Northumberland Fusiliers and cut off the 20th Middlesex and 13th Green Howards, but rearguards, organised by officers like Second Lieutenant Williams and Captain de Quetteville, allowed most of 103 Brigade to reach the river.

Brigadier General Chaplin's men were supposed to cross the Lys west of Armentières but the Germans had already reached the railway bridge. A few brave men swam across but the rest headed into the ruined streets of Armentières. Lieutenant Colonel Misken led the Green Howards to Pont de Nieppe, fighting off groups of Germans en route. Lieutenant Colonel Vignoles and some of the Middlesex found his chosen bridge down, so they made a temporary crossing with a stockpile of timber. The rest of the Middlesex, the Northumberland Fusiliers and the Lincolns crossed the main road bridge. They found Captain Clements guarding the bridge with a company of the 18th Northumberland Fusiliers and Major Russell waiting patiently to blow up the bridge.

Russell had orders to demolish the bridge after 102 Brigade had crossed but he was aware others were still looking to escape, so he stayed long into the night, allowing 103 Brigade to escape. Eventually a group of Germans were seen approaching but they chose to take cover behind boxes of Mills bombs. A few minutes of concentrated fire created a minor explosion and then a larger blast dropped Pont de Nieppe into the river.

The attack north of Fleurbaix aimed to drive 101 Brigade across the Lys, so Brigadier General Gore had asked for help to hold Erquinghem. DuCane deployed 147 Brigade from 49th Division and Brigadier General Lewes sent the 1/4th Duke's to reinforce the front line while the 1/6th and 1/7th Duke's manned the Nieppe Switch.

Lieutenant Colonels Tuck and Lloyd were hard pressed but the 11th and 12th Suffolks held on at La Rolanderie Farm. Lieutenant Colonel Stephenson's mixed group of 15th and 16th Royal Scots were pushed back slowly towards Erquinghem and Major Warr was captured during their dogged defence. Meanwhile, Major Jackson's X Battalion, a mixture of Australian tunnellers, details and stragglers, continued to cover the river bank near Fort Rompu.

There was chaos on the north bank, where the Germans were capitalising on their bridgehead at Bac St Maur. Stephenson had sent Captain Bayliss across the river only to find the 3rd Worcesters falling back, so the Germans could fire into 101 Brigade's flank.

The Germans were also pushing along the river bank and a messenger ran up to X Battalion shouting 'Jerry is over the canal, get back quickly!' Major Campbell headed back to confirm the order and was never seen again, so his subordinates withdrew X Battalion to Erquinghem where they crossed a pontoon bridge. They were followed by Stephenson's Royal Scots.

The Erquinghem bridge was already down by the time the Suffolks arrived, so they began filing across the temporary foot bridges. Unfortunately, the 'Boche came along the north bank so quickly that the bridges had to be destroyed to stop them falling into his hands before all were over. So about a platoon of each battalion fell into the enemy's hands.'

The heroic fighting around Streaky Bacon Farm and La Rolanderie Farm had given time for most of 34th Division to escape. Only a few of Major General Nicholson's men were captured but many died fighting their way back to the Lys. Most of their stories will never be known but the last stand of one brave member of the 34th Machine Gun Battalion eventually reached him:

> *The Germans were held up by a single machine gun so an officer eventually raised a white flag and went forward to ask the team to surrender. He found only one man alive and he refused to give in because he wanted to die with his comrades. The officer could not change his mind, so he went back to his men and the lad fought until he was killed.*

Once across the river, 34th Division's battalions formed a salient around Pont de Nieppe and along the Bailleul railway. The Bailleul road ran behind the front line and it was jammed with people and vehicles:

> *Many very strange sights were to be seen in Nieppe this afternoon; comedy and tragedy were strangely mixed. The parties of refugees flocking down the road... Wounded came streaming through and weary, dirty men searching for their units. Every now and then shells dropped among the buildings and on the road and bullets from the adventurous machine gun intruders whistled by.*

Lieutenant Colonel Sugden's 1/4th Duke's was the last battalion to cross the Lys and 'there were many sad scenes for the inhabitants who had clung to their beloved homes, and even now were loath to quit them. They kept returning amid the shells and bullets to save some specially valued article.'

Captain Farrar's company stopped the Germans reaching the main bridge while Second Lieutenant Clarke covered the temporary bridges. Luck was on Captain Kirk's side when the Germans occupied a farm close to his company: 'Careful observation revealed that a large store of Mills bombs and Stokes shells were in an outhouse against the wall of the farm. Lewis guns were trained on this dump and fired for some minutes without success; but, suddenly, the whole dump blew up completely destroying the farmhouse.' Farrar and Clarke would hold onto the west side of the village until nightfall.

The rest of the Duke's had been unable to reach the 11th Suffolks, south of Erquinghem, so Captain Luty and Lieutenant Machin had fallen back to a railway line. Private Arthur Poulter then repeatedly went out to rescue ten casualties and bandaged up over forty men under fire. Runners could not find Luty with the order to escape across the river, so he withdrew the survivors to the river, only to find the bridges down. One platoon was forced to surrender while the rest made a run for it along the river bank, until they found a bridge to cross: Poulter rescued another two men en route but was wounded making the final attempt; he would be awarded the Victoria Cross.

The Duke's stand had allowed hundreds to escape across the bridges between Erquinghem and Armentières. Only twenty of Luty's men escaped, most of them wounded, and they encountered shocking scenes on the north bank of the Lys:

> *The sight on the Nieppe–Bailleul road that night was such as none of the battalion had seen before, nor any wished to see again. There were practically no vehicles but the whole road was crowded with men hastening to the rear. It was an army in retreat. But the crowd of men was not disorderly; there was no panic. As each one reached his allotted station he quietly fell in, ready to hold a fresh line.*

All along the north bank of the Lys, units were getting the order to withdraw. It was difficult but there was no panic and moves were carried out 'with no little fatigue to the men, owing to the darkness and to the fact the roads were congested with terror stricken refugees who were seeking safety in flight to the north and west'. By the early hours, the brigades of 34th Division and 49th Division were deployed along the Armentières–Bailleul railway, facing south-west with some holding a salient around Pont de Nieppe, facing the Lys. 'The hard-pressed troops knew nothing of what was happening elsewhere. Since midnight all wires had been cut. They were weary but they held on doggedly…'

The mixed group of brigades deployed around Armentières had fought off the Germans but they had ended up in a confused position. The three 34th Division brigades were side-by-side along the Bailleul railway with 147 and 121 Brigades in support.

Major General Nicholson had welcomed the arrival of 88 Brigade, one of 29th Division's brigades, on his right flank. Brigadier General Freyberg VC (awarded for leadership during the 1916 Somme campaign) had marched his men through Bailleul, finding it 'crowded with fugitive civilians and generally in a state of turmoil and confusion'. They had to advance off the road, to avoid the traffic jam, and in open order, in case they encountered the enemy. En route, Freyberg learnt that the Germans were in Steenwerck, so he decided to dig in alongside a line of field guns which were 'firing over open sights with apparently no infantry in front'. The 2nd Hampshires and 4th Worcesters filled the gap between 34th Division and 74 Brigade, completing a solid front facing Steenwerck.

The line was safe for now but the supply wagons were struggling to find their units, leaving men short of ammunition and rations. So the scroungers spent the night searching abandoned canteens and houses for food and a few lucky souls were able to toast their good luck with bottles of champagne. The soldiers also helped themselves to the livestock wandering around the deserted farms.

25th Division and 40th Division, Bac St Maur Back to Steenwerck

Lieutenant General DuCane had wanted the 300 survivors of 40th Division to capture Croix du Bac but Brigadier General Craigie-Halkett pre-empted his order to attack. He advanced while the river was still shrouded in mist but 74 Brigade were stopped by heavy fire. The first counter-attack penetrated between the 9th Loyals and the 11th Lancashire Fusiliers and the second drove back the flanks of the Lancashire Fusiliers and the 3rd Worcesters.

The Germans pushed the three battalions back beyond Steenwerck, 'paying heavily for every yard he gained', taking 119 and 120 Brigades with them. Lieutenant Colonel Martin was reported missing while other officers, including Major Pares and Major Brown, rallied the groups of men scattered among the hedges and ditches. A few Germans drove the 3rd Worcesters from the Bailleul railway line but the 1/4th Duke's helped hold them at bay until 88 Brigade arrived.

Brigadier General Hobkirk had deployed the 300 survivors of 119 and 120 Brigades in the Steenwerck Switch. A midday attack drove the 12th Green Howards (Pioneers) back towards Sailly but the main thrust pushed 74 Brigade north through Steenwerck. It meant the Germans were around both of Hobkirk's flanks, so his men fell back nearly a mile towards Doulieu. The withdrawal had compromised XV Corps' line, but the Germans stayed in the village, allowing Hobkirk's men to retake Steenwerck Switch 'at the point of the bayonet'.

As the tired British soldiers dug in around Steenwerck, they wondered why the Germans had not followed up their success. They would not find out until later that they had been too busy looting.

> *More soldiers piled in, bringing bottles of wine and beer.*
> *Outside in the street whistles shrilled. The officers were*

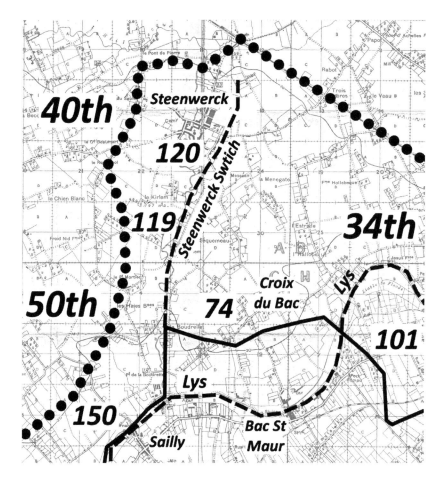

40th Division was driven out of Steenwerck Switch on 10 April. The Germans then looted Steenwerck.

trying to assemble their men again, but nobody paid any heed. Different regiments were arriving by now, but they too followed our example and pretty soon the whole town was filled with men, who for probably the first time in long years, lost the respect for Prussian discipline. On the other side of the street was a large market and grocery store. Other soldiers had already entered there. The place was filled with ham, sausages, cans of delicacies and white bread. Duty was forgotten.

After months of propaganda stating that the Allies were starving, they realised they had been misled. Soldiers were busy eating the fresh food and stuffing the tinned goods into their knapsacks as 'they broke into houses, breaking interiors. They discovered a brewery and started rolling barrels of beer into the street, breaking them open with bayonets and spades, to drink to their hearts content.'

50th Division, Sailly, Estaires and Lestrem
Major General Jackson's three brigades were stretched across 8 miles along the Lys and the Lawe between Sailly, Estaires and Lestrem. His front was strong but he had to deploy the 5th Green Howards to 150 Brigade's left flank, where the Germans were widening their bridgehead around Bac St Maur. But fresh attacks from La Bouderelle pushed Lieutenant Colonel Thomson's men behind the 4th Green Howards and 2nd Scots Fusiliers around Sailly.

The situation was looking bleak for 150 Brigade but help was on its way. Major General Douglas Cayley visited Brigadier General Rees to tell him that 87 and 86 Brigades of 29th Division were marching to the front. The head of the column was already at Neuf Berquin, only 3 miles away, so Rees agreed he would hold on as long as possible.

The Germans forced the issue before the reinforcements arrived and the two Green Howards battalions fell back at 4 pm. They occupied a new line around 1,000 yards to the rear and then 'a great contest for fire superiority developed' during which the timely arrival of a limber loaded with small arms ammunition saved the day. The Green Howards failed to tell the 4th East Yorkshires they were withdrawing and they soon found their flank under attack. The Lewis gunner sections held off the Germans until Captain Barr escaped with many of the East Yorkshires but Major Jackson and his staff were captured in their headquarters shell hole.

Brigadier General Riddell had expected the 5th Northumberland Fusiliers to take over the damaged Pont Levis from the 4th East Yorkshires during the night. But a misunderstanding meant there were only a few Fusiliers guarding the bridge at dawn when German infantry charged across 'under cover of violent artillery fire'. A dozen machine guns around Trou Bayard would stop them leaving Estaires until Major Leathart organised a counter-attack by the 6th Northumberland Fusiliers.

Then 'fierce street fighting took place in which both sides lost heavily. Machine guns, mounted in the upper rooms of houses, did great execution on his troops as they moved up to the attack, until they were knocked out by artillery fire.' Leathart's men could not retake Pont Levis and the Germans

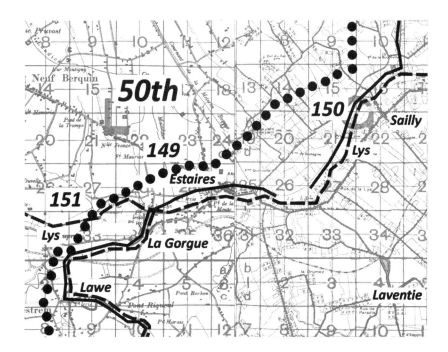

50th Division's left flank around Sailly was compromised while the Germans were able to cross Pont Levis in Estaires on 10 April.

eventually drove them back, so Brigadier General Riddell withdrew 149 Brigade north of Estaires.

Brigadier General Martin's 151 Brigade held the bend in the Lawe canal, near where it joined with the Lys Canal in La Gorgue. The 5th and 6th Durhams stopped the Germans crossing but heavy fire forced them both to withdraw from the bank later in the day.

XI Corps
51st Division, Along the Lawe
Major General Carter-Campbell's Scots were deployed along a 3-mile stretch of the Lawe canal, between Lestrem and Locon. Most were deployed along the west bank but there were bridgeheads at Fosse and Vielle Chapelle. The engineers had been unable to destroy the bridges around the Lestrem loop where 153 Brigade was dug in. The Germans drove Lieutenant Colonel Campbell's 6th Black Watch from Pont de Riqueul early on but the 6th Durhams helped them hold Lestrem. Others

captured Lock de la Rault from Lieutenant Colonel Martin's 8th Durhams but the 7th Gordons stopped the Germans crossing the Lawe south of the loop. Second Lieutenant Scott ordered up a field gun when he saw the Germans digging in close to the stream and the team fired nearly one hundred rounds to drive them away. Captain Richardson's company of 8th Royal Scots would later reinforce the line south of Lestrem.

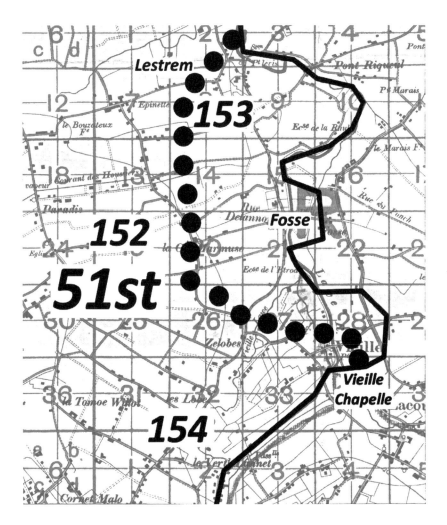

51st Division was driven back from the Lawe Canal between Lestrem and Vieille Chapelle on 10 April.

The German infantry then regrouped while the gunners manhandled their weapons forward, so they could shell the Scots. The evening attack forced the 6th Black Watch and 7th Gordons back, driving the 5th Seaforths from Fosse on 152 Brigade's left at the same time. They were able to cross the Lawe in good order and destroyed the bridge, before rallying on some of the King Edward's Horse.

Captain Christie steadied the 6th Gordons while Lieutenants Stein, Pinckney and Laurenson made sure the rest of the King Edward's Horse held on to Vieille Chapelle. By dusk the Germans had cut off the hamlet. A few of the 6th Gordons collected enough explosives to demolish the main bridge, but there was so much fire directed against the rest of the bridges that the engineers could not reach them.

On 152 Brigade's right, the Germans had crossed the damaged Boundary Bridge in ones and twos and occupied buildings on the west bank of the Lawe during the night. Machine-gun fire raked the 6th Seaforths at dawn and while they stopped reinforcements crossing the stream, they could not drive the Germans back, even with help from a company of the 6th Gordons.

Small parties had used a footbridge to cross the Lawe on 154 Brigade's front during the night and they opened fire on the 7th Argylls at dawn. All day long, machine gun and artillery teams moved their weapons close to the stream but they could not force the Scots to retire. The junction between 51st and 55th Divisions was still intact and Major General Carter-Campbell knew that 61st Division was approaching his beleaguered position.

55th Division, Loisne and Givenchy
General Armin was anxious to drive Major General Jeudwine's Lancashire men back across the Aire canal. There was no attack against the 4th Loyals and 4th King's Own who were holding 164 Brigade's line around Givenchy but there were several against the rest of the division.

The Germans had manhandled captured Portuguese field guns close to the Lancashire front line during the night and they used them to silence machine-gun posts. On 166 Brigade's front the 5th King's Own lost ground around Le Touret and some Germans eventually entered Loisne but the 1/5th South Lancashires helped drive them out. The 5th, 7th and 6th King's on 165 Brigade's front were in high spirits as they stopped attack after attack against Festubert.

Summary, 10 April
There was little air activity in the early morning or late afternoon due to the poor weather but a few contact patrols were able to take off around noon

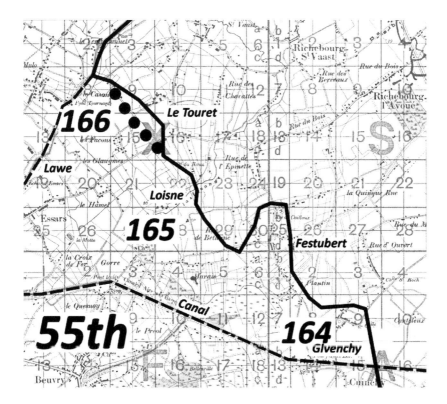

55th Division again held First Army's flank on 10 April, only losing a little ground around Le Touret.

and locate the front line. Many squadrons were busy moving to different airfields because of the German advance but a few managed to fly combat patrols, attacking targets on the busy roads.

Fourth Army's attack north of Armentières had raised a dilemma for Haig and Plumer. Sixth Army's attack had resulted in Second Army's reserves being moved south-west into First Army's area. But Plumer now needed help to stabilise the situation on Messines Ridge. Haig had alerted divisions on the Somme, but they would take time to get to Flanders. He had also messaged Foch for help and he in turn asked General Phillipe Pétain if they could send any reinforcements north. Foch's reply made it clear he did not want the BEF to withdraw unnecessarily because it would encourage the Germans to renew their efforts.

Foch visited Haig during the evening and they agreed the Germans were determined to defeat the BEF, possibly with another large attack on the Somme. The plan was to transfer the 1st Australian Division north to protect Hazebrouck while a reserve of French troops was created near Arras. Haig was encouraged by Foch's promises and he issued a message to let it be known French help was on its way. 'All armies will hold their ground and will employ all their resources to stop any advance on the part of the enemy. French troops are moving north to the assistance.'

Chapter 5

With Our Backs to the Wall

11 April

IX Corps

The early mist lasted until midday, so the British artillery concentrated on hitting roads and likely assembly areas until it cleared. A single division tried to push Lieutenant General Hamilton-Gordon's line off the summit of the Messines Ridge because General Armin had concentrated his forces against IX Corps' right flank. Two would attack Hill 63, while another three waited in reserve to exploit the breakthrough.

9th Division, Wytschaete and Messines

It was difficult to distinguish between friend and foe as the Germans advanced through the dawn mist, so the Scots held their fire until the last minute. All along the line between the Ypres–Comines canal and Messines, 'the attack was broken up by relentless artillery and machine-gun fire, the enemy bolting for shelter in terror-stricken panic.'

On 27 Brigade's front, the 11th and 12th Royal Scots around the White Chateau stopped the Germans advancing out of Hollebeke for the second day in a row. Lieutenant Colonel the Hon David Bruce's 7th Seaforths opened a devastating fire from Damm Strasse, 'cutting deep lanes in the field grey hordes.' The 9th Seaforths (Pioneers) and 8th Black Watch also held on around Onraet Wood on behalf of 26 Brigade.

19th Division, Messines Ridge

Lieutenant General Hamilton-Gordon was concerned about the situation around Hill 63 and Ploegsteert so he met his divisional commanders at Dranoutre during the morning. They agreed IX Corps' right flank would have to withdraw if Hill 63 was lost while 19th Division would have to pull its right back to Wulverghem, at the bottom of Messines Ridge.

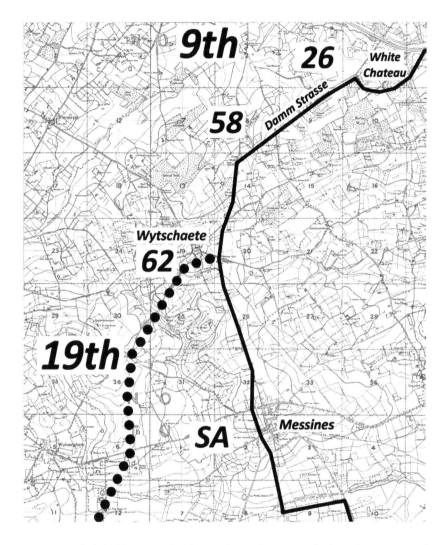

IX Corps' left held on north of Wytschaete but its right lost the summit of the Messines Ridge.

The 2nd Lincolns and 12/13th Northumberland Fusiliers (from 62 Brigade, 21st Division) held onto Wytschaete but a mixed group of 9th Welsh, 10th Warwicks and 5th SWB (Pioneers) were driven back south of the village. This exposed the 2nd South African Regiment's flank but Captain Greene's men held onto the summit of the ridge with help from the 1st Irish Fusiliers and the 12th Irish Rifles (both from 36th Division).

Major General Jeffreys was informed about 25th Division's situation around noon and he warned Brigadier General Cubitt that he had to retire onto 57 Brigade's support line if Hill 63 was lost. But the 4th South African Regiment and 8th South Staffords were already withdrawing from Messines by the time Jeffreys heard the Germans were on the hill. They found the 10th Worcesters, 10th Warwicks and 8th Gloucesters waiting for them in the old British trenches, and they stopped the Germans who were following. It would be dawn before the 9th Irish Fusiliers (also from 36th Division) managed to form a defensive flank across the Douve.

<u>25th Division, Hill 63</u>
Major General Bainbridge's men were in a difficult position with 7 Brigade holding a salient east of Hill 63 and 75 Brigade 2 miles behind its flank. The Germans wanted to drive Brigadier General Hannay's 75 Brigade even further back and the first attack drove a wedge between Major Prior's 11th Cheshires and Lieutenant Colonel Fulton's 9th Cheshires. The second broke through the 6th SWBs and it was down to Second Lieutenant Strong of the 8th Border Regiment to stop them reaching Le Romarin.

The 2nd South Lancashires were the next to be pushed back, allowing the Germans to outflank the 1/4th Shropshires on Hill 63. The situation was precarious but Brigadier General Griffin was told the 1/4th York and Lancasters were being sent up to reinforce the hilltop position, so the three battalion commanders holding the salient agreed to hold on.

Major General Bainbridge then ordered a withdrawal after hearing that an aerial observer had spotted German infantry massing opposite 7 Brigade's salient. The instruction called for outposts to hold the line until dusk while the rest of the men withdrew but Griffin misinterpreted it. The battalion commanders were told to wait, so they could retire under cover of darkness, and the delay resulted in disaster.

The next attack overran the 10th Cheshires, the 4th South Staffords and the 1st Wiltshires, and many men were trapped in the tunnels called the Catacombs under Hill 63. All three battalion commanders were captured as were many of their men; only seventy of the Wiltshires escaped. Major Reade organised those who escaped into the 7 Brigade Battalion.

The loss of 7 Brigade and 34th Division's imminent withdrawal from the Pont de Nieppe salient left Brigadier General Hannay in a precarious position in the Nieppe Switch. It meant the 9th Cheshires and the 8th Border Regiment had to retire to a new line between Le Romarin and Pont d'Achelles during the night.

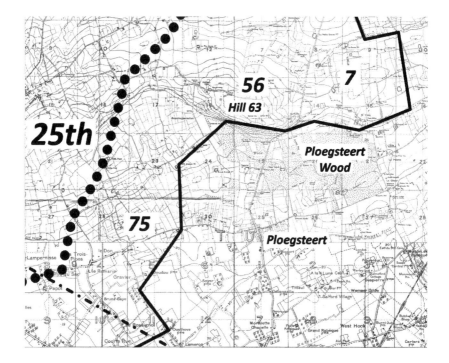

25th Division's right continued to be forced back on 10 April while divisional interference result in a disaster on Hill 63.

XV Corps

34th Division, Nieppe Salient

Major General Lothian Nicholson's brigades were holding a salient around Nieppe. He also had 88 Brigade on his right flank, in contact with 74 Brigade along the Stil Becque stream. The problem was, IX Corps was being driven back towards Neuve Église while the situation around Steenwerck was volatile. So Lieutenant General Beauvoir de Lisle told Nicholson to withdraw his troops through Nieppe to a shorter line around Pont d'Achelles.

The first attack hit 102 Brigade at the head of the salient, pushing Brigadier Thomson's men back to the Nieppe Switch. Captain Dumaresq was never seen again after leading a counter-attack in which 'many Boche were killed and one unwounded prisoner was captured'. But his sacrifice allowed the rest of the 22nd and 23rd Northumberland Fusiliers to fall back to the Nieppe Switch. Brigadier General Hobkirk's 121 Brigade Battalion extended their left flank towards Le Romarin, where 25th Division was falling back. Captain Bryson's rearguard of the 15th Royal Scots allowed the 25th Northumberland Fusiliers and the Royal Scots to escape from the right flank.

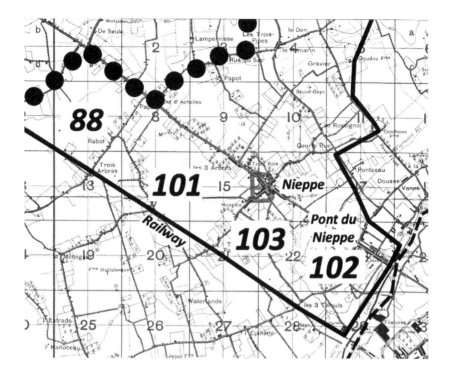

34th Division faced a difficult time extracting itself from the Nieppe salient on 10 April.

On 103 Brigade's front the Germans probed the 1st East Lancashires and 10th Lincolns but one group got behind 101 Brigade on their right. They were about to enter Nieppe when Lieutenant Colonel Richards counter-attacked and closed the gap. A second attempt to drive the 1/4th Duke's from the railway was stopped by 200 stragglers led by 147 Brigade's staff while a counter-attack by Lieutenant Colonel Stephenson's Royal Scots drove the Germans back.

Major General Nicholson gave the order to withdraw to a shorter line around Pont d'Achelles under cover of darkness. Both 147 and 102 Brigades would withdraw along the Bailleul road while 101 and 103 Brigades would follow the railway. The brigade commanders met at dusk to make the final arrangements but 'the night was very dark, detailed maps were scarce, the positions alike of friend and foe were very uncertain and were constantly changing.'

The Germans guessed what was about to happen, so their artillery subjected the Bailleul railway and road to an intense bombardment, forcing companies to move in small groups across country. They then found

German troops holding their rendezvous point at Steenwerck station, so a staff captain had to round them up and take them to a new one.

Brigadier General Lewes had deployed the 6th and 7th Duke's of 147 Brigade across the Nieppe road while the 1st East Lancashires covered their position. Once every one had passed through, the 7th Duke's stayed behind, hoping to catch the Germans, but they did nothing. By dawn 88 Brigade was holding a line around Pont d'Achelles while 102 Brigade extended the line back to Steenwerck station. For the second night in a row, Nicholson's men had escaped Sixth Army's clutches, but as they looked back, 'the whole eastern sky was lit up by burning villages and petrol dumps.'

The Steenwerck Re-Entrant
Brigadier General Freyberg had no idea where the enemy were in front of 88 Brigade until Captain Ozier's company of the 2nd Hampshires found they were still in Steenwerck. There they stayed all day and the Hampshires

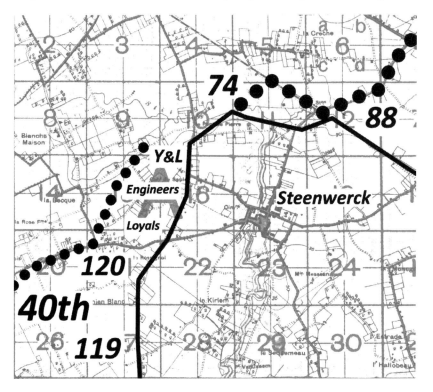

The Germans made little effort to leave Steenwerck on 11 April but they did keep the pressure up either side of the re-entrant.

and 4th Worcesters drove off a half-hearted attack at dusk. Freyberg withdrew his men behind the Stil Becque stream during the night, keeping in contact with 34th Division.

Brigadier General Craigie-Halkett, of 74 Brigade, was in command of a mixed group facing Steenwerck. The 11th Lancashire Fusiliers advanced through the early mist and while Company Sergeant Major Abbott entered Steenwerck, he was soon forced to withdraw. The 1/5th York and Lancasters had joined them just before dawn and the two battalions suffered many casualties as 'the fight was kept up all day, swaying backwards and forwards'.

After two days of fighting, Major General Ponsonby's 40th Division had been reduced to 120 and 119 Brigade Battalions and three engineer companies. An early attack drove them back towards Doulieu, taking Major Nares' 9th Loyals with them, exposing 50th Division's left flank. Major General Jackson sent the 1st Guernsey Battalion, a company of the 2nd Royal Fusiliers and the 1st Lancashire Fusiliers to Le Verrier to help, but they lost many men plugging the gap.

50th Division, Retreat back to Doulieu and Neuf Berquin
The withdrawal from the Lys meant the division was spread too thin because the battalions had suffered heavy losses and they were now in open country. Major General Jackson wanted to establish a better position but he had to maintain contact with the troops to his flanks while driving off attacks. One German division was across at Sailly while a second one had deployed north of Estaires. He did have 87 and 86 Brigades (both of 29th Division) behind his left flank but 31st Division was too far away to help his centre or right.

Brigadier General Jackson had orders to advance 87 Brigade through 150 Brigade's line and counter-attack towards Sailly. But the 5th and 4th Green Howards were 'fighting hard. They held on until practically surrounded and many were captured or left wounded, owing to the impossibility of getting away.' The Germans followed up, engaging the 2nd SWB, the 1st KOSBs and the 1st Border Regiment. The KOSBs 'mowed down attack after the attack' but Major Muir was reported missing, leaving Thwaites in command as the Germans again 'practically surrounded' another position.

Jackson could see no sign of friendly troops to the north, while those to the south-west had withdrawn. His command had suffered heavy losses and while only sixteen of the 2nd SWBs would escape, the KOSBs reported nearly 250 missing and over 200 wounded. Lieutenant Colonel James Forbes-Robertson of the 1st Border Regiment had saved the line several times by riding back and forth, rallying groups of men and directing his

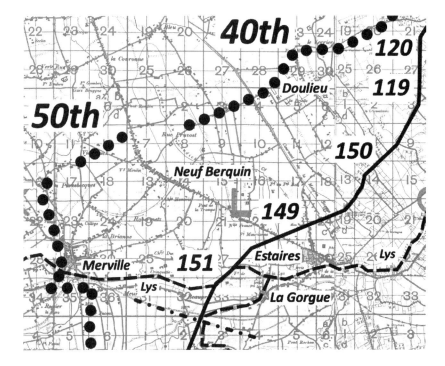

Once Sixth Army was across the River Lys, 50th Division could not hold around Estaires and Merville on 11 April.

officers to danger areas. He led one counter-attack to re-establish the line, continuing on foot after his horse was shot from under him.

The first attack north of Estaires seized Trou Bayard from the 4th Northumberland Fusiliers on 149 Brigade's left flank. Then 151 Brigade was driven back, forcing the 5th Northumberland Fusiliers to fall back astride the Neuf Berquin road. Further fighting in the afternoon was inconclusive but 151 Brigade's withdrawal towards Merville had left Brigadier General Riddell's right flank in danger. After meeting 29th Division's brigadiers, he withdrew the three Northumberland Fusilier battalions north of Neuf Berquin.

The 5th Durhams were driven back slowly towards Neuf Berquin on 150 Brigade's front, so Brigadier General Riddell used the 5th Northumberland Fusiliers to cover the gap across the Neuf Berquin road. The 6th Durhams on the right flank were attacked by 'trench mortars and field guns brought up to close range and snipers firing from behind iron shields'. The Germans penetrated between the two Durham battalions, so the engineers destroyed the pontoon bridge at Beaupré and then they fell back to the bridgeheads in Merville.

The Germans then concentrated on moving reinforcements across the Lys while the 7th Durhams' attempt to drive them back failed. Once enough men had crossed, a new attack was made against the whole of 151 Brigade's line. Some found a gap at Pont de la Trompe but 'the resistance offered along the Neuf Berquin road by the 5th Durhams, which consisted mainly of the battalion headquarters under Lieutenant Colonel Spence, delayed the enemy's advance' for several hours. Spence was wounded as the German machine guns and field guns 'destroyed one post after another', dividing the Durhams into 'small groups of utterly worn out men'.

By the afternoon of 11 April, Major General Jackson had a problem. Both 150 and 149 Brigades were withdrawing north, between Doulieu and Neuf Berquin, but 151 Brigade was retiring west towards Merville. Brigadier General Rees had rallied around 400 survivors of 150 Brigade north of Doulieu. The 4th East Yorkshires assembled under Captain Ralston while the Green Howards gathered under Lieutenant Colonel Thomson.

Jackson instructed Rees to march south and deploy around Pont de la Trompe, alongside Lieutenant Colonel McQueen and the division's engineers. They covered the gap around Neuf Berquin but another attack created a new gap and 'the position now seemed desperate' because Major General Jackson had no reserves to fill it. Field guns were firing over open sights alongside his infantry in a battle which 'was of the hand-to-mouth kind, in which men without maps or overhead direction make what stand they can to cover a continuous retrograde movement'. Despite the problems the Green Howards and East Yorkshires stood their ground until nightfall.

50th Division and 29th Division, The Withdrawal to Doulieu, North of Neuf Berquin and Merville

By dusk XV Corps' centre and right were in trouble because units were mixed up, men had lost their officers and the Germans were too close to the ragged line of tired soldiers. So Lieutenant General DuCane decided to establish a new line, around 3½ miles north of the Lys. It meant the Germans would have to haul everything across the bridges and the congestion would create lucrative targets for XV Corps' heavy guns. DuCane had 31st Division to hand and he instructed Major General Robert Bridgford to deploy his 93 and 92 Brigades west of Steenwerck and Doulieu during the night. Major General Cayley would also withdraw 87 and 86 Brigades north of Neuf Berquin.

A late afternoon attack had cleared Neuf Berquin and the Germans then stopped for the night having found the village wine cellars. One officer

believed 'the only thing that saved us that night was the amount of liquor
the Boche found in Estaires and Neuf Berquin, as I have never heard such
a noise in my life as they made, singing.' A surprise attack by a group of
Northumberland Fusiliers recaptured the north end of Neuf Berquin as the
Germans drank, to create a diversion. Everyone could then withdraw to the
new line and Captain Saltonstall then set up an outpost astride the road, to
stop the Germans leaving Neuf Berquin.

On 151 Brigade's front, the Germans tried to drive the 6th Durhams out
of Merville. They withdrew just before the engineers blew up the last road
bridge around midnight. They had been unable to demolish the railway
bridge south of the town 'but instead of pressing on into Nieppe Forest,
the Germans sacked the wine cellars of Merville and their shouts could be
heard all night'.

31st Division, Reinforcing 50th Division
Brigadier General Williams's 92 Brigade was the first to reach the
battlefield and his men dug in north of Doulieu. Major General Bridgford
had to redirect 93 Brigade towards Steenwerck, after hearing 40th Division
was falling back, but Brigadier General Taylor had to postpone his counter-
attack because it was too dark to organise the infantry and they would have
no artillery support. The delay fooled the Germans, and the 18th Durhams
and 13th York and Lancasters recaptured 40th Division's trenches and
made contact with 74 Brigade north of Steenwerck.

Williams saw to it that the 11th and 10th East Yorkshires completed the
line near Le Verrier but all was not well:

> We were told that when the men in front of us could hold on
> no longer they were to withdraw through our line, leaving us
> to hold up the enemy. But when our patrols went out they soon
> found that there were no British troops ahead of us, though
> there were Germans aplenty.

The final act of a difficult day for 50th Division was the arrival of 31st
Division's third brigade during the night. Brigadier General Butler's 4
Guards Brigade spent the night digging a support line behind Major
General Jackson's right flank. It meant the route into the eastern corner of
the Nieppe Forest had been blocked.

XV Corps Summary
After a day of bitter fighting, Lieutenant General DuCane had authorised
withdrawals to shorten the line. On the left, 34th Division had finally

extricated itself from the Nieppe salient but Major General Nicholson was left with a mixed bag of depleted brigades from four divisions. The centre of XV Corps was now covered by two of 31st Division's fresh brigades and two of 29th Division's battered brigades. The withdrawals had left a large gap north of Neuf Berquin, so the 12th KOYLIs, 31st Division's pioneers, were sent to cover it.

XI Corps
51st Division, West of the Lawe
Four German divisions renewed their attack before dawn. Major General Carter-Campbell's Scots were sheltering in ditches or shell scrapes, knowing there was no barbed wire in front of them. 'They had gone into action considerably deficient of officers and the continuous fighting in the dark had resulted in not only platoons and companies, but also men from different battalions, becoming intermingled.'

Brigadier General Beckwith's 153 Brigade faced Lestrem but the 6th and 7th Black Watch and the 7th Gordons were running low on ammunition. There were no communication trenches and men had to carry everything they needed along muddy ditches or risk their lives in the open.

> *The Jocks were, in spite of their disorganisation, offering a gallant and stubborn resistance but the Germans became bolder as the volume of fire reduced. Forcing gaps through the line, they had pressed their advantage on each flank, bringing up machine guns to very advanced positions. Even light field guns came forward to within very short range.*

There were many casualties as the Scots fell back and officers were targeted as they directed their men to safety.

Brigadier General Dick-Cunyngham's 152 Brigade was holding a narrow salient around Vieille Chapelle on the Lawe. The 1st King Edward's Horse and 6th Gordons had been holding the bridgehead since the battle started but the 5th and 6th Seaforths were being pushed back on both flanks. The Germans focused on the 8th Royal Scots (Pioneers) around La Croix Marmuse on the north side of the salient. They overran Captain Richardson's company before fanning out to the north and south and both Major Humphreys and Captain Fleming were wounded as the Royal Scots fell back.

Machine gun teams began firing from the upper stories of farm buildings so the Scots pointed them out to hidden field guns and they were soon silenced. Company Sergeant Major Dickson had to take command of

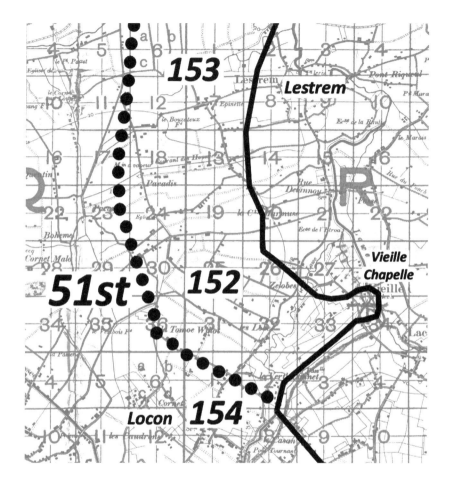

Sixth Army continued to push 51st Division back from the Lawe Canal on 11 April.

the Royal Scots' front line after all his officers were hit, but Major Todd eventually took command of the battalion and gave the order to fall back towards Pacaut.

The Germans moving south from Croix Marmuse took the mixed group of Seaforths and Gordons around Zelobes in the flank, cutting off the men in Vieille Chapelle. The last pigeon message to reach Brigadier General Beckwith from Captain Christie said the situation was 'almost unbearable'. Christie was twice wounded trying to break out of Vieille Chapelle and his small band of survivors fought on until their ammunition ran out mid-afternoon. Their brave stand at Vieille Chapelle had helped the rest of 152 Brigade to make their escape.

The withdrawal of the infantry meant the artillery had to relocate but battery commanders were careful to move their guns back one at a time, so the infantry always had artillery support. Many crews continued firing over open sights until the enemy machine guns were in range, and some of the 8th Royal Scots gave covering fire while others helped load the shells. Once ready, the horse teams cantered forward so the gunners could limber up and escape to new positions.

The continued pressure on 51st Division meant that companies fragmented in small groups of men, often led by a sergeant or corporal, and some were left behind during the retirement. Brigadier General Beckwith was one of the many casualties, and an artillery officer, Lieutenant Colonel Dyson, organised the 200 survivors of 153 Brigade around Pacaut with the help of two British and two Australian artillery officers who had volunteered to lead them.

61st Division, Marching into Battle
The battalions of 61st Division had been marching to the sound of guns all morning and the 2/6th Warwicks and 1/5th DCLIs (Pioneers) were deploying alongside the Scots by the early afternoon. The DCLI had just welcomed a new commander, Major Ward, and his first task was to organise over 420 drafts. They went straight into action and 'the change from the barrack square to the firing line against a well-trained, war bitten enemy was a terrible experience.'

The Germans renewed their attack against 51st Division's flanks late in the afternoon. The 1/5th DCLIs had to fall back when 50th Division withdrew through Merville, across the Lys, and they reformed on the Ancienne Lys stream. The 5th Gordons extended their flank while 153 Brigade straightened out its line around Pacaut. The attack at the south end of 51st Division's line drove the 7th Argylls away from Boundary Bridge but the 4th Gordons held on north of Locon. Lieutenant Colonel Hopkinson's 4th Seaforths' extended the flank north to keep in touch with the 152 Brigade around Pacaut.

Lieutenant General Haking's plan was for Major General Colin Mackenzie's division to relieve 51st Division that night. But he had also sent over one hundred machine gun teams to the Clarence stream, in case the Germans broke through before it arrived. The Vickers guns of the 39th Machine Gun Battalion were deployed between the Lys and Calonne while the 1st Tank Brigade's Lewis guns covered the Clarence stream between Merville and Robecq.

3rd Division, Hinges

Major General Cyril Deverell had already handed over 9 Brigade and his artillery to 55th Division. Lieutenant General Henry Horne instructed him to move his other two infantry brigades to Hinges, where they could support either 51st Division or 55th Division. Deverell was also told to report to Lieutenant Colonel Haking at XI Corps headquarters.

55th Division, Lawe Canal to the Aire Canal

Major General Jeudwine had to extend his left flank as far as the Lawe canal, to relieve part of the beleaguered 51st Division. He had been given 9 Brigade from 3rd Division but it still extended his front to over 5½ miles long. The 'enemy shell fire was terrific: in many parts of the line, and particularly in portions of the Tuning Fork Switch, the breastworks were eliminated.' It meant the line was 'simply a succession of men of mixed units strung out at wide intervals, who had scratched themselves into the ground with their entrenching tools under heavy rifle and machine-gun fire'.

A mid-morning attack pushed the 1/4th South Lancashires (Pioneers) back to the canal near Locon, on 166 Brigade's left flank. Lieutenant Yatman was killed leading a counter-attack with a mixed group of 1st Northumberland Fusiliers, pioneers, engineers and machine gunners but 'a very dangerous gap was filled at a critical moment.'

A mid-afternoon attack captured Cailloux Keep from the 1/5th King's and Festubert East Keep from the 1/7th King's on 165 Brigade's left. Lieutenant Colonel Buckley organised a group of the 1/5th, 1/6th and 13th King's, and Major Keet and Captain Barratt led the counter-attack which recaptured them both. Again the Germans did not try to take Givenchy from 164 Brigade.

Brigadier General Kentish was happy with 166 Brigade's performance but he was disappointed by 'the shelling of our front, support and reserve lines by our own artillery. I am loathe to refer to this, because I do not think that this can ever be helped when fighting is of the open nature it was. I think, however, that brigade headquarters might reasonably expect to be immune, situated as we were 800 yards from the front line at the nearest point.'

Summary, 11 April

The mist cleared by midday and the aerial observers noted that Sixth Army was driving towards Hazebrouck. So far the Germans had advanced 8 miles in just three days and the town was only another 6 miles away. Their infantry had almost reached the Nieppe Forest while their heavy artillery were nearly in range of the rail junction.

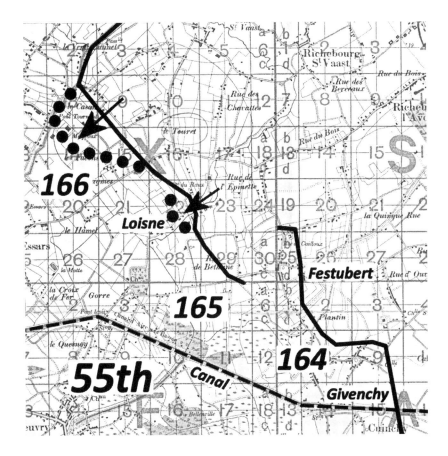

55th Division only lost a small amount of ground around Le Touret and Loisne on 11 April.

Haig visited Plumer during the afternoon and while they agreed that the worst was over, there was still hard fighting ahead. All GHQ's reinforcements would support First Army while Second Army would shorten its line, to create its own reserve. Plumer instructed II Corps, VIII Corps and XXII Corps to withdraw from the Ypres Salient, a place which had cost so many lives to capture only six months before. Haig agreed that XV Corps would transfer to Second Army, leaving Horne to control the battle south of the Lys. It left Plumer in control the front north of the river and he wanted IX Corps to withdraw to a shorter line between Wytschaete, Neuve Église and Steenwerck.

Haig wanted the French infantry divisions west of Amiens to move further north, so he sent his chief staff officer, Major General John

Davidson, to ask Foch. He refused but he did offer to send a cavalry corps north. Haig declined the offer because he thought thousands of horses would interfere with his line of communications. The BEF would just have to stand and fight.

Haig issued a special Order of the Day on 11 April, one which would become known as the famous 'Backs to the Wall' order. The troops knew they were in a tough fight but this was the first sign of how serious the situation was:

> *Three weeks ago today the enemy began his terrific attacks against us on a 50-mile front. His objects are to separate us from the French, to take the Channel Ports and destroy the British Army. In spite of throwing already 106 Divisions into the battle and enduring the most reckless sacrifice of human life, he has as yet made little progress towards his goals. We owe this to the determined fighting and self-sacrifice of our troops. Words fail me to express the admiration which I feel for the splendid resistance offered by all ranks of our Army under the most trying circumstances. Many amongst us now are tired. To those I would say that Victory will belong to the side which holds out the longest. The French Army is moving rapidly and in great force to our support. There is no other course open to us but to fight it out. Every position must be held to the last man: there must be no retirement. With our backs to the wall and believing in the justice of our cause each one of us must fight on to the end. The safety of our homes and the freedom of mankind alike depend upon the conduct of each one of us at this critical moment.*

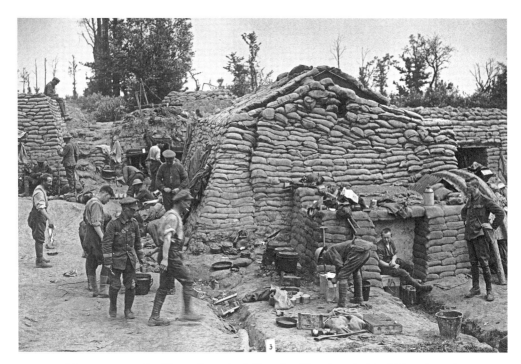

The engineers had been busy building fortifications behind First Army's line.

The artillery had to be ingenious when it came to camouflaging their guns.

Lieutenant General Haking flanked by General Tamagnini and General Costa.

The German heavy artillery move into position near Armentières.

Some of the hundreds of British and Portuguese taken prisoner.

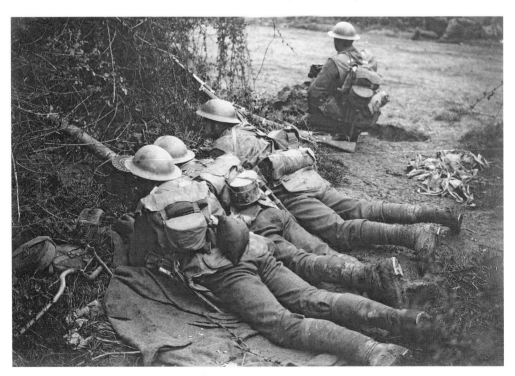

Men had to fight from ditches and hedges during the early stages of the attack.

Reinforcements from 1st Division prepare to move behind I Corps' front.

A young artillery officer gives instructions to his crew out in the open.

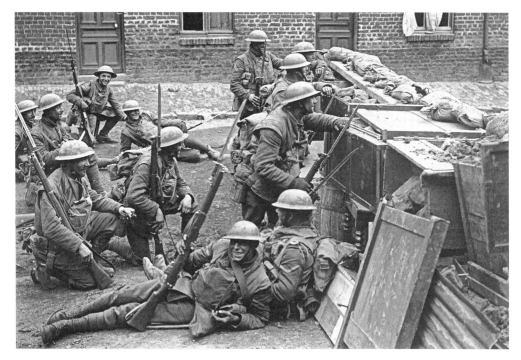

Manning the barricades in the streets of Bailleul, just before it was evacuated.

Men of the 61st Division covering a bridge near Robecq.

Evacuating some of the many casualties on an ambulance train.

Australians dig in after recapturing Villers Bretonneux on 25 April.

A German storm trooper in Pont Arcy on the Aisne.

One of 25th Division's outposts along the banks of the River Aisne.

A few of the many thousands of prisoners taken under guard.

British and French soldiers hobble back to the first aid post side-by-side.

Chapter 6

All Ranks Will Do Their Very Best

12 April

Crown Prince Rupprecht was concerned about the lack of progress and considered whether to call off the attack. He had hoped that the Sixth Army would have reached the St Omer defences by now. General Quast had been told it had been 'a condition of success that the chain of heights [from Kemmel westwards] should already be attained'. Even though 'progress had dropped far behind these expectations' there was still a chance the Flanders hills could be reached if he kept pushing.

There were attacks all along the line but the biggest efforts were directed at two points. One hit IX Corps between Steenwerck and Neuf Berquin and the other was aimed at XI Corps' line, between Merville and Locon. The men had been in action since the first day and brigades were often battalion-sized while battalions were reduced to the size of a company. 'Few men near the front knew what troops were in any neighbourhood beyond their own; even if others were in the same country most of them would be lying under cover or hidden by the hedgerows… All was chaos, no one knew what was happening, or where any troops were.'

There was also confusion behind the line where the supply wagons were trying to deliver food and ammunition to their units. They had to squeeze past crowds of refugees who had suddenly found their homes were within artillery range. 'It was pitiful to see the old French men and women, who had evidently been left behind in the first panic of the civilians, coming slowly along the street, helping themselves with sticks while German shells fell within 50 yards of them.'

The fluid nature of the fighting and the breakdown of established lines of communication made it difficult to track the front line. Aerial observers did their best to monitor the situation but their reports were often out of date. There was clear weather for the first time, allowing the Royal Air Force pilots to fly back and forth over the battlefield from dawn to dusk. More hours were flown, more bombs were dropped, and more photographs were taken on 12 April than on any day since the war had begun.

Second Army
The guns withdrew from the Ypres Salient during the day, a battery at a time, and the infantry followed when it was dark. Supply wagons also worked through the night to remove as much ammunition and stores as they could before dawn. Outposts stayed behind to make it seem that the Forward Zone was still being held in strength, right up to when they too withdrew before first light.

IX Corps
Fourth Army only had one division on Messines Ridge and it 'was apparently content to rest there for a time, and made no further attack'. Brigadier General Tanner's South African Brigade was withdrawn during the night, having stopped the Germans capitalising on the taking of Messines Ridge. The new recruits had shown their 'tenacity in the face of superior numbers and the heavy fighting undoubtedly relieved a serious situation,' but it had cost the brigade nearly 650 casualties.

25th Division, East of Neuve Église
General Armin had four divisions arrayed between Wulverghem and Nieppe, poised to capture the high ground around Neuve Église. It had taken all morning to haul the artillery forward but the observers were then able to bring down accurate fire on 25th Division's line from their new lookout point on Hill 63.

The afternoon attack against 75 Brigade drove the 2nd South Lancashires, the 6th SWBs (Pioneers) and 11th Cheshires back north of Nieppe. Lieutenant Miller led the counter-attack by the 4th South Staffords which restored the line. A second attack during the evening pushed the 4th York and Lancasters and the 4th KOYLIs back, so 148 Brigade was withdrawn to the Green Line during the night. The withdrawals meant the 2nd Worcesters and 16th KRRC of 100 Brigade had to withdraw their flanks back, creating a vulnerable salient south of Neuve Église. The 8th Gloucesters and a company of the 10th Worcesters covered a gap along the Douve stream.

XV Corps
Lieutenant General DuCane had been sent to Foch's headquarters as head of the British Mission, because he was fluent in French. He replaced Lieutenant General Beauvoir de Lisle and found himself responsible

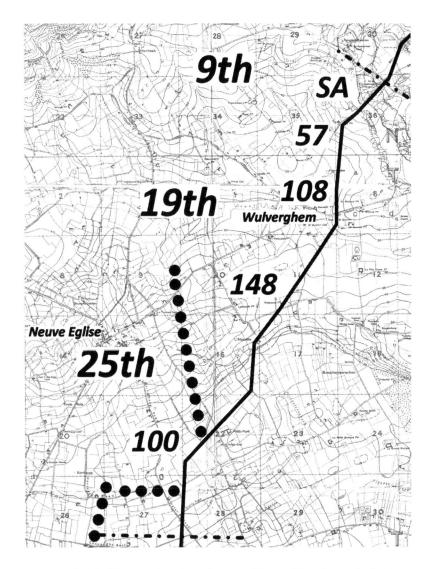

IX Corps' left held around Wulverghem on 12 April but the right flank was driven back towards Neuve Eglise.

for a 9 mile front between Nieppe village and the Nieppe Forest. He commanded a mixture of fresh and exhausted brigades and there had been little time to dig any trenches. All the men could do was find cover in ditches or behind hedges, while field guns were hidden behind cottages and farms. The division and brigade commanders did not think their troops would able to hold on for long against a concerted attack, so they were preparing to withdraw to a new line. Engineers chose the best place to build strongpoints and used stragglers to mark out trench lines (cutting out lines of turf known as spit locking).

There was little artillery fire as the sky lightened, because the German guns were still moving across the River Lys. However, there was plenty of machine-gun fire as six German divisions advanced through the early morning mist.

34th Division, South-East of Bailleul

Major General Nicholson had withdrawn his three brigades into reserve during the night but General Plumer had left him in command of two other brigades south-east of Bailleul. Brigadier General Freyberg's 88 Brigade faced increasingly heavy attacks but the Germans struggled to push their artillery forward from Nieppe to dislodge them. Time and again rifle and Lewis gun fire stopped the infantry advancing but they eventually got behind 1/2nd Monmouths (Pioneers) at Pont d'Achelles. Over 400 of Lieutenant Colonel Evans' men 'who refused to give ground were cut off' and only 150 reached the Newfoundland Regiment who were blocking the Bailleul road.

Lieutenant Moore's men 'fought to the finish, neither he nor his gallant platoon were seen again' and Captain Strong was mortally wounded leading a counter-attack. Their sacrifice had given Lieutenant Colonel Woodruffe time to form a new line across the road. The 2nd Hampshires and 4th Worcesters made sure the Germans did not cross the Grand Becque stream, south of the road, either.

Brigade General Craigie-Halkett's depleted command found itself at the hinge of two attacks. The Germans were intent on pushing 31st Division back and they outflanked the 1/5th York and Lancasters, west of Steenwerck. Major General Nicholson deployed the 16th Royal Scots and 11th Suffolks along the Becque de Flanche stream, but the Germans kept on pushing 31st Division back. The 7th, 6th and 4th Duke's then extended the flank back to Bailleul. Brigadier General Gore had control of the flank and he would later deploy the 9th Northumberland Fusiliers, extending 34th Division's line around the west side of the town.

31st Division, Hoegenacker Ridge

A dawn attack penetrated a gap near Ferme du Bois, between 93 and 92 Brigades. 'A German observation balloon crept unpleasantly near and the air was alive with aeroplanes, which swept low over our lines.' The infantry

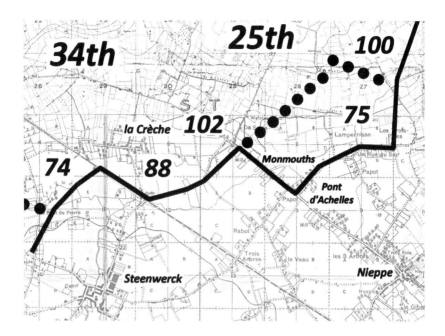

The Monmouths were cut off astride the Bailleul road but the rest of 34th Division held on.

then enfiladed the 13th York and Lancasters to their right and they took the 18th Durhams and the 11th East Yorkshires with them when they retired. Machine-gun fire from Doulieu forced Lieutenant Colonel Headlam's 10th East Yorkshires to abandon their position. 'Successive lines of resistance were held until the Leet [stream] was reached, where we came under the fire of our own batteries.' Some parties became cut off while navigating the ditches and hedges and many had to wade across Meteren Becque, 'a waist deep channel of mud and stagnant water'.

The 15th West Yorkshires and 11th East Lancashires reinforced the line but the enemy 'was now coming on in thick clouds of skirmishers supported closely by mobile trench mortars and light batteries'. Flares told the infantry where to reinforce the line and the artillery where to fire. The attack had left the two brigades isolated and in danger of being overrun, so Major General Robert Bridgford ordered them to fall back to the Bailleul–Hazebrouck railway.

Brigadier Generals Taylor and Williams's men found little cover while the Germans had crossed the railway to the west, and were moving behind the 10th East Yorkshires and 11th East Lancashires. So the two brigades

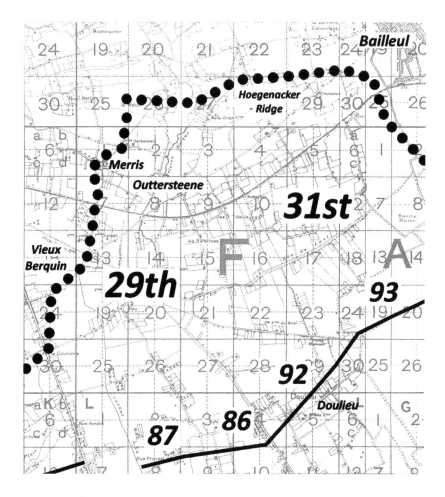

31st and 29th Divisions were forced to retire across the fields and stream to Hoegenacker Ridge, west of Bailleul, on 12 April.

fell back to the Hoegenacker ridge, a long, low hill, south-west of Bailleul. Bridgford's men had fallen back 3 miles but Lieutenant General Hamilton-Gordon had been able to cover the gap which had opened up south of the town.

Brigadier General Gore had deployed his 101 Brigade along the Stil Becque stream north of Steenwerck. Brigadier General Lewes extended the line south of Bailleul with 147 Brigade while Brigadier General Chaplin sent the 9th Northumberland Fusiliers from 103 Brigade to make contact with 31st Division. German cavalry patrols had probed the stream line and Brigadier General Lewes deployed troops into Bailleul after hearing rumours that one group had entered the town.

<u>29th Division, Withdrawal to Merris</u>
Major General Douglas Cayley's position already had a gap on its right flank and then its left flank came under enfilade fire from machine gun teams in Doulieu. The enemy pushed past 86 Brigade's flank, driving the 2nd Royal Fusiliers back towards to Outtersteene. German infantry had also outflanked the 1st KOSBs and they fell back on the 1st Border Regiment who were covering Bleu. The 1st Guernsey Battalion and 2nd South Wales Borderers also had to retire once their flanks had collapsed, taking Lieutenant Colonel Modera's 1st Lancashire Fusiliers with them. Captain Lockwood was left behind during the withdrawal but he fought on until his ammunition ran out; his group then escaped despite being surrounded by the enemy.

Lieutenant Colonel James Forbes-Robertson, 'an officer of outstanding energy and devotion', was in the thick of the fighting with the 1st Border Regiment for the second day in a row. 'He personally superintended the whole of his force, visiting farm after farm, giving orders and ascertaining the position on his flanks.' He again had a horse shot from underneath him but continued on foot until he found a suitable position for 87 Brigade to withdraw to around Vieux Berquin. Forbes-Robertson would be awarded the Victoria Cross for his leadership.

By now battalions were down to a few dozen men and falling back, but the news that the Irish Guards were in Vieux Berquin was 'the first cheering news that we had had for two days'. Stragglers and engineers helped Forbes-Robertson's thin line hold on between Bailleul and Merris until dusk. The fighting then died down and the tired men welcomed the news that the 1st Australian Division was deploying behind them.

Things were confused all along the line south of Bailleul during the night and there were continual rumours that German troops had penetrated the line. Lots of flares made it seem like the enemy were everywhere and 'it was well-nigh impossible for regimental officers to tell the whereabouts of friend or foe.'

XV Corps' Reserves between Bailleul and the Nieppe Forest
<u>33rd Division, Hoegenacker Ridge</u>
Mid-morning Major General Reginald Pinney was told about 31st Division's retirement and he directed Brigadier General Mayne's 19 Brigade to reinforce them. En route they saw 'hundreds of refugees, old men, women and children… wheeling their all in barrows or anything with

wheels and in many cases driving their cows before them. Numbers of walking wounded and stragglers came dribbling back. Those not wounded were collected and absorbed into our line.'

Lieutenant Colonel Seton Hutchison was the 'leader of demonic energy and vehemence' of 33rd Machine Gun Battalion. He went ahead on a reconnaissance and found 31st Division 'in precipitate retreat without officers and saying they had orders to retire'. He half cycled and half begged a lift to get back to his men. He knocked out a driver, stole his lorry and used it to carry his weapons to the spur south of Meteren. He then rounded up all the stragglers he found en route, hitting an officer who refused to help, and used them to stop the Germans reaching Meteren.

Brigadier General Mayne's men found the 18th Middlesex (Pioneers) digging a trench when they moved south of Meteren. During the afternoon Lieutenant Colonel Spens's 5th Scottish Rifles reinforced the line and Captain Kirkwood filled a gap in the line near Hoegenacker mill.

The 1st Scottish Rifles were sent to the right, with instructions to contact the Australians deploying east of Strazeele. The men continued digging well into the night while the horses cantered along the line with ammunition wagons, dropping off boxes for the machine gun teams. The weak link in XV Corps' line around Meteren was safe for the time being.

1st Australian Division, Deployment South-East of Strazeele

Lieutenant General Beauvoir de Lisle was worried the Germans might break through before his reserves arrived and he wanted 1st Australian Division to shore up the line. But rather than push them piecemeal into the gaps, he wanted a new line which the tired troops could fall back through.

The Australians were having a difficult journey north from the Somme. They had reached Amiens to find the station under fire from a German railway gun. One shell nearly hit their train and then planes dropped bombs on the railway sidings. The British engine driver was ready to go but the civilian French station staff had fled. His response when asked to move the train was 'I don't know the points, Sir. I can't start or we might get into worse trouble.' It was several hours before the station staff were found hiding and made to return to work.

Another air attack on St Pol station further delayed the move north and 1 Australian Brigade eventually reached Hazebrouck by dawn. They had a hot meal and dumped their packs and greatcoats, while their officers were given maps with nothing more than a deployment line drawn on them.

They then marched into the unknown. The divisional headquarters had arrived during the night and Major General Harold Walker drove to Second Army headquarters at Cassel, to be told he had to defend Hazebrouck. His three brigades had to create defended locations between Strazeele and the Nieppe Forest.

Captain Blake of 3rd Australian Battalion was the first to locate 40th Division near Merris and his battalion deployed in front of Strazeele with 4th Australian Battalion behind its left flank. Lieutenant Colonel Mitchell's company commanders were told they had to pick 'a line of defence and wait for the Fritzes... They went through empty villages, past empty houses. They were to go along in strict silence but their spirits were up. The men were as proud as punch.' But it soon dawned on them that the situation was critical: 'By Cripes, we are going to be licked... there was nothing between us and the Channel Ports and we felt it was on us!'

The men of 8th Australian Battalion eventually deployed in support of 4 Guards Brigade, south of Vieux Berquin. They had Lieutenant Colonel Herod's 7th Australian Battalion to their right, behind 95 Brigade, and they both had the Nieppe Forest behind them. 'The inhabitants of this part were as pleased as those of the Somme to see the Australians come back; the men met the families and girls on the road, now refugees, who had been known to them, and they were feeling pretty keen on paying some of all this misery back to the Germans.' The Australians had placed another obstacle in front of Hazebrouck but Major General Bridges needed the rest of his division before the line was secure.

50th Division, Vieux Berquin to Merville
Major General Jackson's men had been in action for three days and the weary survivors were strung out between the Vieux Berquin road and the River Lys. Brigadier General Butler's 4th Guards Brigade was behind the division's left flank but there was nothing behind the right and the Nieppe Forest was less than 2 miles away.

Two groups of Northumberland Fusiliers, under Lieutenant Colonel Irwin and Major Temperley, and the Corps Reinforcement Battalion advanced astride the Neuf Berquin road before dawn. There was no sign of 29th Division on their left but Brigadier General Riddell knew that the 4th Grenadier Guards and 3rd Coldstream Guards were close behind.

The Northumberland Fusiliers stood little chance of capturing Neuf Berquin because they had no machine guns and there was only a single battery firing in support. Before long they were falling back, and while they took the 12th KOYLIs (31st Division's pioneers) with them, the

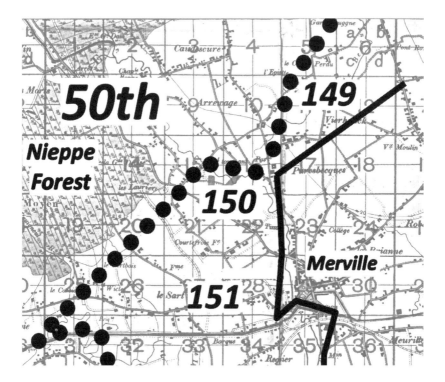

50th Division was forced to abandon Merville after the troops to its flanks fell back.

guardsmen did not budge. 'Many of the troops seem to have known that they were fighting to gain time and enable the Australians to come up.'

Lieutenant Thomson's Green Howards fought astride the Bourre stream, 'taking up and falling back from one position to another, incurring many casualties, but causing great loss to the enemy'. The Grenadier and Coldstream Guards later extended their front towards Vieux Berquin, to cover the ground the Green Howards had lost.

The Durhams of 151 Brigade fought alongside the 7th Black Watch as they were pushed back towards the Nieppe Forest. Lewis gun teams from the 11th Tank Battalion scattered the attackers, while Major Keir launched a counter-attack with stragglers from 50th and 61st Divisions. 'Fortunately, the pressure was not heavy, otherwise the line was so thin and disorganised, and the men so exhausted, that little resistance could have been offered to an assault by heavy masses.' Major General Jackson's shattered command was withdrawn during the night.

5th Division, Covering the Nieppe Forest

Haking had welcomed the arrival of 5th Division at Hazebrouck during the night and it was also late because the railway staff had refused to let their trains leave while Amiens railway station was being shelled. The good news for Haking was that Major General Stephens' division had just returned from Italy and it still had many veterans in its ranks. It had also missed the February reduction to a nine-battalion structure, meaning that twelve full strength battalions were marching forward to take over from 50th Division.

The only problem was that 5th Division's batteries were still on the road, so Major General Reginald Stephens sent his chief artillery officer to organise support. Brigadier General Hussey found chaos at La Motte Château in the middle of the forest: 'the headquarters of three divisions were there temporarily with their lorries and baggage wagons jostled up together in front of the house. All was chaos; no one knew what was happening or where any troops were. It was lucky the place was not shelled.'

Stephens' request to push forward through the forest was granted but his brigadiers were told they would get no assistance. 'There was nothing to be done but to hold on to the eastern edge of the Forest of Nieppe, and that the Division would have to do everything itself. There was no formed body of troops to assist the division and the safety of Hazebrouck and the communications with the Channel Ports depended on it.'

The air was full of rumours of a disaster at the front, including one which stated that German cavalry were roaming the forest. Second Army sent a reconnaissance plane on a mission to check but the observer reported only scattered groups of British soldiers. Brigadier General Jones made sure 95 and 13 Brigades made contact at La Motte au Bois and they then advanced south-east. Major General Stephens 'urged that the line should be in front of the forest and not through it. Indeed, by that time his men had already taken up this line, meeting neither friend nor enemy except a few stragglers of the 50th Division.'

Brigadier General Lord Esmé Gordon-Lennox's 95 Brigade had advanced along the bank north of the Hazebrouck canal. The 1st Devon's deployed astride the Bourre stream and Lieutenant Colonel Worrall sent Captain Veitch forward to hold the lock gates at Pont Tournant. The 1st DCLI deployed on their left flank when it was dark, contacting 4 Guards Brigade around Arrewage. The 1st East Surreys remained in reserve in the forest and they had to deal with the hundreds of refugees from Merville who were looking for food and shelter.

Brigadier General Jones's 13 Brigade also encountered large numbers of refugees, pushing carts and with livestock in tow as they marched through the centre of the forest. The plan had been to drive the Germans back into Merville but the 14th and 15th Warwicks and the 2nd KOSBs were stopped by machine-gun fire as soon as they emerged from the trees. The officers found it difficult to locate the enemy, who were hiding in crops, so they made their men dig rifle pits. The 14th Warwicks were able to capture the Le Vertois brick yards but machine-gun fire from Cornet Malo, across the canal, forced the 15th Warwicks to withdraw their flank. Brigadier Jones had to deploy the 2nd KOSBs to cover the gap.

XI Corps

Horne's memo to First Army echoed that of Haig's 'backs to the wall' message the previous day: 'at this critical period, when the existence of the British Empire is at stake, all ranks will do their very best.'

<u>51st Division, Pacaut back to the Clarence Stream and the Aire Canal</u>
Sixth Army's orders were to bypass the Scots defending Paradis and head for Pacaut Wood, on the north bank of the Aire canal. Major General Carter-Campbell's men were holding a line which 'consisted of few holes hastily excavated in open fields and unprotected by any obstacles, while the country in front was thick with enclosures.' The German infantry crawled forward while it was still dark, overpowering the outposts of the 2/6th Warwicks and while the German trench mortars were accurate, the British bombardment fell short. The Warwicks were overrun and 8th Royal Scots (Pioneers) 'offered lively resistance from his rearward machine-gun nests but one after the other they were silenced and one strongpoint after another was taken.' Many were captured, including Major Todd and Captain Jones, and only a few escaped across the Aire canal when it was dark.

The 5th Gordons were driven back towards Calonne while the 7th Black Watch and 7th Gordons retired on Les Rues des Vaches. Lieutenant Colonel Campbell was killed as the 6th Black Watch fought for Pacaut and they too were forced to retire towards Baquerolles Farm. There was no time to blow up the bridges along the Clarence stream, so the German troops pushed on through the mist. Their 'advance was extraordinarily quick, the troops doing their best to keep on the heels of the retiring enemy. All hostile artillery fire ceased and batteries were found abandoned.' The Scots tried several times to 'improvise lines of defence but, in the absence of officers, these all broke down until the infantry were across the Clarence.' There they linked up with the 5th DCLI.

The headquarters of 153 and 152 brigades were near Le Cornet Malo and Lieutenant Colonel Dyson warned Brigadier General Dick-Cunyngham it was time to leave when the cottage they were using came under machine-gun fire. Dyson escaped but Dick-Cunyngham was captured and the Germans then spread out behind the Scots' flanks and advanced towards the Clarence stream. One party attacked 182 Brigade at Baquerolles Farm while others headed for the bridges at Robecq.

A few Seaforths and Gordons of 152 Brigade formed a flank from 3rd Division's trenches, back to Pacaut Wood. Brigadier General Buchanan organised parties to gather stragglers to cover the bridges west of the wood. He also sent all the pioneers and engineers he could find forward to reinforce 154 Brigade.

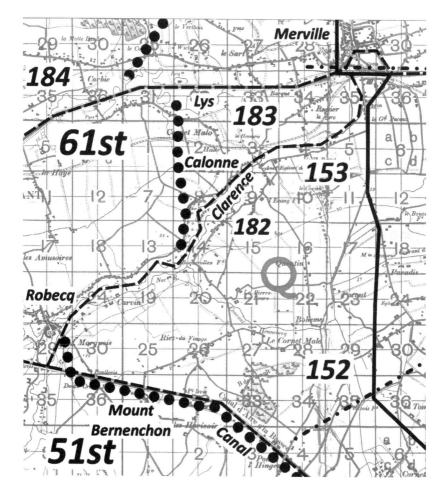

Disaster struck on XI Corps' front on 12 April, as 51st Division was driven back to the Clarence stream.

The Germans advanced so quickly in the mist that they were on top of 51st Division's batteries before they knew it. Lieutenant Colonel Lloyd was warned when the Scots fell back through his battery positions around Calonne. Machine-gun fire and flares showed that the Germans were close, so 'the limbers were brought up at the gallop just as the enemy opened on the position with his artillery'. Most of 12 Australian Brigade's guns escaped towards St Venant but two batteries left it too late and their teams were shot down.

The limbers of 256 Brigade RFA cantered across the Clarence stream, north-east of Robecq, while men rallied by Lieutenant Colonel Dyson and his staff kept the Germans at bay. Sergeant Illidge 'cut out several killed and wounded horses from the different teams, assisted in their hooking up and remained in position until the last gun had left'.

The gunners of 255 Brigade RFA were not so lucky and were taken by surprise west of Pacaut Wood. The limbers were hit by machine-gun fire and a dozen guns had to be abandoned. The rest of the brigade cantered across the canal and Majors Davidson and Jack deployed a gun at each of the bridges. They stopped any Germans crossing with the help of a few men gathered by Major Fairlie.

Sergeant George saw German infantry approaching the Robecq road so he took his limbers forward and warned two batteries that their line of retreat was in danger. A handful of gunners and Warwicks gave covering fire while the batteries raced across the Clarence stream at Baquerolles Farm. A few horses and men were hit but all the guns escaped. The rest of 256 Brigade used another road to escape and all four batteries were soon deployed beyond the canal. The gunners then prepared their guns while their officers rounded up stragglers to man the bridges.

61st Division, Along the Clarence Stream

Major General Colin Mackenzie's division had started to arrive late on 11 April. Lieutenant General Haking's plan had been to relieve 51st Division but the early collapse of the Scottish line meant the South Midland men found themselves in the thick of the fighting, earlier than expected.

Brigadier General Spooner had taken command of the 5th Gordons and 1/5th DCLIs (Pioneers) around Grand Pacaut while the three battalions of his 183 Brigade deployed in support around Calonne. A patrol had discovered that 50th Division had abandoned Merville during the night, so the Gordons had to man the bridges across the Lys. The Germans entered the town before dawn, driving back their bridgeheads before firing across the canal, into their flank. Around the same time, the DCLI found the Germans moving past their right flank and machine-gun fire raked their position, wounding Captains Hodson and Hodge.

Spooner's command began falling back in disorder and the Gordons headed north across the Lys to escape. There they found the 9th Royal Scots and 8th Argylls barring the road in the Nieppe Forest. The DCLI held on until 183 Brigade were driven out of Calonne and they then retired across the Clarence, suffering over 450 casualties. Eventually all the Scots had retired across the stream, leaving 61st Division to hold the front line.

The Germans then turned on 182 Brigade's flank at Baquerolles Farm, where engineers and stragglers held along the Clarence until 184 Brigade arrived around midday. Brigadier General Pagan deployed the 2/4th Ox and Bucks around the farm while Lieutenant Colonel Oates's 2/4th Berkshires covered the bridge at Carvin.

The Scots still had their part to play, because Major General Carter-Campbell made his chief engineer, Lieutenant Colonel Fleming, responsible for gathering all those capable of fighting together. He organised 1,700 officers and men into companies, made sure they had ammunition and deployed them around the Robecq bridges.

I Corps
3rd Division, Defending the Aire Canal
Major General Cyril Deverell had been instructed to relieve 154 Brigade around Locon but the motorcyclist carrying the order to Brigadier General Fisher crashed into a shell hole and had to run the rest of the way. It was dawn before 8 Brigade relieved the Scots and the 1st Scots Fusiliers had to extend their line an extra 1,000 yards before they contacted 152 Brigade.

Fisher had 76 Brigade in support, along the Aire canal and Hamel Switch but the 1st Scots Fusiliers had only just occupied their trench when they discovered the Germans behind their left flank. It had been a day during which 'orders were delayed or received in imperfect form'. All they could do was form a defensive flank where 152 Brigade had once been. Fisher hoped that the 4th Gordons and 4th Seaforths (who they had just relieved) would be able to cover their rear, but he soon learnt that the Germans were in Pacaut Wood, one mile behind his left flank.

Major General Deverell had ridden to the top of Mont Bernenchon and while it was only a low hill, he could see the chaotic situation north of the Aire canal when the mist cleared. He could see fighting along the Clarence stream, the abandoned field batteries of 255 Brigade, the few guns defending the canal and the burning barges sunk by the Inland Water Transport units.

Deverell could also see the thin line of Scots stretching back from 8 Brigade's flank towards Pacaut Wood and the 7th Argylls lined out along

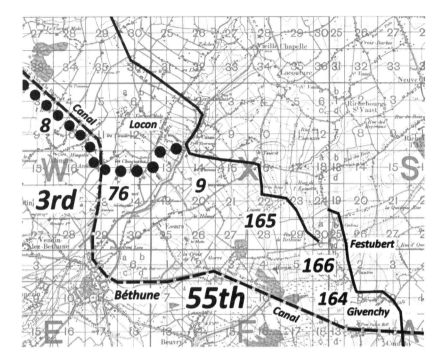

3rd Division was driven back to the Aire Canal on 12 April but 55th Division held on around Festubert and Givenchy.

the canal in front of Hinges. Lieutenant Colonel James and the 170 remaining men of the King Edward's Horse were moving forward to man the bridges and they were all that he had to hold them until the 1st Gordons and 8th King's Own arrived.

An early afternoon attack drove the Scots of 154 Brigade out of Pacaut Wood, forcing the 1st Scots Fusiliers to fall back. Lieutenant Colonel Gillatt's 2nd Royal Scots were also driven from Locon, resulting in 8 Brigade withdrawing behind the Aire canal. Parties of 4th Gordons and 4th Seaforths held on but 'what happened has never been recorded' because no one returned. Major Jobson was just one who lost his life holding off the Germans until dusk. The last stands made the Germans decide against advancing beyond Locon and instead they attacked the bridges on 3rd Division's front. But they failed to capture Avelette drawbridge from the 1st Gordons or Pont Tournant from the 7th Shropshires.

Major General Deverell had been expecting reinforcements from 4th Division and he directed 11 Brigade's three battalions to the Aire canal between Robecq and Pacaut Wood. Brigadier General Wade's men spent a difficult night digging in and 'no one had the slightest idea where the enemy was…' There were no attacks but 'the gun fire that could be heard from every direction might as well have been that of German guns as well as British.'

55th Division, Festubert and Givenchy
Sixth Army had given up trying to dislodge the West Lancashire men, preferring to shell their position instead. During the evening Captain McSwiney and Lieutenant Ellis made a combined attack with the 1/10th King's and 13th King's and they recaptured Route A Keep 'in a brilliant little counter-attack'.

Changing the Front
As Haig spoke with Clemenceau, GHQ staff were reorganising the Lys front to suit the developing battle. The boundary between the Second and First Armies was changed to counter Sixth Army's drive towards the Nieppe Forest. General Plumer would hold the line north-east of the forest while General Horne was in charge of the area south of it. A midday order from GHQ made Lieutenant General Haking responsible for the line from the Nieppe Forest to Robecq. It also meant that XV Corps was now under Second Army.

Foch's headquarters called GHQ during the day to tell them that a corps of cavalry was heading for St Omer, to reinforce Second Army. GHQ had also directed Lieutenant General Charles Kavanagh to shift the British Cavalry Corps behind First Army, as Foch had suggested.

Prime Minister Clemenceau's Visit to GHQ
While First Army was fighting for its life, Prime Minister Georges Clemenceau and his Minister of Munitions, Louis Loucheur, visited Horne and then Haig. They were worried about the safety of the Bruay coal mines, the main source of coal south-west of Béthune. French industry would grind to halt if they were lost. Clemenceau had been told that First Army was holding on but he was concerned that the BEF was running out of reserves. Haig said he faced around twenty-three German divisions while he only had a few understrength divisions left and they were busy absorbing replacements.

Haig asked Clemenceau for French and American divisions to be deployed to Flanders before his line broke. He also asked for lowlands around the Dunkirk area to be flooded as quickly as possible, to secure the coastal flank. Clemenceau knew that General Henry Wilson had already asked Foch for the same things, so he politely suggested making the requests through the correct military channels.

Chapter 7

A Sanguinary Struggle in Some Old Bayonet Fighting

13 and 14 April

By now Crown Prince Rupprecht realised that Georgette would not 'develop into a breakthrough operation on a big scale; it was too narrow, and, in particular, was restricted by the failure on its left wing'; that was at Givenchy. Both Fourth and Sixth Armies were far behind schedule. They were now going to focus on breaking First Army's line at two points. Fourth Army would attack Neuve Église on IX Corps' front and Sixth Army would try and enter the Nieppe Forest on XV Corps' front.

Mist and low cloud stopped air support on the fifth and sixth days of the battle so the British heavy artillery concentrated on shelling the congested roads. Instead ground observers established lookouts in church towers and set up a rudimentary flash spotting system to locate the German howitzers. The German gunners often manhandled their field guns as far forward as they dared to silence the machine guns. However, 'they suffered proportionately heavier losses than the infantry' and the supply wagons found it difficult to get ammunition to their forward positions.

There were attacks all along the line between Wytschaete and Robecq but the German infantry complained that 'the opposition of the enemy was extremely stubborn everywhere. He defended himself especially by means of skilfully built machine-gun nests, which could only be spotted at the last moment.' It was noted that teams deployed their weapons to flank the approaches to the infantry trenches, forcing the German infantry to cross deadly kill zones.

IX Corps
The retirement of IX Corps' right flank had left Lieutenant General Hamilton-Gordon responsible for a huge 15-mile-long sector. Fourth Army was to capture Ravelsberg Ridge west of Neuve Église while Sixth Army

was looking to follow up on its success of the previous day by advancing west of Bailleul.

19th Division, Wulverghem

Fourth Army's attack did not affect 19th Division. However, 25th Division's retirement behind the Douve stream resulted in the 7th Sherwood Foresters withdrawing from Wulverghem.

25th Division, Neuve Église

Fourth Army had three divisions poised to seize Neuve Église from the mixed group of units serving under 25th Division. Artillery observers would then be able to direct the heavy guns from the hill at targets across the Douve valley. Major General Bainbridge had Brigadier General Baird's 100 Brigade east of the village and Brigadier General Green-Wilkinson's 148 Brigade to the south-east. He had deployed a company of the 10th Worcesters to cover a gap on his left flank but he had been unable to cover the gap on his right.

A surprise attack through the pre-dawn mist overran 75 Brigade's composite battalion and some of the Germans turned west against 34th Division. Others found Brigadier General Hannay's men had rallied on the 9th HLI, covering Neuve Église. The rest overran 16th KRRC's headquarters before engaging the 2nd Worcesters' rear while they faced a frontal attack. But the Worcesters fought back-to-back, killing many and capturing fifty prisoners, including a battalion commander. Some of the Worcesters fought their way back into Neuve Église, where they garrisoned the Mairie (town hall) with some engineers.

The stand by the Worcesters and 16th KRRC resulted in a group of Germans being trapped behind 100 Brigade, so they attacked the 1/4th York and Lancasters' rear, on 148 Brigade's left. The Yorkshire men kept them at bay until a counter-attack by Major Wingrove's 1/4th Shropshires scattered them, removing the threat to Neuve Église.

Brigadier General Stansfeld was ordered to send two battalions of 178 Brigade's Sherwoods forward to recapture Neuve Église but their patrols discovered the Worcesters in the village. They also found the 148 and 100 Brigades were still east of the village but there was a huge gap in the line between Neuve Église and Crucifix Corner. Major General Bainbridge sent 71 Brigade (from 6th Division) forward and Brigadier General Brown deployed the 2nd Sherwoods and 1st Leicesters, in case Neuve Église was lost.

During the night, Lieutenant General Hamilton-Gordon sent his senior staff officer, Brigadier General Maxwell-Scott, to talk to Major Generals

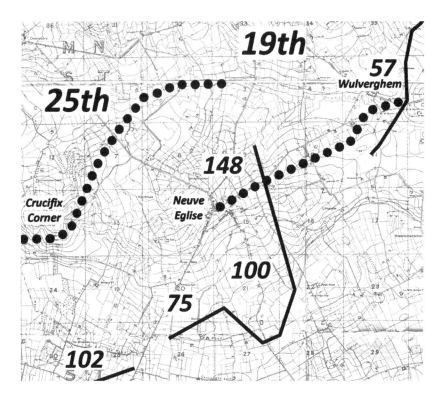

IX Corps only just held onto Neuve Eglise in confused fighting but its line was split in two on 13 April.

Jeffreys and Bainbridge. Jeffreys wanted to recapture Neuve Église hill but Maxwell-Scott disagreed because an attack could be costly. After hearing the results of the discussion, Hamilton-Gordon told Jeffreys he could withdraw west of Wulverghem if his position was in danger.

Major General Bainbridge discovered that his command split into two parallel lines during the night. The survivors of 148 and 100 Brigades were holding a line between Wulverghem and Neuve Église but there was then a large gap back to 71 Brigade between the Douve stream and Crucifix Corner. Fortunately, the Germans were equally disorganised and the Worcesters were able to escape from Neuve Église early on 14 April. It was late in the afternoon before the Germans attacked but the 2nd Sherwoods and 1st Leicesters stopped them.

The Germans withdrew when it was dark, allowing General Bainbridge to withdraw his exposed forward line. The 2nd Worcesters and 16th KRRC evacuated the Neuve Église area while the 4th York and

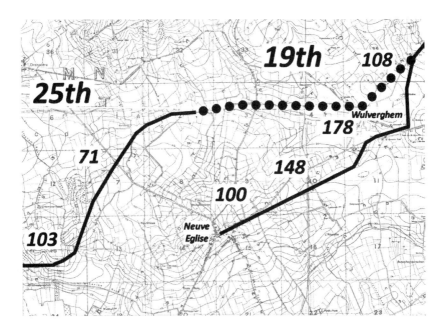

25th Division held on around Neuve Eglise on 14 April but it was time to withdraw to the Douve stream during the night.

Lancasters, 4th KOYLIs and 4th Shropshires withdrew across the Douve; Brigadier General Stansfeld's Sherwood Foresters closed the gap west of Wulverghem.

34th Division, South-East of Bailleul and the Ravelsberg Ridge
Major General Lothian Nicholson had six brigades and they were all weak after three days of hard fighting. They faced six divisions and it was only a matter of time before the numbers started to tell, so the engineers were preparing a position on Ravelsberg Ridge to fall back to, 2 miles to the rear. The infantry stopped the early morning probes but observers guided the German gunners onto their targets as soon as the mist cleared before waves of infantry surged forward.

Nicholson's first problem occurred on his left flank, where a pre-dawn attack had exploited the gap next to 25th Division. Some of the Germans who overran 75th Brigade Battalion fell on 102 Brigade's flank, north of the Bailleul road. Fortunately, the German barrage had fallen short, scattering the frontal attack, so the 23rd Northumberland Fusiliers were able to concentrate on the threat to their flank.

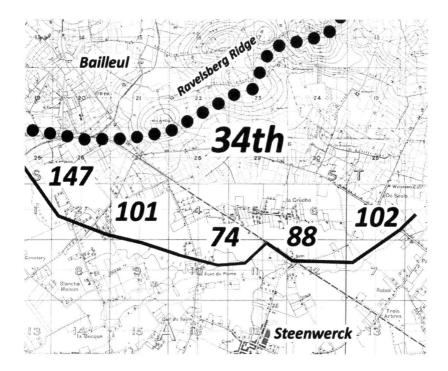

After a hard day's fighting 34th Division's mixed command were forced to withdraw to Ravelsberg Ridge.

Lieutenant Pigg's company of Fusiliers held on until Nicholson deployed the 25th Northumberland Fusiliers and then the Newfoundland Regiment stopped the Germans getting behind his line. Captain Clift's men 'caught a column of Huns in mass' and he then rallied all the stragglers to block the gap in the line. A final attack along the Bailleul road was stopped by the 22nd Northumberland Fusiliers but a single shell wiped out Lieutenant Colonel Studd's staff.

Both 74 and 88 Brigades held on along Stil Becque stream and the 2nd Hampshires and 4th Worcesters stopped the Germans reaching La Crèche. Major Brown was wounded when the Germans attacked the 11th Lancashire Fusiliers on 74 Brigade's right but Captain Beswick made sure they held on around Pont de Pierre and the 3rd Worcesters stood alongside them. A big attack across the Stil Becque stream in the afternoon drove the 11th Suffolks and 16th Royal Scots of 101 Brigade and the 7th and 6th Duke's of 147 Brigade back a short distance.

Major General Nicholson was worried about the situation around Neuve Église on his left flank. The enemy would be able to enfilade his position if they captured it from 25th Division. He considered withdrawing to the Ravelsberg Ridge but Lieutenant General Alexander Hamilton-Gordon instructed him to hold on a while longer because reinforcements were moving up.

Brigadier Generals Thomson and Freyberg were becoming increasingly concerned about the open flank and they discussed how they would withdraw when it was dark. But it was difficult to communicate their worries to General Nicholson because they were relying on runners to take their messages to the divisional headquarters. Hamilton-Gordon eventually allowed Nicholson to withdraw to the Ravelsberg Ridge at dusk, starting with the threatened left flank.

Rumours that the Germans had broken through 88 Brigade proved to be untrue and everyone was relieved when the order to pull back reached the front line. One by one the companies withdrew, each one leaving a Lewis gun team behind to keep the enemy at bay. Brigadier General Thomson's men climbed the east end of Ravelsberg Ridge to find 103 Brigade holding Crucifix Corner. But Brigadier General Freyberg's men had to remain in the front line and the 2nd Hampshires and 4th Worcesters deployed along the rest of the ridge. Brigadier General Craigie-Halkett's 75 Brigade also stayed in the front line and the 3rd Worcesters and 11th Lancashire Fusiliers had to dig in around Mont de Lille.

Brigadier General Gore's 101 Brigade only had a short distance to withdraw to the south edge of Bailleul but the town 'was incessantly strafed and, at times, was almost hidden under a pall of red brick dust and shell fumes'. One large-calibre shell hit the cellar where 74 and 101 Brigades had their headquarters. A shaken Craigie-Halkett was dug out of the ruins but Gore was killed and Lieutenant Colonel Stephenson had to take command of 101 Brigade.

Major General Nicholson's men spent the night entrenching, which was 'hard work for weary men, many so tired they fell asleep while trying to dig'. Fortunately, the Germans were as tired as his own men and they made no effort to locate the new line during the night. By the early hours of 14 April battalions from seven different brigades were lined out along the Ravelsberg Ridge and around the south side of Bailleul.

The Germans wanted to capture the highest point on the ridge, and a pre-dawn assault hit 103 Brigade's line around Crucifix Corner. The 9th Northumberland Fusiliers 'drove off the Boche, deceiving them as to their numbers by their loud shouts'. Lieutenant Rowe was then killed leading 'a sanguinary struggle in some old bayonet fighting' while Lieutenant Vignoles' battalion staff helped regain their trenches.

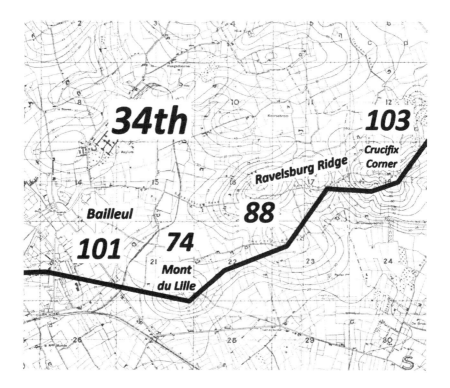

34th Division's mixed command drove off all attempts to take Ravelsberg Ridge.

For the rest of the morning, 'the enemy was observed dribbling troops forward', using ditches and hedges to get closer. The bombardment was weak and the Lewis gunners stopped the German infantry climbing the slope. The British artillery then hammered the shallow jumping-off trenches as the Germans regrouped. No ground had been lost but casualties were mounting and Nicholson was running out of reserves.

A second attack drove 75 Brigade Battalion from the north side of Crucifix Corner. At one point there were so many Germans on the ridge 'it seemed to our men as if they were fighting in a hollow square with the enemy practically all around them.' Major Reade then 'made a magnificent counter-attack', taking one hundred prisoners, but Lieutenant Colonel Fulton was killed and Major Busfield had to take command of the 9th Cheshires. A third attack in the afternoon was stopped and Crucifix Corner remained in 75 Brigade Battalion's hands.

It was the same story all along Ravelsberg Ridge as the elite Alpine Corps threw its weight at the depleted battalions of four brigades. The

9th Northumberland Fusiliers, 10th Lincolns and 1st East Lancashires of 103 Brigade held onto the east end of the ridge. Ground was taken from the 2nd Hampshires and 4th Worcesters only for men from 88 Brigade to recapture it. The 3rd Worcesters, 11th Lancashire Fusiliers and 5th York and Lancasters lost Mont de Lille in 74 Brigade's sector. But Second Lieutenant Ward 'cleared the crest of the hill, driving the enemy down the steep slope' with some of the Lancashire Fusiliers and the 9th Loyals.

On 101 Brigade's front, the survivors of the 15th and 16th Royal Scots under Major Osborne and Lieutenant Colonel Tuck's 11th Suffolks stopped the Germans entering Bailleul from the south-east. Second Lieutenant Kitson was killed when the Germans captured a steam mill from the 1/4th Duke's, but the 1/7th Duke's stopped the enemy penetrating 147 Brigade's line, south-west of the town.

Battalions were the size of companies commanded by captains and companies were the size of platoons led by lieutenants but 'neither shell nor bayonet could move' them. Two brigades from 59th Division arrived at dusk and prepared to take over from Nicholson's battered battalions. After five days of fighting the survivors were looking forward to a rest.

33rd Division, Hoegenacker Ridge

After falling back 3 miles the day before, Major General Bridgford was relieved that the Germans needed time to reorganise before attacking again. His men connected their rifle pits as the German infantry edged forward and reported the British positions to their artillery. Afternoon attacks drove the Corps Reinforcement Battalion and the 1st Queen's back a short distance but they stopped the Germans reaching Meteren. The 5th Scottish Rifles withdrew alongside after dusk while the 'flaming thatch of the cottages lit up the country around'.

The first attack on 14 April hit 19 Brigade's line at dawn, driving the 1st Queen's back towards Meteren. They were 'reinforced by a brave advance of some men of the New Zealand Entrenching Battalion supporting the demonic Hutchison's machine-gunners of 33rd Machine-Gun Battalion. Some of 31st Division's men remained in the line to help and Lieutenant Colonel Tilly of the 15th West Yorkshires was killed leading them. The 1st Scottish Rifles held onto the rest of the line and 5th Tank Battalion's crews reinforced Brigadier General Mayne's position with forty Lewis guns during the night.

XV Corps

31st Division and 29th Division, Vieux Berquin

The burning buildings in Bleu silhouetted the infantry advancing towards the survivors of 86 and 87 Brigade north of Vieux Berquin before dawn.

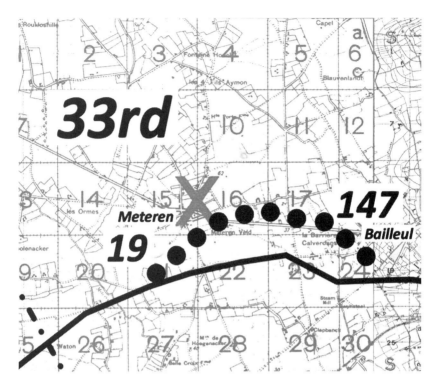

33rd Division had a desperate struggle for Meteren, west of Bailleul.

Rifle and machine gun fire scattered the first two attacks but a third one forced the outposts to retire. Machine gun teams then moved forward and enfilade fire forced Major General Cayley's men back towards the Australian line in front of Strazeele.

The 12th KOYLIs (Pioneers) fought to hold onto Vieux Berquin but the German artillery and machine gun teams worked together to make the ruins untenable: 'The German field-guns were brought up to close range, so they fired direct on the British posts. Shortly after noon an outburst of intense machine-gun fire on the left told where part of the outflanked KOYLIs was trying to retreat across the fields.' The British guns shelled the village as soon as they heard the news, driving the enemy back to the church. Cayley's battered battalions were withdrawn during the night, leaving the Germans facing the fresh Australians who had spent the past twenty-four hours digging in.

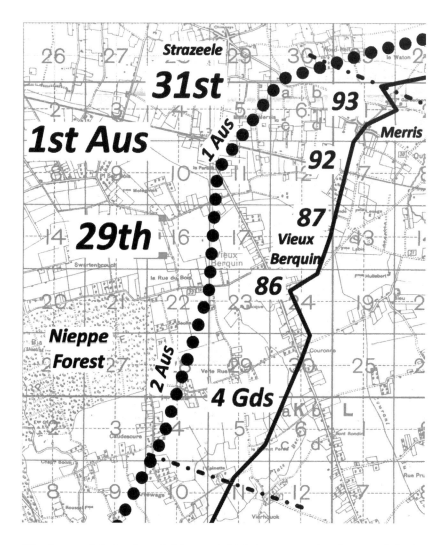

The battered brigades of 31st and 29th Divisions fought on while 1st Australian Division blocked the roads to Hazebrouck on 13 April.

The line held by the 4 Guards Brigade, south of Vieux Berquin, was too long for the guardsmen and there was too little artillery but they stopped the waves of Germans advancing from Neuf Berquin. Only forty of Captain Thomas Pryce's 4th Grenadier Guards had survived the night but they repeatedly thwarted attempts to advance along the Vieux Berquin road.

He eventually led a bayonet charge to drive the enemy back but only one man returned and the rest were never seen again. Pryce was posthumously awarded the Victoria Cross.

The 3rd Coldstream Guards stopped an armoured car with machine-gun fire but they could not stop the Germans penetrating their flank next to the Grenadier Guards. A company of the 2nd Irish Guards sent forward by Lieutenant Colonel Alexander to plug the gap was wiped out, so the headquarters of the Coldstream and Grenadier Guards joined in the fight. The guardsmen refused to retire onto the Australians, who were digging in behind them; only 250 survived to escape at nightfall.

The heroic defence around Vieux Berquin had given the 1st Australian Division time to deploy and dig in as reported in Haig's despatch: 'The performance of all troops engaged in this most gallant stand, and especially that of the 4th Guards Brigade, on whose front of some 4,000 yards the heaviest attacks fell, is worthy of the highest praise. No more brilliant exploit has taken place since the opening of the enemy's offensive, though gallant actions have been without number.'

1st Australian Division, Strazeele and the Nieppe Forest

Lieutenant General de Lisle had stuck to his plan of letting 1st Australian Division form a new line in front of Hazebrouck. The first four Australian battalions had deployed between Strazeele and the Nieppe Forest, taking cover in ditches and behind hedges, on 13 April. They spent the night scraping out trenches but they 'could not be dug deep, on account of water, and consequently the support companies had to build themselves breastworks of turf and earth piled between wattled stakes. For the support line, where it ran through the forest, the best defence was the concealment given by the trees.'

The rest of 1 and 2 Australian Brigades had deployed during the night and they started building lines of defence, blocking the roads leading to Hazebrouck. On the Strazeele road the 12th Australian Battalion dug in at Bourre with the 10th Australian Battalion behind it. Meanwhile, the 6th Australian Battalion had deployed through the north-west corner of Nieppe Forest, with 5th Australian Battalion behind it. The main fear was that the German artillery would hit the forest with gas shells but it was shrapnel which mortally wounded Lieutenant Colonel Day as he rode through the trees reconnoitring the ground in front of his position.

Major General Harold Walker was given command of XV Corps sector but he was receiving reports of British soldiers falling back 'thoroughly demoralised'. Patrols were also discovering that the area in front of the Australian line 'was alive with Tommies digging in for their lives all over

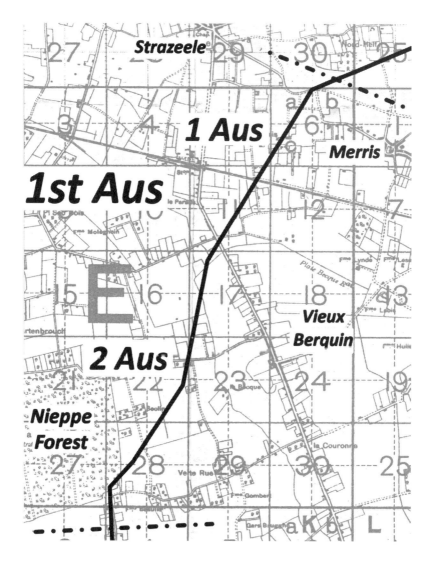

1st Australian Division stopped all attempts to advance past the north side of the Nieppe Forest.

the place'. Walker wanted it cleared before dawn and General de Lisle agreed the survivors of 31st and 29th Division would withdraw through the Australians. They were relieved to be in reserve after three days in action but Walker was happy for the 4 Guards Brigade to hold onto Caudescure on his right.

It was some time before the German patrols discovered that XV Corps had abandoned its line around Merris, Vieux Berquin and Arrewage. The first contact on the morning of 14 April was made when a battalion made the mistake of marching across 8th Australian Battalion's front 'with no attack patrols ahead of its front'. Captain Fox's men let them 'march without alarm within 20 yards, when Lieutenant Colonel Mitchell's Victorians blazed at them from every barrel and continued to pour a withering fire into the Germans, whose survivors panicked and fled.'

The enemy artillery began shelling Strazeele at dawn as 3rd Australian Battalion watched 'miles of infantry slowly but surely goose-stepping towards them. Officers on grey horses were riding up and down the column.' A barrage by no less than twenty-eight brigades of artillery was 'splendidly effective, shells bursting right over the Germans'. But they kept coming and 'the Lewis gunners and machine gunners had such targets as were seldom presented to them.' One of Lieutenant Colonel Moore's men said it was 'like firing into a haystack; one could not miss.'

The Germans tried to get close to the Australian line for two hours but the few that did were driven away by Lieutenant Prescott. There were further attacks and while the German officers tried to get their men forward, they lacked spirit and often refused to leave their trenches. Every time, the Australians 'allowed attacks to come close before giving the order to fire, then meeting them with intense bursts which had demoralising effects'.

First Army
XI Corps
5th Division, Covering the Nieppe Forest
Major General Stephen's men had spent the night creating a defensive line east of the Nieppe Forest but it had been difficult. Some men had dug rifle pits but water appeared by the time they were only knee-deep and they had few sandbags. Others dug themselves into ditches, using hedges to hide their movements while a few converted cottages into strongpoints. The high crops in the fields made it difficult to see much, so patrols had to keep the enemy at bay while working parties erected fences with what little barbed wire they had.

The artillery observers struggled to see anything, so the guns concentrated on hitting the roads and villages. Occasionally the enemy were spotted observing from a cottage, so flares were used to set the thatch roof on fire and a howitzer battery would be given the coordinates; a short bombardment would demolish the building.

Astride the Bourre stream, 95 Brigade stopped all attacks towards Caudescure. The 1st Devons held on but the Germans forced a gap between the 1st DCLIs and the Guardsmen, on the left. Regimental Sergeant Major Willis led a counter-attack but half of the Cornish men were hit as the line swung back. The Germans spent all afternoon trying to exploit the gap but the 12th Gloucesters helped hold the line. The 14th Warwicks lost Le Vertois in the centre of 3 Brigade's sector and Lieutenant Colonel Quarry was killed during the counter-attack which retook it.

Major General Stephens welcomed his artillery after the gun teams had covered 65 miles in just twenty-four hours but his supply wagons had still not turned up. Scroungers had gone in search of anything useful and they found the Inland Water Transport Depot's abandoned stores and an old army ammunition dump in Aire. They hauled wire, tools and over two million bullets to the front in two abandoned lorries they had 'borrowed'. Rather than reprimand anyone, Lieutenant General Haking's message was 'well done 5th Division'.

An intense barrage early on 14 April cut the front line off from their support companies for a time. One hit 95 Brigade's headquarters, seriously

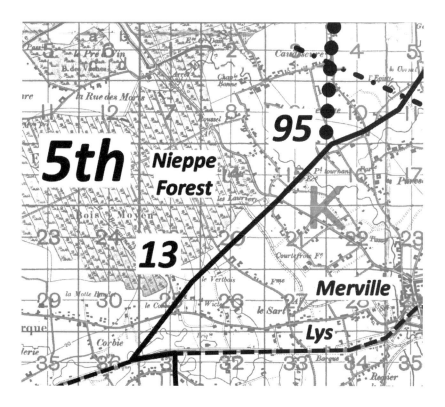

5th Division held on into front of Nieppe Forest.

wounding Brigadier General Lord Esmé Gordons-Lennox and his brigade major. The attack was directed against Lieutenant Colonel Norton's 1st DCLI, north of the Bourre stream, but machine guns from the 95th Machine Gun Company 'played great havoc with the German infantry'. Captain Meyrick was wounded directing enfilade fire from the 1st Devons' position while a later attack against the Devons was stopped. The two battalions had plenty of ammunition and concentrated machine-gun fire drove back an armoured car and shot up a battery of guns before it could deploy.

The Germans made three attempts to drive the 14th and 15th Warwicks but a company of the 1st Devons helped them hold on. 'Some of the men had to go through water right up to their waists' but Captain Honywill's charge retook the lost ground around La Vertois. The counter-attack warranted thanks from Brigadier General Lord Esmé Gordons-Lennox with the words, 'the Devons have never failed me yet…' Meanwhile, 'a bold dash' by Captain Pringle saved the 2nd KOSBs' line on the north bank of the Lys canal.

61st Division, Along the Clarence

Major General Mackenzie had a mix of battalions under his command dug in between the Lys canal and Robecq. The 2/5th Gloucesters stopped the advance from Cornet Malo, south of the canal, but the Germans did not attack the 2/7th Warwicks because the Clarence stream crossed their front. It was a different matter for the 2/4th Oxford around Baquerolles Farm and the 2/4th Berkshires covered Robecq. The Germans tried several times to drive them back from the stream but they failed. 'A satisfactory feature of this attack was that it was driven off by the infantry alone and largely by rifle fire from small isolated posts. This had a very stimulating effect on the newly joined drafts.' The 1,500 Scots serving under Fleming's Force took over the defence of Robecq during the night.

The 8th Argylls and 9th Royal Scots stopped several attacks from Cornet Malo on 14 April while the Ox and Bucks again stopped the Germans crossing the stream around Baquerolles Farm. For the second day in a row Mackenzie's command had stopped Sixth Army south of the Nieppe Forest.

I Corps
4th Division, Aire Canal

Sixth Army's plan was to drive 4th Division out of Robecq and to take Mont Bernenchon from 3rd Division. However, the German soldiers were so tired and harassed by enemy action that the attack across the Aire canal failed to materialise. 'Packed together, they suffered heavily from the

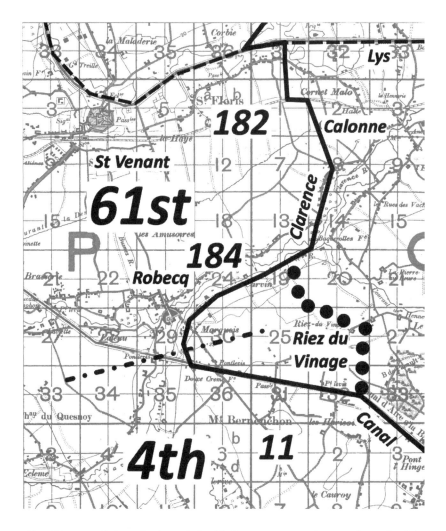

61st Division did not budge while 4th Division gained ground north of the Aire Canal.

bombs and machine-guns of enemy aeroplanes and from the enfilade fire of enemy batteries.' It was clear the German soldier 'had very little idea where he was and his units were very mixed up and disorganised'. The only attack which materialised failed to drive Lieutenant Colonel Johnston's 7th Shropshires away from Pont Tournant in the afternoon.

Major General Torqhil Matheson's 4th Division took over the Aire canal line between Robecq and Hinges from 3rd Division. The 1st Somersets and

1st Rifle Brigade established outposts on the north bank during the night and they reported that the Germans were disorganised. Brigadier General Wade moved the 1st Hampshires and the Somersets across in ones and twos during 14 April and they took cover in houses and ditches on the far side. The British artillery opened fire at dusk and the assault companies attacked while the support companies rushed across the bridges en masse. Thirty minutes later the attack went in.

The Hampshires reached their objective with few casualties but the Somersets were pinned down until Captain Osborne led the support company into Riez du Vinage. A counter-attack from Pacaut Wood was met with rifle and Lewis gun fire and 'it was estimated that casualties to the extent of 40 per cent were inflicted on the enemy: half the remainder ran away, and the other half ran forward with their hands up and surrendered.'

The rest of the Somersets faced fierce opposition from the direction of Pacaut Wood and it was eventually left to the artillery and machine-guns to drive the Germans out. The Rifle Brigade 'had some good musketry practice from the canal at the Boches who were bolting from various houses'. The Somersets would capture around 130 prisoners and recover a dozen of 51st Division's field guns which had been abandoned on 12 April.

55th Division, Festubert

A three minute hurricane bombardment hit the area north-west of Festubert before the 13th King's charged and captured a battered Keep A. Elsewhere patrols exchanged rifle and machine-gun fire, while artillery observers sought out targets. Cease fires were called regularly because 'stretcher bearers were permitted to come and go in broad daylight.' On one occasion snipers let 'a party of peasants enter a farm and return with a cart full of live-stock'.

Summary, 13 and 14 April

It was quiet during the nights across the Lys plain and it was the first opportunity for many to sleep properly since the battle began. Parts of IX Corps line had moved little around Neuve Église while the rest had fallen back to a prepared line on the Ravelsberg Ridge. The troops on XV Corps front had fallen back through the Australians. Meanwhile, XI Corps front had stablished along the Clarence stream while I Corps was secure behind the Aire canal.

Haig and his Chief of the General Staff, Lieutenant General Herbert Lawrence, were joined by Lord Milner, the War Cabinet's representative, at Foch's headquarters in Abbeville on the morning of 14 April. They were there to discuss the Lys battle and strategy on the Western Front with

General Foch and his chief of staff, General Maxime Weygand. Lieutenant General DuCane was the chief liaison officer.

Haig reported the BEF had suffered around 26,000 casualties in the first three days of the battle and it had run out of reserves. He also thought the French reserves were too far away to be of any assistance. Foch refused to relieve British divisions while the battle was ongoing because the recent experience on the Somme had shown that such a manoeuvre was far too risky. That aside, he thought the Germans had reached the limit of their advance and announced, *'la bataille d'Hazebrouck est finie'* – 'the battle of Hazebrouck is finished'.

Haig submitted a written request for help but Foch was worried the Germans would switch their attention back to the Somme and he issued orders accordingly: 'In the case of a powerful attack forcing back the Allied line between Arras and Albert, it is of the highest importance that the enemy should be definitely stopped on the line Arras-Monchy au Bois-Fonquevillers-Colincamps…' Foch instructed General Paul Maistre to be ready to support the BEF with the French Tenth Army if General Sir Julian Byng's Third Army got into difficulties.

Haig and Foch had agreed the line in Flanders should be shorter and the Belgian Chief of the General Staff, Lieutenant General Cyriaque Gillain was instructed to withdraw his army in line with the Second Army. Plumer also discussed another withdrawal from the Ypres Salient with his corps commanders. The Forward Zone would remain in the same place but the Battle Zone would withdraw towards Ypres over the next twenty-four hours.

Chapter 8

Hold On *Coûte que Coûte*

15 to 17 April

Mist and low cloud again interfered with aerial operations. Little happened on the ground either, because Fourth Army and Sixth Army were relieving infantry battalions, moving up artillery batteries and stockpiling ammunition. Fourth Army resolved to capture the Ypres Salient on 17 April and Operation Tannenberg had three objectives. It would hit the Belgians and British north and south of Ypres, while following up on the success at Neuve Église by capturing Kemmelberg. Meanwhile, Sixth Army would keep pushing either side of the Nieppe Forest.

It was also the time that French troops started arriving in the Lys area. The relieving units soon noticed the different artillery tactics as French batteries deployed behind the British line. They noted that 'the constantly changing and brief, but correspondingly more vehement, bombardments of the French artillery were particularly unpleasant.' They were a complete contrast to 'the little changing British bombardments, which lay always on the same spot.'

Belgian Army, West of Houthulst Forest, 17 April
The German guns started shelling the Belgian line between Merckem and Langemarck at dawn and the infantry attacked at 8 am. General Armin wanted to cross the Yser Canal as the north part of a pincer move to cut off Ypres. The Belgians were driven back at Blankaart Lake and Kippe, and the storm troops then turned south-east, in an attempt to roll up the line.

Two strongpoints at Draaibank stopped the Germans getting to the British trenches at Langemarck while a counter-attack recaptured Kippe. Artillery and machine-gun fire, supported with strafing planes, meant that the infantry had retaken the whole position by dusk. The Belgians were so confident about their situation that they relieved the 30th British Division on the Pilckem ridge.

XXII Corps

Lieutenant General Alexander Godley held the southern half of the Ypres Salient with a Forward Zone around 2 miles in front of the Battle Zone. While 6th Division had outposts at Polygon Wood and Hooge, east of the town, 21st Division covered the area around the Comines railway and canal, to the south-east. General Armin planned to seize the high ground around St Eloi and Wytschaete, at the south end of the Salient, as part of Operation Tannenberg. Fourth Army would then be in a good position to drive north-west, cutting off the Ypres Salient.

9th Division, Wytschaete and Spanbroekmolen, 16 April

Major General Tudor's men were holding the line between St Eloi and Spanbroekmolen, south-west of Wytschaete, with his own 26 Brigade and 64 and 62 Brigades of 21st Division. After a quiet day on 15 April, the German artillery opened fire before dawn on 16 April and gas shells forced the men to don their masks while high explosive shells knocked out the communications network. The division had just been handed over to XXII Corps and the heavy artillery had not had time to include its front line in their list of targets.

The first attack hit Wytschaete where Brigadier Gator's 62 Brigade had endured a particularly heavy bombardment. The barrage hit the 1st Lincolns a little longer than it did the 12/13th Northumberland Fusiliers and then 'the fog hid the approach of the enemy and companies did know they were attacked until the enemy appeared at close quarters.'

The Germans penetrated the line and then wheeled left and right, but 'the battalion stood firm and fought it out to the last. No officer, platoon post or individual surrendered and the fighting was prolonged.' Captain Neilson was killed but Captain McKellar commanded the rearguard as Major Gush evacuated all the wounded. The 12/13th Northumberland Fusiliers swung their right flank back but only one hundred of the Lincolns escaped. The 7th West Yorkshires were overrun around Spanbroekmolen and the huge crater created on 7 June 1917 was lost.

Around noon a second attack against Damm Strasse was stopped by the 8th Black Watch and the 5th Camerons. 'The Germans withdrew to Pheasant Wood, leaving their wounded where they fell.' A second attempt to penetrate 26 Brigade's line also failed.

Major General Tudor was anxious to retake Wytschaete but he had to postpone a counter-attack because the mist cleared. The 7th Seaforths and some of the 39th Composite Brigade advanced late, missing the creeping barrage, but they still cleared Wytschaete Wood. Lieutenant Colonel

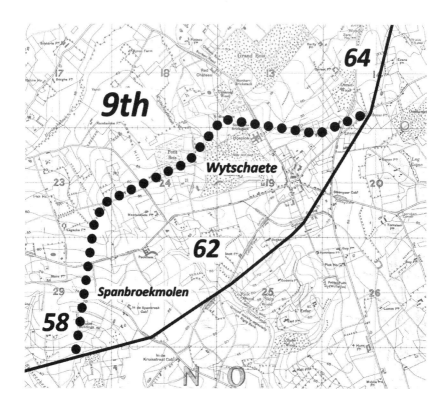

9th Division lost the high ground around Wytschaete and Spanbroekmolen on 16 April.

Bastard's 'fine leading and Captain Reid's daring made sure the attack went home under very heavy machine-gun fire from the front and right flank.' The rest of 39th Composite Brigade and the 2nd Lincolns could not take Peckham craters because of enfilade fire from Spanbroekmolen, so the 1st East Yorkshires and 6th Wiltshires had to form defensive flanks facing the salient.

IX Corps

General Plumer was determined to hold the line because he thought a withdrawal would boost the enemy's morale while having a bad effect on his own men. He did, however, recognise that the thin line of exhausted men were in a precarious position on the Ravelsberg Ridge. So he had instructed Lieutenant General Hamilton-Gordon to put his reserves to work digging new defensive lines.

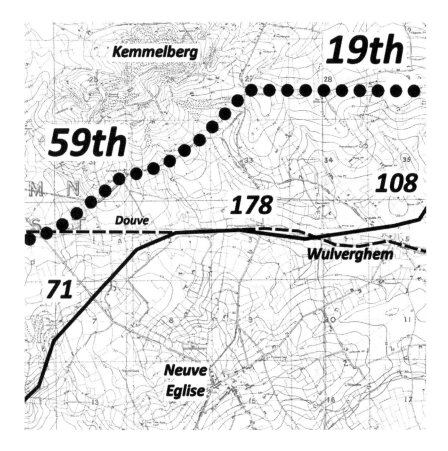

19th Division had to withdraw to the Meteren–Kemmel Line once Spanbroekmolen and the Ravelsberg Ridge had been lost.

19th Division, Between Wytschaete and Kemmel, 15-17 April
Major General Jeffrey's line along the Douve stream was under observation after the loss of Neuve Église and the 12th Irish Rifles beat off an attack early on 15 April around Wulverghem. That evening the 6th Wiltshires withdrew because Spanbroekmolen had been lost. The rest of 19th Division's line was now under observation, so 108 Brigade had to withdraw from Wulverghem while 178 Brigade abandoned the Douve stream. The loss of the Ravelsberg Ridge meant 71 Brigade had to pull back to the Kemmel–Meteren Line. For the next two days the Germans located targets along 19th Division's line, south of Kemmel, ahead of Operation Tannenberg.

Jeffrey was in command of 18 Brigade and Wyatt's force, as well as his own weakened brigades. The German guns began shelling Kemmelberg at dawn on 17 April, missing the front line trenches. A couple of hours later, German infantry advanced in extended order only to be stopped by artillery and machine-gun fire directed from the hill. But they had given their position away by firing, so the German guns hammered 19th Division's position for another hour while the infantry moved closer in small groups.

Brigadier General Cubitt coordinated the defence as the 9th Welsh, 10th Warwicks and 8th North Staffords stopped several attempts to reach Kemmel. Both Aircraft Farm and Donegal Farm were captured from the 7th and 2/6th Sherwoods, so Brigadier General Stansfeld reinforced 178 Brigade's front with the 2/5th Sherwoods.

59th Division, Ravelsberg Ridge, 15 April

After six days in action, 34th Division's soldiers 'were very weary, terribly short of sleep and hardly able to keep awake'. Major General Cecil Romer's division was to relieve them but it had only recently been engaged in the Somme battle and it had absorbed a lot of replacements into its ranks. There was a shortage of officers to control the inexperienced replacements and it took all night to complete the relief. Brigadier General James's 177 Brigade took over the Ravelsberg Ridge while Brigadier General Stansfeld's 176 Brigade was covering Bailleul. At dawn on 15 April the two brigades found themselves holding a maze of trenches and shell holes scattered with the bodies from the previous day's fighting.

The trenches were shallow, they had no camouflage and very little wire. They had been dug on the front slopes, so the occupants could see across the Grand Becque valley, and the German artillery now knew exactly where they were. The ground was dry enough to dig deeper but the morning bombardment was so intense that hundreds of men were hit. The 2/6th North Staffords had been reduced to just a handful of men by the time the attack was made. Even the back areas were given a dreadful pounding and one officer wrote, 'green Kemmel hill was turning brown before our eyes' as shell after shell exploded on the slopes.

An early attack from Wulverghem drove the 12th Irish Rifles back and Major Waring was killed leading the 1st Irish Fusiliers' counter-attack. Two companies of 9th Irish Fusiliers covered the gap until they were surrounded at dusk and many were killed or captured trying to escape. The 7th, 2/5th and 2/6th Sherwood Foresters stopped the Germans pushing 178 Brigade's line back from the Douve, west Wulverghem. 'In some cases these youths were put to the severest test almost before they knew their officers by sight and they emerged from it with quite astonishing credit.'

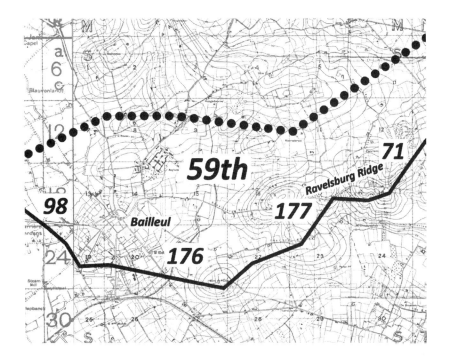

59th Division was driven off the Ravelsberg Ridge on 15 April.

The brunt of the attack hit 177 Brigade and it drove Lieutenant Colonel Day's 4th Lincolns from Crucifix Corner. Major Spurrell led the counter-attack by the 9th Norfolks but Captains Byrne and Failes were killed in the face of the 'great strength of infantry and machine guns brought up by the Germans'. Some forced the Norfolks back along Clapham Road while others turned against the rest of the Lincolns.

Captains Stephenson and Wilmshurst were wounded leading the Lincolns' 'stands and retirements, in which hand-to-hand fighting was a frequent occurrence'. The 2/5th Lincolns were then attacked in the flank and Lieutenant Colonel Roffey was killed 'in desperate fighting at close quarters'. One 'Lewis gun section went down fighting to the bitter end, having emptied its magazines into the closely packed ranks of the enemy at very close range.' More Germans then charged the front of the Lincolns and they rolled up 177 Brigade's line.

Patrols sent forward to find out what was happening discovered the enemy were where the Lincolns should have been, so the 'battalion headquarters personnel were organised into fire units'. Brigadier General

James ordered the 6/7th Scots Fusiliers (Pioneers) to form a defensive flank, to stop the Germans reaching Mont de Lille which overlooked Bailleul; they failed.

Brigadier General Cope's 176 Brigade held a difficult position along the forward slopes east and south of Bailleul. But 177 Brigade's line 'then crumbled' after the Germans drove the 2/8th North Staffords from Mont de Lille. All the officers could do was to tell their men to escape from the firing line and head for the rally points before they were overrun.

The loss of Mont de Lille precipitated a general retirement late on 15 April. Lieutenant General Hamilton-Gordon confirmed the withdrawal of 71 Brigade back to the Kemmel–Meteren Line while 59th Division fell back behind it. Major General Nicholson had to alert all the units reporting to 34th Division and their 'enjoyment was rudely put to an end' after only twelve hours rest. Two companies of the 9th Northumberland Fusiliers deployed to cover the retirement but there were chaotic scenes. 'The strength and position of the enemy, as well as the lines on which he was advancing, were not known and there had been no time to form an organised outpost line.' Virtually everyone escaped but German patrols were soon probing the Kemmel–Meteren line, using flares to direct reinforcements to gaps in the British line.

The retreating men skirted Bailleul in the darkness, to avoid the exploding shells and falling masonry. Men from the 2/8th North Staffords, 2/6th South Staffords and 9th North Staffords assembled at Brigadier General Cope's headquarters on the Locre road. Several hundred stragglers gathered at Lieutenant Colonel Sugden's rally point on the St Jans Cappel road. The rest of the North Midland men were allowed to pass through the Kemmel–Meteren Line, so they could organise themselves in reserve. Nicholson's weary soldiers grimly noted that they 'again became the front line troops'.

Brigadier General Mackenzie was sure that the German infantry would assemble around the asylum north-east of Bailleul, so he asked IX Corps' heavy howitzers to shell the area at regular intervals. He was right and an aerial observer reported the complex was surrounded by hundreds of bodies the following morning.

34th Division, Back in the Line North of Bailleul, 16 and 17 April
The retirement of the 59th Division from the Ravelsberg Ridge had left the six weak and tired brigades under Major General Nicholson once again in the front line. His order 'called on his troops to hold on *coûte que coûte*' (at all costs) until the French arrived. They faced Bailleul and the British bombardment created 'a cinema picture of the Great Fire of London, with steeples and houses crashing down one by one into a sea of smoke and flame'.

Observers on Mont Noir directed the heavy artillery against any groups of infantry seen around Bailleul while small arms fire stopped all the probes against the outpost line. Short bombardments heralded two late afternoon attacks against 34th Division's line. One nearly drove the 2nd Worcesters from Hill 70, north-east of Bailleul, until the 9th Northumberland Fusiliers' counter-attack restored the line. The second, against 147 Brigade's line north of Bailleul, was stopped by the 6th and 4th Duke's.

The German guns began shelling the trenches on the forward slopes of Mont Rouge and Mont Noir at dawn on 17 April, 'shifting the barrage backwards and forwards'. A counter-barrage hit the infantry as they assembled on the Ravelsberg Ridge while Major General Nicholson's

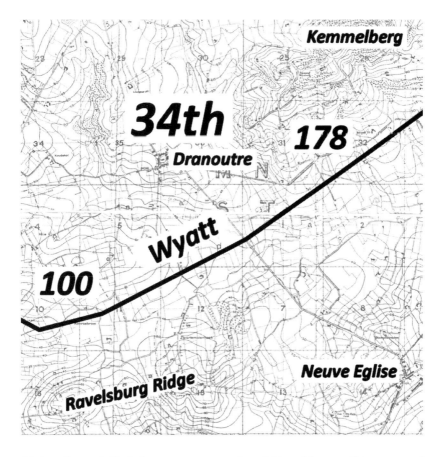

Major General Nicholson once again found himself controlling a mixed group of brigades on 16 April.

men dealt with the rest: 'The attacking waves were cut down by furious machine-gun fire… The foremost waves were compelled to return to their jumping-off trenches, suffering severe losses. There the troops lay the whole day under the heaviest fire, whilst British aeroplanes circled above them and shot them down. The bombs tore great gaps in the ranks.'

A few outposts were captured south of Dranoutre and Lieutenant Macdonald was killed leading the 6/7th Scots Fusiliers' counter-attack, but neither they nor the 1/5th York and Lancasters could retake them. Artillery fire broke up the Germans advancing towards 103 Brigade and the 9th Northumberland Fusiliers, 10th Lincolns and 1st East Lancashires drove the survivors back. There was another bombardment before 74 Brigade was attacked, but the artillery again helped the 3rd Worcesters and 11th Lancashire Fusiliers stop it. The men of 34th Division had fulfilled General Nicholson's command to hold on at all costs.

The constant shelling of Bailleul had turned the ruins into a death trap, so the Germans decided against moving troops through it, so there were no attacks against 101 Brigade or 147 Brigade. The men of 89 Brigade of 30th Division would take over the line north of Bailleul during the night and it was reinforced by forty-eight Lewis gun teams from 13th Tank Battalion.

33rd Division, Meteren, 15 to 17 April

There was no attempt to capture Meteren on 15 April but Major General Pinney became concerned when he saw a large number of flares around Bailleul during the night. He correctly guessed they had been fired by the enemy, as they moved across Ravelsberg Ridge. He was told the town had been abandoned and was given permission to withdraw the 1st Middlesex and 2nd New Zealand Entrenching Battalion east of Meteren, so they connected the original trench to the new line north of Bailleul.

The overnight move left a gap in the line and the Germans rushed Captain Warburton's company to the 4th King's left flank early on 16 April. The Middlesex were also driven out of Meteren so a company of the 2nd New Zealand Entrenching Battalion reinforced the line. It ended up with them all being surrounded, and while Sergeant Morrin led some to safety, over one hundred were captured; the largest number of New Zealand prisoners taken in an action during the entire war.

The Germans were rolling up the King's line, so the 1st Middlesex moved up from 98 Brigade's reserve. Heavy fire stopped them entering Meteren, so they formed a new line north of the village while the Lewis gunners stopped the enemy getting behind the 5th Scottish Rifles' flank. A few engineers of the 11th Field Company counter-attacked and stabilised the rest of the line, but plans were afoot to recapture Meteren.

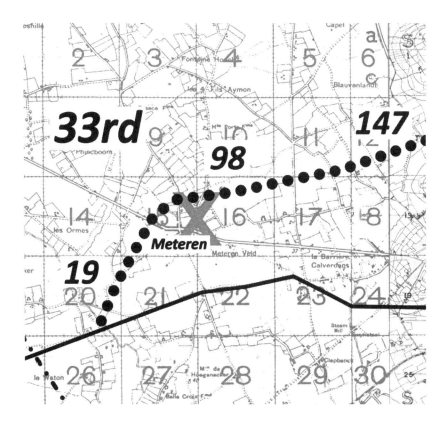

33rd Division had been driven out of Meteren by 16 April.

Lieutenant Colonel Sasse's 1st Australian Battalion relieved the 5th Scottish Rifles west of the Meteren Becque stream and took advantage of the supporting barrage to improve his position in front of Merris. French Chasseurs Alpins 'advanced some hours later, but wisely limited their effort to the relief of the British troops whom they found just short of the village'.

The 2nd Argylls soon spotted the Germans moving from hedge to ditch towards 98 Brigade's line, north of Meteren, on the morning of 17 April. The Lewis gun teams of 5th Tank Battalion made sure they 'were beaten off well away from our line by excellent shooting.' The 1st Middlesex held on north and west of Meteren but there was a problem when French troops took over some of their trenches because they were driven back before they had settled in. Captain Warburton was killed as the 4th King's helped retake the lost ground.

XV Corps

1st Australian Division, Strazeele to Caudescure, 15 to 17 April

Both the 8th and 3rd Australian Battalions stopped the probing attacks from Vieux Berquin early on 15 April. Their camouflaged machine gun teams were positioned to create interlocking fields of fire. The division's artillery had also arrived and Brigadier General Anderson had deployed his batteries in the Nieppe Forest. So had Brigadier General Bennett's 3 Australian Brigade, and his four battalions were digging in around Hazebrouck.

The Germans spent 16 April trying to locate the Australians' line but it was clear they had failed when the artillery opened a 'terrific' barrage against Brigadier General Lesslie's 1 Australian Brigade the following

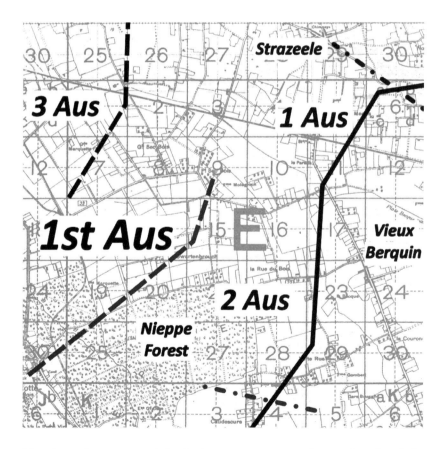

The Australians stopped Sixth Army getting past the north side of the Nieppe Forest

morning. They 'shot at pretty well everything marked on the map, farms, cross-roads, villages, even some hedges' south of Strazeele. But they soon stopped firing because their ammunition was running short.

Lines of infantry started moving north in short rushes an hour later, only to be met with a 'deluge of fire' by the 1st and 4th Australian Battalions and Captain Kirkwood's men of the 5th Scottish Rifles. The machine-gun fire was so intense in places that many Germans 'could not leave the jumping-off line'. Others moved forward by rushes as they 'watched their barrage waltzing away from them into the Australian back area'.

To the south, 3rd Australian Battalion observed the German officers 'leaping out of the trenches and trying to induce their men to follow, but the barrage of the defending artillery and the fire of small arms was so intense that the infantry standing along the trenches would not leave their shelter'. Major Burrett later said that he had 'never seen the men so cheerful and confident'. Another attempt before dusk failed and Lesslie would later report that he estimated the enemy had suffered between 1,500 and 2,000 casualties. Even the Germans admitted 'the field was sown with dead and wounded. Enemy machine-guns from the flank had mown down whole ranks.'

XI Corps
5th Division, Covering the Nieppe Forest
An attempt to advance astride the Bourre stream on 15 April was scattered by artillery fire and the 1st DCLI and 1st Devons stopped anyone entering the Nieppe Forest. No further attacks were made against 5th Division.

61st Division, Between the Nieppe Forest and Robecq, 15 to 17 April
The German artillery kept up their daily bombardments of the roads around the Nieppe Forest and St Venant but there was little infantry action. An evening attack on 15 April failed to drive the 2/4th Ox and Bucks back from the Clarence stream around Baquerolles Farm. Lieutenant General Haking's men were getting the upper hand and it was plain to see that the German infantry were struggling:

> *The plight of the enemy in the front line was not enviable; he lived in cubby-holes in the ground with a thin line of wire in front, and often had to go rationless, as the ration parties could not approach the front line through our machine-gun and artillery fire; his daily morale was getting lower. Hardly a night passed without a raid being carried out by our infantry, or prisoners being brought captured by a patrol, or deserters coming in.*

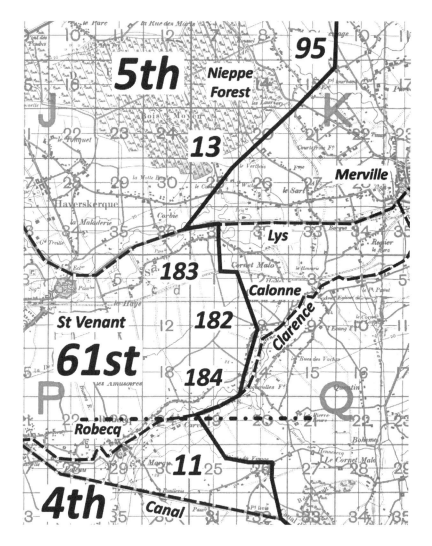

The German Sixth Army's attack had stalled between the Nieppe Forest and the Aire Canal by 15 April.

It was difficult for the Germans to organise themselves – 'the dead lay thick in the fields in front and stretcher bearers were constantly seen at work.' It was difficult to bring up ammunition and hauling their field guns forward was nigh on impossible because there was so little cover. As a consequence the attack against XI Corps' line dwindled to just a couple of attempts to seize tactical points.

I Corps

4th Division, Robecq to Hinges, 15 April

At dawn the 1st Somersets spotted dozens of Germans in full marching order moving forward in twos and threes towards Riez du Vinage on 11 Brigade's front. 'Every available rifle and Lewis gun was brought to bear on all Germans seen and severe casualties were inflicted on them. If a serious counter-attack was intended, it was nipped in the bud and never developed. The German stretcher bearers were busy for the remainder of the day.' The 1st Hampshires failed to clear the area south of Baquerolles Farm before nightfall.

Major General Matheson was anxious to widen the bridgehead on the north bank of the Aire canal, to make it easier to launch an attack. So his engineers pushed a pontoon bridge across the waterway during the night, giving 10 Brigade three bridges to use. Pacaut Wood was shelled and bombed and then Brigadier General Green's men charged across the canal.

Some of the Somersets entered the wood from the west, only to find that Lieutenant Colonel Officer's 2nd Duke's had been pinned down crossing a drawbridge. The pontoon bridge had been hit so wagons carrying replacement parts had to be brought up at a gallop to replace the damaged section. The 1st Warwicks crossed Pont d'Hinges under heavy fire, only to run into large numbers of Germans assembling for their own attack. Green's brigade had suffered over 250 casualties and the survivors had to dig in around Pacaut Wood, with the canal dangerously close to their backs.

Summary, 15-17 April

There were concerns that the Germans could drive IX Corps back and take Kemmelberg, because it was only half a mile behind the front line. Observers would be able to see Second Army's rear if they reached the summit of the highest hill in the area. General Plumer was already discussing with GHQ how to withdraw back to St Omer while Haig had again asked Foch for reinforcements to help hold the Flanders hills.

Haig was also asking the French to open the coastal locks to flood the low-lying land around Dunkirk and St Omer but Foch was refusing because the salt water would ruin the land. Instead Foch visited Plumer on 16 April, to hear about Second Army's position around Mount Kemmel first-hand, and the situation sounded grim.

On 17 April, CIGS General Sir Henry Wilson met Foch at Second Army headquarters to discuss future arrangements. Wilson was determined to force a decision from the French and he said the BEF was considering pulling back when the inundations were ready, some 15 miles to the west. That would result in the Belgians withdrawing to Veurne and Bergues, so they could keep a token foothold in Belgium. Second Army would continue the line south-west to St Omer while First Army would withdraw to a line through Aire, connecting with the current front north of Béthune.

Foch said he wanted the British to fight for Ypres, the Flanders hills and Hazebrouck. Wilson countered by saying Plumer's advice was that Second Army could not hold on if the Germans kept up the pressure. While General Armin seemed to have plenty of reserves left for Sixth Army, the BEF had none. So he again asked Foch to provide some and this time he relented.

Wilson told Plumer to submit a plan for withdrawing from Flanders, for approval after the meeting. Meanwhile, Foch visited the Belgians to see how they were faring after the attack between Merckem and Langemarck. He also spoke to King Albert, President of the Senate, Paul de Favereau, and the Army's Chief of Staff, General Cyriaque Gillain. Next he went to Dunkirk to visit General Henri Putz, Commandant Supérieur du Nord. The message to them all was that extra French divisions were going to be sent north to reinforce the BEF.

Haig was visiting Plumer to find out how he was fairing but there was little good news. They spoke about the successive defensive lines Second Army could hold and how to move the enormous amounts of stores back to the St Omer. They were sensible ideas but there were too few men available to carry them out.

Haig then visited XXII Corps headquarters to discuss the loss of Wytschaete. Lieutenant General Godley complained that the French had not helped him out. It was a similar story of woe at IX Corps headquarters, where Lieutenant General Hamilton-Gordon reported his troops were tired and struggling to hold on.

The BEF's adjutant general, Lieutenant General George Fowke, had reported the losses since 21 March during the day. There had been around 210,000 casualties in just twenty-five days, over ninety per cent of them infantry. They were losses from an already under-strength army which had been fighting constantly for nearly a month. Despite Prime Minister Lloyd George's promises to send replacements for the losses, only 114,000 men had been received so far and many were young men. One of the Australians who saw the BEF's replacements wrote: 'For two days companies of infantry have been passing us on the roads. Companies of children, English children; pink faced and round cheeked, flushed under the weight of their unaccustomed packs, with their steel helmets on the back of their heads and the strap hanging loosely on their rounded baby chins.'

Chapter 9

From That Moment, We Had Them Cold

18 to 24 April

The German objectives appeared to have changed because Fourth Army tried to capture Kemmel while Sixth Army tried to advance past the south side of the Nieppe Forest. It led the Director of Intelligence, Brigadier General Cox, to believe they were just probing the BEF's line to draw the French reserve north, so they could resume the attack on the Somme and take Amiens.

XXII Corps
9th Division, Wytschaete

The Germans overran the South African Brigade's outpost line north of Wytschaete only for Brigadier General Tanner's men to recover it soon afterwards.

IX Corps
59th Division, Kemmel

Sixth Army had spent the past few days moving up guns and stockpiling ammunition but it had not been easy. Horses and men had to move everything across the Lys and then hide it on the flat, open fields. The Royal Air Force's observers had no difficulty locating targets for the artillery and the destruction of many dumps delayed the attack. The obvious preparations also meant that the British and French soldiers were on their guard.

General Armin was determined to take Kemmelberg but his pre-dawn assault failed miserably because the German artillery fired short, hitting Fourth Army's shallow jumping off trenches. The observers could not adjust their range in the dark because the mist hid the infantry's SOS signals. So the German infantry had to endure two hours of shelling from their own guns before the range was extended onto 59th Division's trenches. It was several hours before the infantry were in a fit state to attack and when reports that Donegal Farm and Aircraft Farm had been lost turned out to be false, it was clear that both the South Midland and French troops had held on.

XV Corps
<u>1st Australian Division, Covering Steenwerck</u>
Brigadier General Bennett's plan was for the 3rd Australian Brigade to recapture Meteren in two stages. Small parties from Lieutenant Colonel Rafferty's 11th Australian Battalion and Lieutenant Colonel Elliott's 12th Australian Battalion crept forward behind hedges during the early hours of 23 April. Captains Holyman's company approached from the east while Captains Andrew and Jorgenson cleared the west end of the village; they all fired green flares when Meteren was theirs.

The attack the following night had no preliminary bombardment but the Germans spotted 10th and 9th Australian Battalions crossing the fields in the bright moonlight. 'Flares went up from all parts of the German front; machine-guns opened from a large house known as the chateau, at the western end of the village, and also from behind the hedges.' Successive companies were pinned down by machine-gun fire and calls for artillery support went unnoticed. As dawn approached, both Lieutenant Colonel Jacob and Lieutenant Colonel Coleman had to withdraw their men, having suffered over 150 casualties.

XI Corps
<u>61st Division, Clarence Stream</u>
General von Quast wanted to extend the foothold across the Clarence stream, ready to advance south of the Nieppe Forest. The artillery hit the battery positions for four hours with high explosive and gas shells and then fell silent for three hours, to conserve ammunition. An intense barrage at 8 am was the sign for the assault troops to form up, and ten minutes later it started creeping forward. The 2/6th and 2/7th Warwicks stopped them advancing west of Calonne while Sergeant White of the 2/5th Gloucesters recaptured Baquerolles Farm near the Clarence stream.

Major General Mackenzie's men had again stopped Sixth Army. Major Barrett's 2/4th Oxfords and Lieutenant Colonel Lawson's 2/5th Gloucesters attacked the salient south of Baquerolles Farm, on 23 April, capturing over 120 prisoners.

I Corps
Sixth Army's main attempt was against Lieutenant General Arthur Holland's line along the Aire canal, and Quast's objective was to threaten the Béthune coalfields. The German artillery opened fire at 3 am and while the field guns showered the trenches with shrapnel, the howitzers shelled the villages and road junctions around Hinges and Essarts with high explosive. At 4 am the field guns started firing short

intense bursts at regular intervals and the infantry advanced in the mist an hour later.

<u>4th Division, Along the Aire Canal</u>
Sixth Army was determined to cross the Aire canal and take Mont Bernenchon and Hinges. On 12 Brigade's front, Captains Robinson and Clarke stopped the attack against the 2nd Lancashire Fusiliers north of Riez du Vinage. However, the German infantry captured the south end of Pacaut Wood from the 2nd Seaforths, allowing them to overrun the 1st King's Own right company. But the rest of the battalion held on and they managed to recapture Riez du Vinage.

The 2nd Seaforths' posts in Pacaut Wood were overrun but the enemy were unable to reach Pont d'Hinges. Engineers launched pontoons and footbridges on bladders onto the canal but the 2nd Duke's made sure no one reached the south bank. Instead, over one hundred Germans found themselves pinned down along the north bank and they surrendered at dawn; some were ferried across while others chose to swim.

The 2nd Essex made a surprise attack on 19 April and they captured 150 prisoners around Riez du Vinage. They also removed a number of elderly villagers on stretchers; they had endured ten days of battle. The following night, patrols from 11 Brigade crossed the Aire canal using a damaged bridge and ferries.

At dawn on 22 April the 1st Hampshires ran across three pontoon bridges which had been pushed across the canal during the night. The German counter-barrage came down only minutes after zero and Captains Causton of the Hampshires and Trevor-Jones of the Rifle Brigade were killed leading the advance along the rides in Pacaut Wood. Second Lieutenant Abbott's company of Hampshires cleared the east side of the wood while Lieutenant Colonel Fellowes' 1st Rifle Brigade captured sixty prisoners in the south end. The area was then subjected to a counter-barrage and Colonel Armitage was killed organising the Hampshires' defence of the wood.

<u>3rd Division, Astride the Lawe Canal</u>
Major General Deverell's men remained dug in astride the Lawe canal. None of the German assault troops reached 3rd Division's trenches during their early attack on 18 April.

<u>1st Division, Festubert and Givenchy</u>
Major General Peter Strickland's division had taken over 55th Division's sector around Festubert and Givenchy just before the attack early on 18

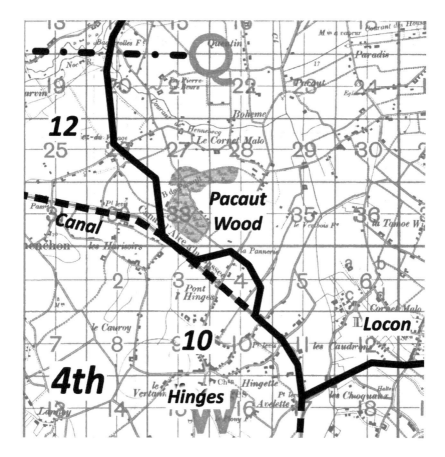

Again 4th Division stopped Sixth Army crossing the Aire Canal.

April. Route Keep A's garrison were knocked out by the barrage, allowing the Germans to attack the Tuning Fork Line behind it. An injured Captain Fowkes made sure the 1st SWBs stopped them getting behind the 1st Gloucesters in Festubert. But some of the Gloucesters were cut off at the south end of the village until a small group of signallers, cooks, orderlies and batmen drove them off.

Lieutenant Ainsworth's company of the SWB spotted some of the enemy wandering around lost in the mist, and 'from that moment, we had them cold.' Brigadier General Morant's men were then treated to a display of pyrotechnics when a shell hit an ammunition dump, setting off hundreds of flares. Lieutenant Colonel Taylor thought the explosions were another attack, so he deployed his battalion staff to meet the imaginary threat. He then called down a barrage and some of the 2nd Welsh and 1st Camerons surprised the Germans crawling back to their own lines.

The gas barrage which hit 1 Brigade's line around Givenchy kept Brigadier General Thornton's reserves underground. Lieutenant Burton's men held Moat Farm while Captain Cooke fought on in Givenchy Keep on the 1st Black Watch's left flank. The German storm troops overran the right company and Captain Sinclair's men 'were overcome by superior numbers' at close quarters when they emerged from their tunnel. Lieutenant Stephen's men were trapped underground, with the water level rising, but they only surrendered when a flamethrower team reached their dugout.

Some of Captain Arbuthnott's men manned their trenches during a lull in the bombardment, only to be hit by a fresh burst of shellfire. The wounded crowded around the tunnel exits, stopping the reserves getting out, and they were all taken prisoner. It was down to Lieutenant Valentine to keep the Germans away from the battalion headquarters with a captured German machine gun.

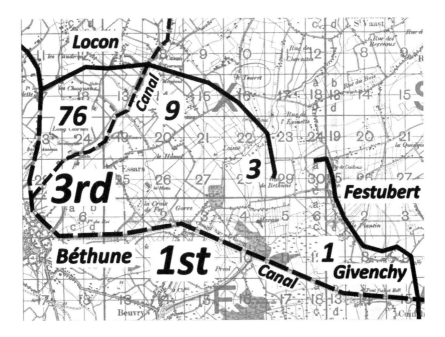

1st Division had a fierce battle for Givenchy and Festubert on 18 April.

The area north of the La Bassée canal was then quiet for several days with action reduced to sniping during the day and shelling all night. Patrols often found the German sentries asleep at their posts and they 'winkled them from their cover' before returning with their prisoners. The 1st SWB seized Route A Keep while the 1st Northants captured ground west of Festubert on 20 April. The Germans retook it two days later but 55th Division returned on 24 April and the 1/10th King's took the strongpoint the division had lost two weeks earlier.

Preparing the Next Attack
After ten days on the offensive, OHL suspended attacks in Flanders for several days. The lull was welcomed by the soldiers at the front but it worried the Allied generals. Haig's staff thought the Germans wanted to capture Hazebrouck but General Phillipe Pétain's staff thought they wanted to seize Amiens. In fact, General Armin was preparing to capture Kemmelberg from the British Second Army. The hill rises over 100 metres above the Flanders plain and he thought its capture would allow observers to see across the British rear. So Fourth Army's guns spent the next five days pounding the Kemmel area.

General von Quast's plan was still to advance either side of the Nieppe Forest, aiming for Hazebrouck. Late on 21 April, Sixth Army's artillery started hitting the Nieppe Forest with gas shells until the undergrowth reeked of mustard gas. The nightly gas bombardments made the forest a dangerous place to be but 5th Division's chief medical officer, Lieutenant Colonel Hewetson, took a number of steps to reduce casualties. Teams roamed the wood, neutralising concentrations of gas, while stretcher bearers were deployed on roads and rides, to warn troops marching through. Other stretcher bearers were on standby to evacuate anyone who was affected.

There were gas bombardments of other parts of the line and one on 20 April caused 700 casualties in 3rd Division trenches around Locon; 'every precaution was taken, helmets being adjusted and the trenches sprinkled with chlorine of lime after the bombardment.' The high number of casualties was attributed to the lack of wind and the hot sun which had encouraged the gas to seep out of the ground and clothing.

Early every morning the British and Australian artillery fired barrages at the German front line, just in case troops were assembling ready to attack. Observers then spent the day locating targets for the artillery, and the infantry carried out evening raids, looking for prisoners or papers. The biggest haul came when two men were captured with an entire company's mail and it was studied to try and work out when the next attack would be made. Many of the prisoners spoke about an imminent attack and that the objective was Kemmelberg. On 24 April there was evidence that the elite Alpine Corps had just taken over the trenches facing the hill.

French Reinforcements

Having heard all the opinions and seen the British situation, Foch made plans for the days to come. He decided to increase the number of infantry divisions in Flanders, so they would take over IX Corps' line covering the Flanders hills. General Henri Putz's *Commandement Supérieur du Nord*, the established French command in Flanders, would be replaced by the *Détachement de l'Armée du Nord* (DAN), under General Antoine de Mitry. He ordered General Paul Maistre to move French Tenth Army north, to support First Army between Robecq and Béthune. He also told General Joseph Micheler to move French Fifth Army north of Amiens, behind General Henry Rawlinson's Fourth Army. Foch instructed his generals to cooperate with the British before leaving Flanders on 18 April; he would not return until the battle for the Lys was over.

Foch and Haig's plan was for French troops to take over Second Army's right flank. General Antoine de Mitry visited General Plumer. He was introduced to General Félix Robillot and the three discussed arrangements for relieving IX Corps in the Kemmel sector. Robillot took responsibility for Kemmelberg but Lieutenant Colonel Bousfield's Defence Force would remain on the hill until the French were familiar with the trenches. General Valentin's 133rd Division would relieve IX Corps' three exhausted divisions (34th, 25th and 19th) by dawn on 21 April. The French troops found themselves holding a 6-mile-long sector in front of Kemmel, Dranoutre and St Jans Cappel. The British guns would stay on for as long as they were needed.

Georges Clemenceau visited Haig on 22 April to offer more French troops that could take over from the Belgians, reducing the number of nationalities around Ypres to two to ease the logistics situation. However, Haig had just received a letter from Foch stating he was sending all the divisions north he had asked for. It made it clear he wanted Generals Plumer and Gillain to produce a defensive plan in case Ypres was lost, and he also wanted Horne to build more defensive lines between the Nieppe Forest and Béthune. It was a sensible suggestion but GHQ had no spare troops to prepare them. Haig's reply again asked for the flooding around St Omer to be speeded up, by opening the sea locks.

The Threat of a New Attack

General Plumer issued orders to Second Army to improve its defences between Ypres and the Nieppe Forest. Lieutenant General Godley was told to retake Wytschaete and General de Mitry was to seize Spanbroekmolen and reconsider recapturing Neuve Église. Meanwhile, Lieutenant General de Lisle was to take Meteren and push the Germans away from the north-east corner of Nieppe Forest. But snow and then hail, followed by low clouds and cold, damp conditions made the work difficult.

The French spent the next two days settling in but Hille Farm, south-west of Dranoutre, was lost on the evening of 23 April. General Robillot wanted to advance his line across the Douve valley, to push the Germans away from Kemmelberg, but the first attempt late on 24 April failed. A few hours later the German artillery opened fire as the offensive everyone had been waiting for began.

The Royal Navy Raids on Zeebrugge and Ostend
Early on 23 April, Saint George's Day, ships of the Royal Navy attacked the ports of Ostend and Zeebrugge. The plan was to block the harbour entrances so ships and submarines could not attack the British convoys in the English Channel. The Ostend raid was a failure while Zeebrugge harbour was only partially blocked and an alternative shipping channel was soon opened. The raid shocked Crown Prince Rupprecht's headquarters but no changes were made to the plans for a new attack towards Kemmelberg.

Chapter 10

Every Yard of Ground Must Be Contested

25 to 29 April

A number of prisoners taken by the French during the evening of 24 April told their questioners that the German bombardment would start early the following morning. A thick mist covered Kemmelberg when Fourth Army's guns opened fire on the French positions at 2.30 am. They pounded the British and French batteries and communication centres with short, intense concentrations of gas and high-explosive shells. Many of the French batteries had been deployed close together behind Mont Rouge and Scherpenberg and the crews suffered badly from the bombardment. The British batteries were rather more spread out and while the immediate impact for the shelling was less, there was so much gas around that the gunners had to wear their masks until midday. The number of casualties per battery would be recorded as the highest of the war so far.

The German guns fell silent at 4.30 am only to start again thirty minutes later. Every howitzer, field gun and trench mortar hammered XXII Corps' trenches facing Oosttaverne and Wytschaete and DAN's trenches between Spanbroekmolen and Dranoutre. It had caused confusion and destruction all along the allied line before the German assault troops surged forward at 6 am.

XXII Corps
9th Division and 21st Division, St Eloi to Spanbroekmolen
Lieutenant General Godley's men held a salient and while 26 Brigade covered St Eloi, 64 Brigade faced Wytschaete and 27 Brigade faced Spanbroekmolen, next to the French. They had also been busy building the Vierstraat Line and the Cheapside Line, as Plumer had wanted. Major Generals Henry Tudor and David Campbell had divided them into brigade sectors with a battalion in each; two companies manning the trenches and

two companies ready to counter-attack. General Armin wanted to drive them from the north end of the Messines Ridge, so his artillery could fire at the road and railway connecting Poperinghe to Ypres.

The 5th Camerons stopped the attack towards St Eloi but the two companies of the 7th Seaforths had to form a defensive flank for 26 Brigade as the Germans advanced towards Vierstraat. When the 'ammunition began to run short, several men dashed forward to deserted dumps in full view of the enemy and brought back bandoliers of cartridges.' Captain Bennett's trench mortars scattered a second attack at midday while the Scots collected ammunition and filled belts for the machine gun teams.

Brigadier General Croft's men had presented a 'stone wall defence' but he had to withdraw them to the St Eloi craters after dusk because of the breakthrough to the south. Two companies of the 6th Leicesters and 39th Division's No 1 and No 3 Battalions were sent forward and they formed a defensive flank around Voormezeele, connecting St Eloi and Dickebusch Lake.

Flame thrower teams broke through the 1/6th West Yorkshires and the 1st East Yorkshires on 64 Brigade's front, hardly anyone escaped through Bois Quarante and Grand Bois to the Vierstraat Line. The two battalion headquarters were 'encircled by hordes of Germans' in Grand Bois but they put up 'a gallant fight'. By mid-morning Brigadier General Headlam could also see that 27 Brigade was falling back, exposing his right flank.

The 1/5th West Yorkshires eventually fell back onto 9th Scottish Rifles in the Vierstraat Line because the battalions to their flanks were driven back. The Germans followed up and drove the 1/7th West Yorkshires out of Vierstraat but part of Lieutenant Colonel McCulloch's 9th KOYLIs stopped them in Cheapside. They even made a counter-attack so the gunners could rescue three abandoned field howitzers from Vierstraat.

The barrage had wiped out the 12th Royal Scots' support companies but enough men survived in 27 Brigade's front trench to stop the Germans advancing from Spanbroekmolen. However, the French had fallen back on their flank and a wounded French battery commander reported the bad news to Brigadier General Croft. As soon as the mist lifted everyone could see the enemy were 'pouring down towards Kemmel and turning north they cut off the whole of the Royal Scots. Hordes of field grey figures swept down from all sides on the devoted battalion, which fought until it was practically wiped out.'

The Royal Scots headquarters formed a defensive flank but less than one hundred men would escape. The 6th KOSBs two front companies were 'virtually annihilated after a fierce resistance' in the Vierstraat Line. They lost half their men, including Major Wilkie and his headquarters, while falling back onto the rest of the 9th KOYLIs.

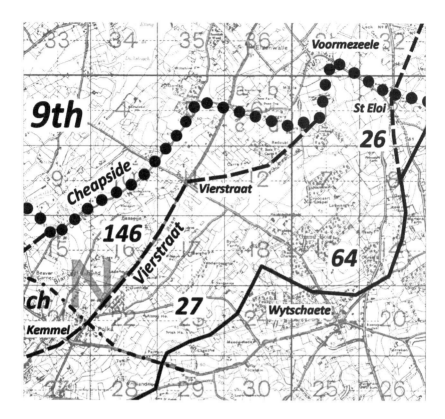

9th Division struggled to hold Cheapside after losing its Outpost Line and the Vierstraat Line.

As soon as Lieutenant General Godley heard of the disaster from Major General Tudor, he sent all his reserves to reinforce the men in Cheapside. The 8th Black Watch and 13th Tank Battalion's Lewis gunners were joined by cavalry, cyclists and motorbikes armed with machine-guns. The Black Watch and the KOSBs captured over fifty Germans each when they counter-attacked.

Major General Neville Cameron was told to send 147 Brigade (49th Division) to look for the French flank, and Brigadier General Lewes's men found them at La Clytte, some 2 miles behind the original line. It meant they had to cover the one-mile gap to 9th Division's flank in Cheapside.

Détachement de l'Armée du Nord (DAN), Kemmelberg

The main focus of the German attack was Kemmelberg, just behind the DAN's line. General de Mitry was holding an 8-mile sector with four divisions. While 28th Division held the trenches south-east of Kemmelberg, 154th Division was to the south-west. The line facing Bailleul was held by 34th and 133rd Divisions but the attack would brush past them.

The French had not been impressed with the British trenches, but that is not surprising, considering they had only held the position for ten days. There were no dugouts or strongpoints, the wire was patchy and all the work had been carried out with the enemy close by. The front line was on the forward slopes of Mount Kemmel, making it an easy target, so artillery fire often smashed entanglements and flattened trenches before the troops could complete them.

Late on 24 April, 28th Division made an attack south of Kemmel, and while it was a partial success, it led to the undoing of the French. There had been over one thousand casualties, so the reserves were moved forward to reinforce the new position. The advance had stopped around half a mile short and the German barrage was far more effective than usual because the French infantry were caught in the open. The French artillery did not know their infantry were pinned down short of the objective, so their counter-barrage fell behind beyond the German assault troops when the attack began at 6 am.

A 5-mile length of line was overrun in no time at all and while the troops on the flanks headed for Kemmel and Dranoutre, the Alpine Corps climbed the slopes of Kemmelberg. A few strongpoints and machine-gun posts fought on but the rest of the line fell back in disorder taking the support troops with them. The Kemmel Defence Force had been busy digging a communication trench when the attack started and the Germans were on the hill before they realised what was happening. Lieutenant Colonel Bousfield was defending his headquarters dugout when the local French commander told him to cease fire.

The Alpine Corps reached the summit of Kemmelberg in less than an hour, catching many reserve troops in their tunnels. They chased the retiring French down the slope and finally came to a halt along the Kemmelbeek stream at the foot of Scherpenberg. German patrols found 162 Brigade's batteries deployed along the road called the Milky Way, east of La Clytte. Most of the British crews fired until the last moment before escaping but a few had to disable their guns and fall back. Some were recovered with the help of 147 Brigade during the night.

All communications across DAN's front had been cut by the bombardment. The commander responsible for Kemmelberg first heard the Germans were on the hill when an aeroplane dropped a message at his headquarters. A runner would deliver the news to the commander

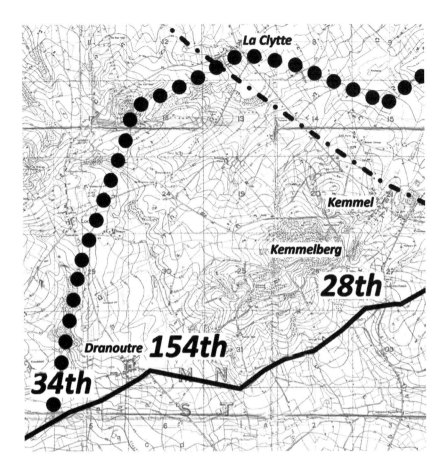

The Alpine Corps took advantage of the DAN's confused state to rush Kemmelberg.

responsible for Scherpenberg and he then heard that the field artillery in his area was under machine-gun fire.

Two French battalions were deployed in a thin screen between Locre and La Clytte, while 147 Brigade covered the gap to Cheapside. They were soon reinforced by stragglers, cavalry and rear area troops. The French and the British were too weak to drive the Germans back but they had stopped them taking Scherpenberg and Mont Rouge.

The Alpine Corps had advanced 2 miles. The two German divisions on the left of the attack bypassed Dranoutre in the mist and they had formed a defensive flank stretching back from Locre. Between them, they had taken around 3,000 prisoners in just a few hours.

<u>Summary, 25 April</u>
The loss of Kemmelberg in such a short time was a total shock. Early rumours were dismissed but reports were soon being forwarded by French officers. Even so, it was late in the afternoon before they were confirmed and the Allied guns started shelling the hill. The good news was that the hill did not give unlimited views of the Allied rear area because of the undulating nature of the terrain. The Germans would have to take Scherpenberg and the adjacent hills before they could see right across the British rear.

Plumer immediately drove to General de Mitry's headquarters when he heard about the attack. Although they talked about making a counter-attack, Second Army only had the depleted 25th Division to offer. News about the loss of Kemmelberg reached De Mitry's headquarters after Plumer left, and the confirmation message did not reach Second Army headquarters until the evening. By then Plumer also knew that XXII Corps had lost the Vierstraat Line, so they had to reconsider their plans. The only good news, as far as Haig and Plumer were concerned, was that De Mitry and his staff were now genuinely concerned about the Flanders situation.

De Mitry attached 39th Division to General Robillot's command but it had to march over 10 miles to reach the front while Lieutenant General Alexander Godley was waiting for 25th Division to join XXII Corps. The plan was for the two divisions to attack from La Clytte towards Kemmelberg during the early hours of 26 April.

26 April
XXII Corps
Lieutenant General Godley wanted 39th Division to secure the line east of Voormezeele but the main attack was going to be against Vierstraat, in conjunction with the French. The plan was for 25th Division to advance alongside French 39th Division from La Clytte. The left flank would be covered by 49th Division while the French 154th Division covered the right. Zero hour was set for 3.30 am, four and a half hours before the German attack was due to start.

It rained all night, making it difficult to deploy, and then mist formed as the preliminary barrage hit the German line. Men became disorientated as they tried to find their way forward even though the battalion and company commanders led the advance on foot, and they soon lost the creeping barrage as they plodded forward in the rain.

<u>39th Division Composite Brigade, Voormezeele</u>
Brigadier General Hubback's men were aware that the enemy was preparing to attack. A message asking for help never reached 26 Brigade's

headquarters, while the early morning fog hid the SOS flares. The Germans had pushed past the 16th Manchesters on the Bluff and overrun No 2 Composite Battalion around St Eloi by the time the artillery knew the front line was under attack.

Lieutenant Colonel Wynne's 2nd Bedfords formed a defensive flank north of the canal while Second Lieutenant Page held onto the Bluff until late in the afternoon. The rest of 39th Division Composite Brigade stopped a later attack towards Voormezeele but it was several hours before Major General Cyril Blacklock knew reserves were required. Fortunately, the 6th Leicesters held on to the Spoil Bank until the 1st West Yorkshires arrived.

49th Division, Attack on Vierstraat and Kemmel

The early hour of the attack and the miserable conditions meant the attack towards Vierstraat was a fiasco. The 9th Scottish Rifles and the Otago Mounted Rifles never got their orders to advance. The 4th and 5th York and Lancasters did get their instructions but they could only advance a short distance before they were forced to fall back to 148 Brigade's trenches. On 147 Brigade's front, the 9th KOYLIs advanced an hour late towards Kemmel, only to find no one on their flanks, so they withdrew to a safe distance. The 1/4th Duke's decided to go no further than Cheapside because the KOYLIs had not moved and they could see no one where the French were supposed to be. The German attack at 8 am drove all of Major General Cameron's men back to their start line. The 9th Scottish Rifles defended Ridge Wood during the afternoon while the 4th and 5th York and Lancasters held onto Cheapside.

25th Division and French 39th Division, Advance from La Clytte to Kemmel

The advance towards Kemmel was no better. Brigadier General Griffin's men came under fire as they crossed the Kemmelbeek, so 7 Brigade drifted south and lost touch with 49th Division. Lieutenant Colonel Stewart and all the other officers of the 4th South Staffords were hit but Lieutenant Miller continued to lead his men forward, taking seventy prisoners. Brigadier General Craigie-Halkett led 74 Brigade across the flooded stream and into Kemmel village but the French advanced late and did not get beyond their front line. All of Major General Bainbridge's men were soon falling back.

A combination of bad weather, poor planning, bad artillery support and a lack of coordination had doomed the attack to failure. One battalion commander went as far as to call it a 'discreditable affair', but they had disrupted German plans to capture La Clytte and the Scherpenberg. The

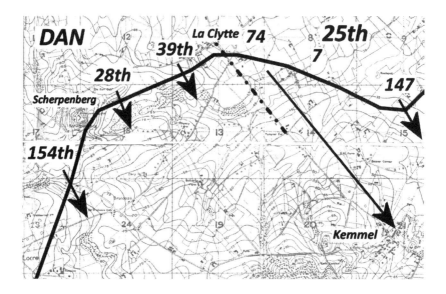

The hasty Allied counter-attack towards Kemmel failed in the dark and rain.

only place Sixth Army's attack began as scheduled was at Locre but the French held onto the village.

The Withdrawal to the Cheapside Line

General Plumer became aware that 21st Division was struggling to hold the Spoil Bank and a breakthrough along the Comines canal would endanger the Ypres Salient. So he decided to pull Second Army back during the night. Lieutenant General Claud Jacob withdrew his outpost line from the Steenbeek stream around St Julien and Frezenberg. His troops fell back to the Ypres ramparts, the ancient walls which surrounded the ruined town. Lieutenant General Godley pulled back his outposts from either side of the Menin road. His new line would be the Cheapside Line, south-west of the town.

While the plan to evacuate the Ypres Salient made tactical sense, Foch was concerned that the British Second Army was preparing to withdraw towards Poperinghe. The loss of Kemmelberg and now the prospect of giving up Ypres prompted him to contact General Philippe Pétain to ask for more reinforcements.

Summary, 26 April

The first report to reach Second Army headquarters said the French had lost Mont Rouge and Scherpenberg but Haig's chief of staff, Lieutenant

General Sir Herbert Lawrence, reassured General Plumer that 'the situation is never so bad, nor so good, as first reports indicate'. He also had to tell Plumer that GHQ had no more troops to give him. It eventually turned out that the Germans had not taken Mont Rouge; in fact Brigadier General Bethell could see no troops on the hill.

The Alpine Corps had failed to clear Locre at the foot of the Scherpenberg and they had been forced off Hyde Park hill. General André Massenet asked Major General Bainbridge for help to secure the area east of Mont Rouge but two attempts by the 2nd South Lancashires were abandoned because the French could not advance.

Lord Milner and General Wilson were holding a crisis meeting at GHQ. Haig reported that there were still around fifty German divisions behind the Western Front and that there were disagreements over where they were going to strike next. He thought the Fourth Army could try again to dislodge Second Army from Ypres or push First Army back from Béthune. Then of course, there was always the danger of a new thrust toward Amiens. Milner and Wilson were due to meet Foch the following day and Haig wanted them to ask him to relieve XXII and II Corps. That would extend the French sector in Flanders and release several divisions to add to GHQ's reserve.

27 to 29 April
<u>39th and 9th Divisions, GHQ Number 1 Line</u>
The Germans spent the next two days relieving infantry units and hauling ammunition to the batteries. Voormezeele was probed on the afternoon of 27 April, and later that night the enemy infiltrated the village while Brigadier General Currie's 89 Brigade was taking over the line. They also captured the Spoil Bank on the Comines canal from the 6th Leicesters on 110 Brigade's front; they took Lock 8 the following day.

The German artillery started firing gas shells at the British batteries at 3 am on 29 April and two hours later they switched to hitting XXII Corps' trenches with high explosive. The main attack fell on Brigadier General Currie's 89 Brigade's line in the Voormezeele Switch at 5.40 am. The 17th King's were driven back to the GHQ No 1 Line and 'the enemy got through on both flanks, practically surrounding two companies. A Company was surrounded and captured after severe fighting.' The 19th and 18th King's were shelled out of their outpost line but the Germans suffered many casualties and 'numbers of the enemy were picked off as they endeavoured to get back to their own lines.' An attack against the 9th Royal Scots 'was utterly defeated' because the barrage had missed the Lewis guns, which had been placed well out in front of Ridge Wood. The South Africans also stopped the attack from Vierstraat.

<u>49th Division, Cheapside</u>
The brigades serving under 49th Division endured an intense bombardment and 'rarely has heavier fire heralded an attack', but it too did not knock out the Lewis gun teams deployed in front of Cheapside. Their fire raked through the assault troops and then the German 'barrage came down on the top of them. First a few rose up and bolted and then the remainder fled in panic.' Both 148 and 147 Brigades stopped the afternoon attacks, as did the 8th Border Regiment which was covering La Clytte.

Further Defensive Plans
The withdrawal to the Cheapside Line was the straw which nearly broke Second Army's back, and General Plumer had issued the following message to II Corps and XXII Corps on 27 April:

> *Every yard of ground must be contested and all ranks must understand this: successive rear lines were in the course of construction, but every opportunity must be taken to strengthen and improve the front lines: local counter-attacks should be made freely, if possible from a flank, strongly supported by machine guns: the artillery policy of counter-battery, harassing and annihilating fire must be vigorously maintained.*

While that was the message to the troops, Plumer knew that Second Army could be driven back again if the Germans kept pushing. A secret memorandum to Lieutenant Generals Claud Jacob and Sir Alexander Godley outlined where they should prepare defensive lines in case they were. He was, however, adamant that they had to help the French hold the last line of the Flanders hills.

The following day GHQ told Second Army to plan a more comprehensive defensive scheme to protect the Channel ports. The German guns were searching for targets while the trench mortars were hitting the front line defences. Prisoners and deserters were all sure that Fourth Army was preparing another offensive. It was not; Operation Georgette was over.

Chapter 11

Look Out, Jerry Tanks About!

Villers Bretonneux, 7 to 25 April

Fourth Army

The German offensive on the Somme had ended on 5 April with General Sir Henry Rawlinson's Fourth Army holding on in front of Amiens. Lieutenant General Richard Butler's III Corps took over the front and his men made 'a series of lively counter-attacks, which for the most part affected the German positions on either side of the Luce [stream]'. Both sides wanted to improve their situation but the Second German Army postponed their plan to capture Villers Bretonneux until they had enough troops and guns.

Meanwhile, Fourth Army was preparing to 'clean up the woods and ravine north and north-east of Hangard', while the French would 'clear the Germans from part of the west side of the [River] Avre'. They could then advance to reach a line between Warfusée, Démuin and Moreuil. But Hangard Wood, on the boundary between the two armies, had to be taken first.

7 April, 2nd Australian Division, Hangard Wood

Charles Bean, the Australian Official Historian, explains the absurdity of a senior officer drawing a line on a map and writing a few lines of orders. Hours later a young officer had to work out how to reach the line without getting his men killed.

> *[The attack] is a particularly interesting example of the way in which an operation, readily sketched with a sweep of the pencil by higher authority, and formulated in a fluent order – Fourth Army to clean up woods and ravine north and north-east of Hangard – came to the test of all military operation orders with some harassed company commander standing in the dawn among the bullets on the actual country and wondering how he could fulfil there the designs implied in his instructions.*

Operations which looked feasible on a large-scale map spread on a table looked completely different when viewed through binoculars from a shallow trench while under fire.

At dawn on 7 April, Brigadier General Smith's 5 Australian Brigade waited for a barrage which never started. Captain Wallach was one of many wounded when the 19th Australian Battalion eventually advanced through the north half of Hangard Wood. Lieutenant Storkey stumbled upon a large group of Germans but his six men 'got in quickly with bombs, bayonet and revolver', killing thirty and capturing fifty. Captain Portman's company of the 20th Australian Battalion had cleared the south side of the wood, but Captain Wallach's objective was covered in scrub so he withdrew to where he could see his front. Portman's position was hit by counter-attacks and enfilade fire, so he too withdrew.

A larger attack against Lancer Wood, Hangard Wood and Moreuil Wood was postponed because the French were not ready. The Germans recaptured Hangard village from the French on 12 April, so the Australians poured machine-gun fire into the ruins while Captain Macdonald's company of the 7th Queen's Own advanced up to it. Lieutenant Colonel Frizell's 10th Essex (both battalions from 18th Division) then captured 120 prisoners in the rest of the village, in cooperation with the French.

On 15 April, Lieutenant Colonel Murphy's 18th Australian Battalion secured the area south of Hangard Wood while French troops cleared the village cemetery. The Germans countered by taking Bois de Sénécat on the high ground south of Hangard, so they could overlook the Allied positions. The French retook the wood but General Rawlinson and his commanders wanted to secure Villers Bretonneux's right flank before the Germans tried to reach Amiens again.

A prisoner revealed to his interrogators that there was a plan to capture Villers Bretonneux, so Major General Talbot Hobbs was instructed to draw up a counter-attack plan for 5th Australian Division. The alarm was sounded when Villers Bretonneux, Bois l'Abbé and Cachy were hit by 20,000 gas shells early on 17 April. Many of the 6th London Regiment and 33rd Australian Battalion were sent to the rear, suffering from the effects of the mix of mustard, phosgene and sneezing gas. The gas bombardment continued for several days and the number of casualties rose to over one thousand. All the while, aerial observers spotted more and more enemy batteries and 'little square objects, thought to be waggons with trench mortar ammunition'. The men on the ground also noted the German batteries were registering their targets.

On the morning of 21 April a red Fokker Dr.1 triplane flew low over the Morlancourt ridge, as the German ace Baron Manfred von Richthofen chased Canadian pilot Lieutenant Wilfred May. Another Canadian pilot, Captain Roy Brown, had been tailing the Red Baron but he pulled away as the other two flew along the Somme valley. 'As the two rose to clear the hill east of Corbie, Richthofen turned and then swerved and crashed, shot through the region of the heart, evidently by some bullet from the ground.' Various studies have attributed the fatal shot to different Australian soldiers.

24 to 27 April 1918
Villers Bretonneux

Several prisoners stated that an attack against Villers Bretonneux would begin early on 23 April while others said it had been delayed by twenty-four hours. There was talk of a prolonged gas bombardment before the infantry advanced and there was mention of a number of the new German tanks.

Aerial observers saw the storm troops assembling on 23 April and the British and Australian artillery opened fire on the packed trenches while the Royal Air Force dropped bombs on the rear area. The bombardment started at 3.45 am and high-explosive and gas shells hit Fourth Army's batteries, roads and rear areas, before switching to the front lines just before zero hour.

Three miles behind the German lines, thirteen A7V tanks (another one had broken down) assembled at Wiencourt. They moved forward during the bombardment but found it difficult to navigate around Marcelcave in the pre-dawn mist. The right group of three headed directly for Villers Bretonneux while the left-hand group drove towards Cachy. The centre group of six tanks headed for the gap between the two villages.

III Corps
8th Division, Villers Bretonneux

Major General William Heneker's division held the line in front of Villers Bretonneux. Brigadier General Coffin's 25 Brigade was north of the main road but the large volume of gas shells used in the preliminary bombardment had forced the 2nd East Lancashires to evacuate Villers Bretonneux. The German infantry were disorganised when the barrage fell short but the tanks broke through 23 Brigade and turned north behind 25 Brigade. Both Lieutenant Colonel Hill's East Lancashires and the 2nd Rifle Brigade's right were overrun, but Major Mostyn-Owen's left held on. Rather than counter-attacking, Lieutenant Colonel Griffin made the 2nd Berkshires form a defensive flank facing the north side of Villers Bretonneux.

Brigadier General Grogan's 23 Brigade was 'surprised by the tanks suddenly appearing through the fog' south of the main road. One tank

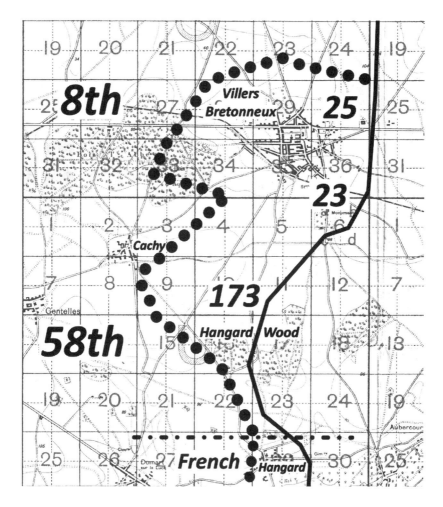

8th Division lost Villers Bretonneux while 58th Division was driven from Hangard on 24 April.

'emitted long jets of lachrymatory gas. A modern and terrible form of dragon, indeed, breathing from its nostrils not fire but an element with which it was no less difficult to contend!' German flamethrower teams dealt with the forward companies but the support line held on for several hours. The 2nd West Yorkshires abandoned the railway station after the German infantry drove Major Ingham's men from the village. Lieutenant Kennington organised the survivors after they fell back to the reserve trench and Major Drew's 2nd Middlesex followed.

The 2nd Devons were the counter-attack battalion but the first Lieutenant Colonel Anderson Morshead knew about the attack was when a tank 'came right up to his battalion headquarters, blew away the parapet and then drove away'. Another three tanks then scattered his left company. One tank deviated around a sunken road but the other two poured fire into the rest of the Devons. Anderson Morshead's men had 'dealt with such German infantry as had appeared at their front very effectively but tanks were another matter'.

The German infantry followed the tanks through the gap in 8th Division's line and entered Bois d'Aquenne. Lieutenant Colonel Davidge's 1st Worcesters had to fire from the back of Cachy Switch to stop the enemy leaving the south side of the wood behind the 6th Northants. One tank became stuck in the wire and Whippet tanks 'went full steam ahead to meet the enemy. [They] dashed to and fro among the Germans, shooting and crushing them down.' Major Shepherd's men 'brought in the tank as a trophy'.

Second Lieutenant Butler had lost one of his guns to shell fire but he had stuck by his other after the infantry fell back. He fired at the five tanks approaching Villers Bretonneux and the 'Boche infantry scattered like rabbits.' The tanks disappeared from view but one reappeared only 200 yards away, so Butler turned his gun round to face it: 'the tank still came on. Then when it was about 100 yards away, our first round was fired; it fell short. The second round burst right on top of the tank. There was a large cloud of smoke and the tank turned round and went into a dip, just as our third round burst under its tail.' By the time Butler withdrew his gun the team had fired 1,100 rounds in seven hours.

The first rumour of a breakthrough by tanks reached divisional headquarters around eighty minutes after the attack began but it was another hour before Major General Heneker was sure that Villers Bretonneux had fallen. Four tanks were deployed to drive the Germans from Bois d'Aquenne but fresh troops would be needed to recapture Villers Bretonneux.

58th Division, Hangard Wood
Major General Albemarle Cator had 173 Brigade in the front line. The 3rd London Regiment stopped the German infantry advancing north of Hangard Wood but four tanks drove them back to the Cachy Switch. The 2/2nd London Regiment swung back a defensive flank and Brigadier General Worgan sent his counter-attack battalion forward to fill the gap between the two battalions. Lieutenant Colonel Symonds was one of the many hit when the 2/10th London Regiment came under fire from Hangard Wood.

The Londoners stopped the Germans reaching Cachy and Lieutenant General Butler gave 54 Brigade (18th Division) to 58th Division, to reinforce III Corps' flank. But the 2/4th London Regiment were still driven out of Hangard Wood at dusk, forcing the 2/2nd and 2/10th London Regiments to fall back to Cachy Switch.

Major General Heneker had given three Mark IV tanks, commanded by Captain Brown of the 1st Tank Battalion, to 23 Brigade. They were about to run over the men holding Cachy Switch when one jumped out of the trench and shouted through the flap of one tank, 'look out, Jerry tanks about!' Lieutenant Mitchell could see a 'squat looking monster approaching, with two waves of infantry following. Farther to the left and right crawled two more of these armed tortoises.' The two female Mark IV tanks were immediately hit and their crews withdrew because they were only armed with machine guns:

> *Mitchell fought a duel with the Germans, manoeuvring so as to bring first one gun and then the other to bear upon it. Eventually [he] took the risk of stopping, so as to give his gunner a better platform, and at once hit the opposing tank three times in succession. Its crew left it, and he then turned to fire case shot at the infantry, and to shoot at the two other German tanks, which were still advancing. As soon as he fired at one of these, it turned and made off, and, to his surprise, the third followed it.*

Two more of 1st Tank Battalion's tanks joined Lieutenant Colonel Moore's 1st Sherwoods as they cleared Cachy. They drove south of Bois l'Abbé before turning north into Bois d'Aquenne where the male tank was disabled by shell fire. The female tank would go on to help the 2nd East Lancashires advance north of Villers Bretonneux.

Mitchell's tank was hit by artillery fire but he saw seven Whippet tanks driving pass the north end of Cachy as he withdrew. An aerial observer dropped a message for the tank pointing out were the enemy were resting in a dip in the ground just in front of Cachy. The tanks raced towards the position and the Germans 'scattered in all directions'. They 'then turned upon groups of the enemy in shell-holes, chasing them, firing at them, even running down some and crushing them'. Gunfire from the German tanks and field-guns knocked out four of the Whippets but they had inflicted 400 casualties and the advance towards Cachy had been stopped. The three surviving tanks returned with 'their sides splashed high in blood'.

Night of 25 April, The Counter-Attack

By midday, III Corps had stopped the attack west of Villers Bretonneux. Major General Hobbs had offered 15 Australian Brigade to help 8th Division but Lieutenant General Butler said his own troops could retake the village. General Rawlinson disagreed, he wanted to take it as quickly as possible, before the Germans dug in. Major General Ewen Sinclair-Maclagan was instructed to send 13 Australian Brigade from 4th Australian Division to make the counter-attack. He also ordered Major General Richard Lee to send 55 Brigade from his 18th Division to help.

Major General Heneker wanted a surprise night attack because the artillery had not had time to silence the machine gun teams around the village. Heneker was put in charge but he had to coordinate three brigades from three divisions and none of them from his own. To make matters worse, half of the British soldiers were 'untried youngsters under the age of nineteen'. The two Australian brigades would make a pincer attack on Villers Bretonneux and three tanks would then help the 2nd Northants and the 22nd DLI to clear it. Meanwhile, 54 Brigade would retake part of Hangard Wood on the right flank.

The plan was an attack at 10 pm with no preliminary bombardment and it was hoped the clouds would hide the full moon. There was no time to coordinate a creeping barrage, so the gunners would shoot at specific targets around the village before lifting beyond the objective. There were concerns because 'an improvised counter-attack in the dark is a ticklish business; the only guide to direction was the barrage and this was soon confused by the German counter-barrage.' The fact that the planning and deployment had been rushed only added to the complications.

The final plans were issued late because Brigadier General Glasgow rightly insisted on finding out what was happening at the front first. As he drove back to his headquarters the car passed his brigade; they 'were marching full of confidence, helmets cocked, cigarettes in mouths'. But Glasgow thought, 'poor chaps, they are in for a tougher time than they realise.'

Heneker had wanted the attack to start at 8 pm but Glasgow wanted 10.30 pm, saying, 'if it was God Almighty who gave the order, we couldn't do it in daylight. Your artillery is largely out of action and the enemy has all his guns in position.' They had compromised on 10 pm and 'the sky became rimmed with glare' when the guns opened fire. Captain Billy Harburn's words to his company of the 51st Australian Battalion summed up the mood: 'The Monument is your goal and nothing is to stop you getting there. Kill every bloody German you see, we don't want any prisoners, and God bless you.'

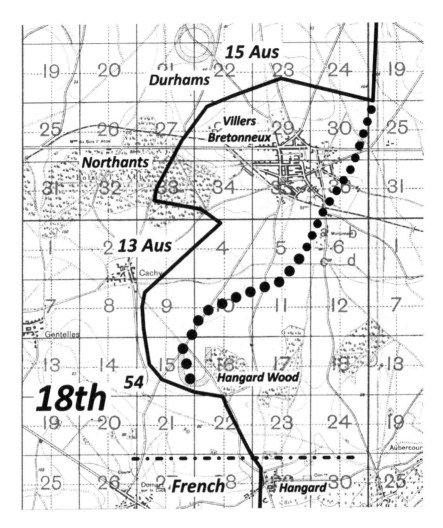

15 and 13 Australian Brigades had captured Villers Bretonneux with a pincer attack by early on 25 April.

> The whole field was soft . . . and covered with men hurrying
> forward in what looked like disorder. The lights [flares] died
> out and I plodded forward with a thin line of men about me
> into the dark. Again the lights sprang up in front of us and an
> officer shouted "still". I could see a long single line of men
> standing motionless as far as I could see in either direction,
> and, as the light faded, the darkness in front started to tap,

tap, tap, and bullets whistled round as the line shuffled forward with rifles at the ready like men strolling into fern after rabbits. The whistle of bullets became a swish and patter, and boys fell all round me, generally without a sound.

Both Heneker and Glasgow had changed Brigadier General Elliott's original plan of attack so the battalion commanders had returned from 15 Australian Brigade's headquarters late, delaying zero hour by nearly two hours. The night was very dark and 59th and 60th Australian Battalions moved slower than expected while one company lost its way.

The officer leading the 59th Battalion shouted 'charge' when the German machine guns opened fire and the whole line went forward 'in one great rush, yelling and cheering'. Flares and burning buildings cast an eerie light as Elliott's men pushed on to the Hamel road north of Villers Bretonneux. Two companies of the 57th Battalion then began looking for 13 Brigade on the right flank.

The marking out parties had discovered German troops, north of Villers Bretonneux, inside Bois d'Aquenne, and 51st and 52nd Australian Battalions set off ten minutes late from a line west of the intended start line. Lieutenant Colonel Christie's 51st Australian Battalion was pinned down by enfilade fire from Bois d'Aquenne so Lieutenant Clifford Sadlier's bombing group entered it and silenced six machine gun teams. All the bombers were killed but the advance was able to continue and a wounded Sadlier would be awarded the Victoria Cross. Lieutenant Colonel Whitham's 52nd Australian Battalion found some the 2nd Devons and the 1st Worcesters still holding a trench and they shouted words of support: 'Give them hell, Aussie, they have knocked us rotten.'

Christie's men again came under fire as they struggled through the wire covering Cachy Switch. Two machine guns gave covering fire as Captains Harburn and Cooke blew their whistles, hoping it would get the line moving again. They were right but the 'next day the wire was lined with the dead of the two battalions.' As the Australians closed in on their objective, there was 'a wild yell and the line went at them' as the Germans either surrendered or ran.

Whitham's men also reached their objective but they had to pull back their right flank after the 7th Bedfords withdrew and then had to stop a counter-attack. Meanwhile, 51st Battalion had been unable to find 15 Australian Brigade because the Germans were still holding on in Villers Bretonneux. Lieutenant Colonel James's 22nd Durhams had advanced late due to the change in orders and they could not reach the northern outskirts of the village. Lieutenant Colonel Latham had been mortally wounded as his men crossed the wire protecting Cachy Switch but Major Forster made sure the 2nd Northants contacted 13 Australian Brigade. The men 'would watch for the places from which the flares were coming and would then rush and capture them at the point of the bayonet'.

The German artillery had no idea where to shell so their infantry finally withdrew down the railway cutting between the two Australian brigades. Some put their hands up when they saw 51st Battalion but Captain Harburn gave the order 'No prisoners'. His company was so weak, he 'did not know what to do with them'.

18th Division, Hangard Wood

Brigadier General Sadlier Jackson's battalions lost touch with each other because the moon clouded over as 54 Brigade advanced towards Hangard Wood. Captain Browning's company of the 7th Bedfords fell back being hit by an accurate barrage. Captains Kingdon, McBride and Lawrence were killed and their men soon found themselves surrounded. Many were youngsters in their first battle but Second Lieutenant Tysoe decided to hold on after Private Hughes found a stack of abandoned ammunition boxes.

Lieutenant Colonel Hickson's 7th Queen's Own suffered heavy casualties because 'the enemy held forward shell hole posts which had entirely escaped our artillery barrage.' They came under fire as soon as it became light because the 9th London Regiment had been unable to hold onto Hangard Wood, and they too fell back.

The following morning a German sergeant major approached under a white flag and explained that the Bedfords were surrounded by no less than two divisions. Second Lieutenant Tysoe and Company Sergeant Major Kirby refused to surrender but the German insisted, so Company Sergeant Major Burles led him back to the battalion headquarters blindfolded. Burles was wounded en route and the German was found wandering around, still blindfolded. Tysoe and Kirby held on until they were relieved by French Moroccan troops during the early hours of 26 April.

25 April, Villers Bretonneux

Major General Heneker was determined to secure the line east of Villers Bretonneux before it was light and Brigadier General Grogan was told to gather as many men as he could find. Three tanks helped the 2nd West Yorkshires and the 2nd Devons to clear Bois d'Aquenne in the pre-dawn mist. The Germans ran and 'the fugitives were heavily punished by the rifles and Lewis guns of the Devons in the Cachy Switch as they emerged from the wood into the open.' The West Yorkshires and the Devons eventually contacted the 22nd Durhams at the east end of the village while Major Forster captured the railway station with the 2nd Northants.

At first light, 57th Australian Battalion and the 2nd Berkshires resumed clearing the area while the Northants helped the Durhams mop up the ruins of Villers Bretonneux. Between them, they had taken over 470 prisoners and 60 machine guns. Brigadier General Glasgow sent the 50th Australian Battalion forward but machine-gun fire from the Monument stopped them filling a gap in the line south of the village. Captain Pascoe would use some of the 2nd Rifle Brigade to close it. At the same time three Whippet tanks cleared a trench west of Hangard Wood, allowing the 9th London Regiment and 7th Queen's Own to close up 18th Division's line.

26 April

Foch now told General Debeney to cooperate with Fourth Army. Rawlinson and Debeney decided that the Moroccan Division would clear the ground south of the Monument while 58th Division cleared Bois de Hangard with 18th Division's battalions. The decision was taken to advance before dawn because it was thought the Germans were planning their own attack. There would be no preliminary bombardment and Whippet tanks would accompany the Moroccans advance.

General Albert Daugan's French colonial troops were 'in superb condition and the troops impatient to attack' but their Australian guides 'were of no help whatever, being completely ignorant as to the position of the elements to be relieved'. It was a disaster in the making and the French Tirailleurs stumbled on the German front line, which was further west than expected, before they deployed. 'The swift advance of masses of French infantry in daylight across the open plateau before Cachy was watched with admiration by the astonished Australians to whom the operation seemed, as it was, plainly suicidal.'

A counter-attack soon drove the Moroccans back; they had suffered over 3,450 casualties between the Monument and Hangard Wood. The 10th Essex and 7th Queen's retook part of Hangard Wood at the same time but French troops could not take the village. The attack by the Moroccans brought the fighting around Villers Bretonneux to an end.

Chapter 12

Rats in a Trap

Deploying on the Aisne

Haig was worried about the BEF's precarious situation. His left had just been pushed back towards the rail centre at Hazebrouck in Flanders; his centre was protecting the Béthune coalfields and the city of Arras; his right was guarding the important rail junction of Amiens on the Somme. Despite pleas to General Sir Henry Wilson, the CIGS, for extra men, and the promises by the War Cabinet to provide them, the BEF was dangerously below strength. It had been short of men before Operations Michael and Georgette and it was even more so now. Haig only had fifty-nine divisions and forty-three of them had been engaged in the Somme battle while another twenty-four had fought in the Lys battle; meaning some had been mauled twice in less than a month.

The BEF had suffered around 260,000 casualties in just one month; on average 8,500 a day or 4,400 from every division. They had been replaced by only 133,000 men, many of whom were either teenagers with no battle experience or those who had recently recovered from their wounds. The BEF had also lost a huge amount of artillery in the two German offensives and many divisions and heavy artillery brigades were still short of guns. On a positive note, the BEF had enough ammunition and nearly 600 tanks available. The British and Empire soldiers were also in good spirits because they had defeated the best efforts of their enemy to break them.

The French Army was also under strength, having suffered 100,000 casualties supporting the BEF on the Somme and in Flanders. General Pétain had asked for an additional 200,000 men at the beginning of April and while there were plenty of men who had been mobilised for service in the interior available, it would be July before the French Army was back up to strength.

Foch argued that the British armed forces had mobilised or had earmarked for service around 1,400,000 men who were still employed in Great Britain. He believed only 100,000 were needed to keep all the BEF's divisions in the field, even if they only held quiet parts of the line. That would allow the stronger divisions to join the General Reserve he wanted to assemble.

Haig supported Foch's idea and spoke to the War Cabinet while Clemenceau contacted Lloyd George. Foch eventually got the CIGS, General Wilson, to agree to send extra men to France and Flanders every month. It would take time to organise and the BEF had to reduce eight of its weakest divisions to cadre strength in the meantime. That involved reducing units to a core of experienced men while the rest were transferred to other units. Some of the cadres would train American troops, while others would serve on the lines of communication.

The Roulement

Foch, in his role as *Généralissime* of the Allied Armies, was considering how to make the most of the Allied divisions. He recognised that the BEF had borne the brunt of the fighting over the past month, that many British divisions needed time to recover, and that Haig was unable to give them the time. He also recognised that many French divisions were still fresh and large sectors of the French line were traditionally quiet.

Foch planned to move some of the tired British divisions to the French front, allowing French divisions to move to a threatened area of the front. All he had to hope was that the front line divisions could hold on long enough for them to make the journey. So far they had; but only just. Foch and Haig agreed in principle to swop divisions in a *roulement*; Pétain was against the idea – he was overruled.

Foch's message to Haig explained how he would like to establish a reserve of around fifteen French divisions behind the BEF. In return he wanted a similar number of tired British divisions to move to the French front. Both Haig and the War Cabinet's representative, Lord Milner, agreed to send four divisions straight away. The only proviso was that the British and French troops would maintain their own corps' sectors because their logistics were very different. Lieutenant General Hamilton-Gordon, who had just come out of the line after nine days fighting with IX Corps, was sent to French Sixth Army headquarters to discuss the details. The plan was to start the roulement as soon as possible and 50th Division headed for the Aisne on 25 April.

The American Expeditionary Force

General John J. Pershing, commander of the American Expeditionary Force, had agreed that headquarters, infantry, machine guns, engineers and signal units would be shipped first because the artillery and logistics units took up too much tonnage. The troops transported in British ships would train with the British while those carried in American ships would go to the French. So more British merchant ships were found in response to the Lys offensive.

Pershing and Lord Milner signed a deal in London on 21 April guaranteeing that the units from six divisions would be sent to the British in May. Six days later, the Allies met to discuss the transfer of the American divisions and Clemenceau complained about the Anglo-American deal until it was explained to him.

So far the equivalent strength of eight divisions, or 450,000 officers and men (American divisions were double the size of British and French divisions), were in France but only one division was in the trenches. Another three were ready to enter the line, one was in training and another was about to start training. The equivalent of two divisions were employed on rear area activities and the lines of communications. Another 200,000 officers and men would have arrived by the time the Germans attacked on the Aisne, on 27 May.

Both the British and the French representatives wanted the American divisions to reinforce their understrength divisions but Pershing was adamant that they would be grouped together as an independent American Expeditionary Force. Pershing's view was respected and it was agreed that the American infantry and engineers would be withdrawn from the BEF's sector as soon as possible, so that the divisions could be formed and deployed. The problem was it would take three months before the AEF was ready.

The Supreme War Council
The members of the Supreme War Council met for the fifth time on 1 May, the first time since early March, but the recent German offensives on the Somme and in Flanders did not take up much of their time. Instead they agreed to disband the Executive War Board and give *Généralissime* Foch control over the Italian front; they also discussed moving troops from Salonika to the Western Front. The General Reserve was also discussed and while both Haig and Foch wanted to increase the size of it, neither had any spare divisions.

The issue of deploying French troops behind the BEF was not discussed until the Inter-Allied conference in Paris on 6 May. Problems about coordinating supply and logistics were considered but they would not be resolved before the next German attack on the Aisne. In fact, most of the two-day conference was spent talking about the deployment of the American troops.

What Would the Germans Do Next?
A message intercepted on 1 May said that German Sixth and Fourth Armies were putting their attacks in Flanders on hold but that raised more questions than it solved. They still had nearly eighty divisions in reserve and some had not been engaged yet. Would they renew the attack in Flanders or on the Somme to try to destroy the BEF? Or would they choose a new location along the French front and try to reach Paris?

The American Army's Intelligence Branch had told the Supreme War Council that the Aisne sector could be attacked. It had been quiet for over six months but many German divisions had been reported in the area. Pétain and Haig were sure the Germans would renew the offensive between Arras and Albert while Foch now believed they would renew the attack across the Lys valley.

Ludendorff was in fact planning to attack the Aisne with Operation Blücher-Yorck, a large diversionary attack across a 35-mile front between Soissons and Reims. OHL (*Oberste Heeresleitung*) expected that an advance across the Aisne and Marne rivers would threaten Paris. Pétain would then pull reserves south from Flanders and they could renew the attack against the weakened BEF.

General Max von Boehn had been planning Seventh Army's attack against the French Sixth Army, which included Lieutenant General Hamilton-Gordon's IX Corps. The plan was to push the French and British troops off the Chemin de Dames and cross the River Aisne. The storm troops would then advance south another 20 miles to the River Marne. General Fritz von Below's First Army would take Reims to the east.

False preparations were being made across a wide front around Arras to make the British think they were going to be attacked again. The British aerial spotters noticed dumps, roads and other signs of a build-up. Meanwhile, the German gunners were firing gas bombardments and registration shoots to make it look like an attack was imminent.

Boehn and Below would eventually assemble forty-one divisions but there were delays because the infantry battalions were waiting for replacements while the artillery batteries and supply companies needed more horses. The soldiers' *aufmarsch* to the front was carried out over a series of nights, stopping in the Samoussy and Coucy forests during daylight hours.

The two German armies were only facing nine weak divisions of the French Sixth Army and the three under-strength divisions of IX Corps. Everyone was optimistic and Major Fritz von Unruh, IV Reserve Corps' Chief of Staff, said 'our preparations were so thorough that, if the information of their weakness in numbers was correct, we should overrun

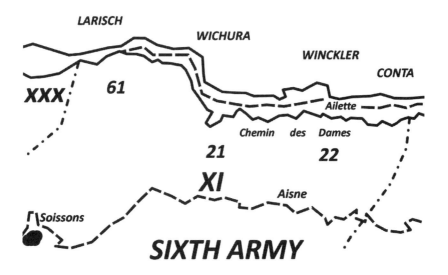

The French Sixth Army held the Chemin des Dames in strength, high above the Aisne and Ailette valleys.

the English.' Their intelligence was right because the Allies did not notice anything unusual until it was too late.

With the Lys offensive at an end it was important to keep track of the German reserves. However, the Allies had no idea where around forty-five divisions were. The railway system behind the enemy lines meant that large numbers of troops could be quickly switched from front to front, particularly around the salient which struck a huge arc between Arras, Amiens, Soissons and Reims. There were still differences of opinion over where they would attack next.

The French Intelligence Bureau had suggested that there could be a large attack across the Aisne but aerial observers had seen no signs and prisoners knew nothing. Foch also had his suspicions that the Germans could attack the Aisne, to pull reserves south, but Pétain remained convinced that the British were still the target. Brigadier General Cox, head of GHQ's Intelligence Branch, reported that divisions and heavy artillery had been spotted moving south and finally Haig believed the Aisne could be attacked, even though there was little evidence.

Taking Over the Aisne Front

The staff of the British IX Corps' headquarters reached the Aisne on 26 April and they found themselves in 'trenches shadowed by green trees and the Bois de Beaumarais gay with flowers and singing birds...' It was a welcome change after fighting in the muddy ditches across the Lys plain. The volume of shelling and sniper fire was so little that the Germans referred to the area as 'the sanatorium of the west' – a place where soldiers could rest after a battle.

The front line ran west to east, approximately 5 miles north of the River Aisne. It followed the Chemin des Dames, a narrow, steep sided ridge which separated the Aisne and the Ailette valleys. The BEF had captured it back in September 1914 and while the Germans had seized it several months later, the French retook it in October 1917.

The ridge was held by General Denis Duchêne's Sixth Army in the spring of 1918 and 50th Division took over the Californie Plateau on 8 May. Then 8th Division entered the trenches opposite Juvincourt by 13 May and 21st Division occupied the salient north of Berry-au-Bac two days later. Lieutenant General Alexander Hamilton-Gordon's headquarters opened in Jonchery and IX Corps took over from the French XXXVIII Corps two days later. Both 19th and 25th Division soon arrived in reserve.

All of the divisions had been engaged on the Somme or the Lys and the Aisne was 'a haven of delight' after 'the bleak north, with its mud and water-logged trenches'. Despite the amiable surroundings, the British soldiers were far from impressed by the French trenches. Major General David Campbell said 'he was not satisfied and [21st Division] could not hold the position for 24 hours'. The departing French commander replied that he had held it for two years, but Major General Henry Jackson was concerned to hear that a French officer had told his staff, 'you are rats in a trap. If you keep quiet all may be well.'

Anglo-French Cooperation

Pétain had laid down the principles for a greater flexibility in defence at the end of 1917. He only wanted a few troops to hold the Forward Zone, to limit the losses incurred in the initial onslaught. The outposts would delay and disrupt the attack, giving units time to man the Battle Zone where the main battle would be fought.

But some generals thought Pétain's proposal was bad for morale because it involved abandoning ground. This would be particularly true along the Chemin des Dames and General Denis Duchêne protested. So Pétain allowed the French Sixth Army to man its Forward Zone in strength

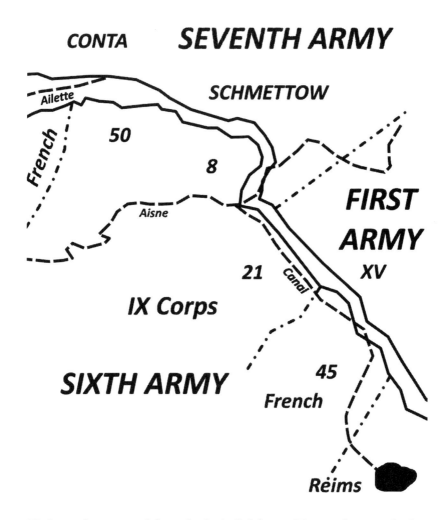

IX Corps front ranged from the high Californie Plateau down to the low ground around the canals.

on the proviso that 'none of the divisions placed in reserve were to be brought north of the Aisne.'

Foch had reinforced Duchêne's view during the battle of the Lys, stating that 'no ground can be lost… It is a matter of defence foot by foot.' Foch repeated his message after the loss of Kemmelberg, emphasising that the Allies had to protect France's coalfields and rail junctions. So Foch and Pétain had different views on how to defend.

The three commanders of IX Corps' divisions were far from happy and they expressed their feelings at a conference on 15 May. Major General William Heneker said holding troops in the Forward Zone 'was contrary to what all the British divisional commanders had learnt up north during the battles we had been in'. Lieutenant General Hamilton-Gordon agreed it made tactical sense to man Forward Zone with as few men as possible. He passed his views to General Duchêne only to be told, 'you English have learnt up north how to retreat, I will teach you to stand.' Hamilton-Gordon contacted GHQ with his concerns but there was no time to address them before the Germans attacked.

The State of the Defences
No man's land was over one mile wide on IX Corps' left, where 50th Division held the Californie Plateau, but it was only 250 yards wide where it crossed the Aisne valley, in front of 8th Division, and where 21st Division was deployed along the Aisne–Marne Canal.

The French handed over three lines of defence to Lieutenant General Hamilton-Gordon; the French referred to them as the First, Intermediate and Second Positions, the British called them the Forward Zone, the Battle Zone and the Rear Zone. The French were proud of their fortifications but the British soldier thought they left a lot to be desired. The Forward Zone had far too many trenches, some of them abandoned, making it easy for intruders to penetrate the defences. There were plenty of gun emplacements but they had been built months before and the German artillery knew exactly where they were.

The Battle Zone was on average one mile behind the Forward Zone and it consisted of a belt of strongpoints which used machine guns and field guns to cover the gaps. There were also a number of '*centres de resistance*' on the spurs north of the River Aisne or the wooded heights west of the Aisne–Marne Canal. The Rear Zone or Green Line was a mix of abandoned trenches and half-built strongpoints. It was south of the Aisne behind 50th Division and 8th Division's line, which meant they had to abandon the entire north bank if the Germans broke through. However, it was only one mile behind the 21st Division's Battle Zone on the right.

The three divisions had all deployed their three brigades side-by-side. Two battalions were split between the Front and Battle Zones and too many men were deployed too far forward. The third battalion was held in reserve, in the Rear Zone, and in some cases this meant it was south of the River Aisne.

The Aisne heights were quiet but aerial observers eventually spotted signs that an offensive was imminent. Ground observers saw dust behind the German line during daylight hours and moving traffic could be heard during the night. Lieutenant General Hamilton-Gordon expressed his concerns at the corps commanders' meeting on 24 May. He thought it was unwise to deploy so many untrained recruits in the front line with inadequate reserves. Major General Sir Edmund Guy Bainbridge's comments about the men of 25th Division explain the concerns:

> *These reinforcements, largely composed of the nineteen-year-old class, who had been training for the last nine months in England, were most excellent material, but the absence of older men suitable for promotion to NCOs rank was, in some units, a serious disadvantage… Owing to age and physique, some of these immature boys were quite incapable of carrying the weight and doing the work required of an infantry soldier in the line: their presence in the ranks rendered them a danger to their units.*

General Duchêne had no answers and GHQ had no time to remedy the problem before the attack started.

The German Air Force took to the skies in force on 24 May, to prevent Allied reconnaissance patrols crossing no man's land. A few long range reconnaissance flights by French squadrons and No 52 Squadron RAF slipped past the enemy fighters but they reported nothing of significance.

The German gunners started checking their ranges the following day as they registered their targets. French and British patrols discovered that night that the Germans were determined to stop them roaming around no man's land. Early on 26 May, German wireless traffic stopped and then jammers were switched on at dusk to interfere with the Allied communications.

All the signs were there and they were confirmed by information taken from two prisoners seized by the French on the afternoon of the 26th. They said there would be a bombardment lasting two and a half hours before a pre-dawn attack and it would take place either early on 27 or 28 May. General de Maud'huy informed Hamilton-Gordon and he in turn gave instructions to his divisional commanders. Units moved to their battle stations all long Sixth Army's and IX Corps' front as soon as it was dark, while the French and British artillery fired at roads and tracks behind the enemy lines. Major General Bainbridge's 25th Division was returned to IX Corps during the evening, ready to deploy along the Green Line, but Hamilton-Gordon had specific instructions not to move it across the Aisne.

The French and British troops along the Chemin des Dames had been given a warning but there was insufficient time to prepare before the barrage started soon after midnight. Across no man's land, storm troops from twenty divisions were waiting to cross the River Ailette and climb a steep slope to the front line. Around 5,200 artillery crews waited silently under their camouflage nets and many guns were trained on the 1,350 French and 240 British guns dug in along the north bank of the River Aisne.

The German Barrage
Oberst Georg Bruchmüller had again been chosen to plan the preliminary bombardment. The front had been static for so long that the German artillery knew where most of the Allied guns were located. So the guns and trench mortars hit every target in range with ten minutes of gas shells, starting at 1 am. Many batteries then fired gas and high explosive shells at every Allied battery for sixty-five minutes. Others hit roads, headquarters and communications centres across Sixth Army's rear area while the trench mortars hammered the Forward Zone.

The hour-long barrage smothered the battlefield with gas, forcing everyone to put their masks on in the dark, creating 'at the very start an irremediable confusion and moral effect'. At 2.15 am, the long-range gun batteries switched to targets along the Vesle and Aisne rivers, to catch reserve units on the move. The medium guns continued counter-battery fire while the field guns and trench mortars completed their destruction of the Forward Zone and the wire.

The bombardment had kept the French and British troops under cover while the German engineers bridged the Ailette and the storm troops climbed towards the Chemin des Dames. Wire was smashed, trenches were flattened and strongpoints were blown in all along the Allied line. Communications to the front had been cut, machine-gun posts had been knocked out and battery positions had been smashed.

The Germans' guns started firing a protective barrage along no man's land at 3.40 am and a few minutes later it began creeping forward. The waves of storm troops followed as close as they dared, guided by the line of explosions made by high explosive shells. The dust and gas thickened up the pre-dawn mist and the Allied soldiers did not see their enemy until they were upon them.

Seventh Army had been given twenty British Mark IV tanks which had been captured near Cambrai the previous November. They were useful for tearing holes in the Allied wire but it took them time to negotiate the trenches and shell holes. The storm troopers were soon far ahead of the tanks, leaving behind the few which were still running to help clear up any few pockets of resistance.

Chapter 13

All Hands to the Pumps!

27 May

Sixth French Army

The attack by the Seventh German Army engulfed a 21-mile wide front held by XXI Corps. On the left, 61st Division was dug in along the south bank of the Ailette but the storm troopers had soon bypassed or silenced them. By nightfall the Germans had advanced around 6 miles, travelling half the distance towards the important town of Soissons on the River Aisne.

The main part of the attack was aimed at the summit of the narrow ridge overlooking the Ailette, known as the Chemin des Dames. The assault troops quickly overran the Outpost Zone and 21st Division was driven back across the River Aisne between Vailly and Pont Arcy. The left managed to form a flank around Chassemy but the right was pushed beyond the River Vesle east of Braine, an advance of around 11 miles. However, the main thrust was made against 22nd Division's sector and the Germans quickly crossed the Aisne between Pont Arcy and Maizy, threatening the British IX Corps' left flank. The advance was relentless and by nightfall troops were 2 miles beyond the Vesle stream, west of Bazoches. Seventh Army had advanced an impressive 14 miles, rupturing the French Sixth Army's centre.

Time and again the rapid retreat meant the orders to blow up the bridges did not reach the engineers in time and 'parties were caught at work by the enemy... all initiative was forbidden by the defence plan. Moreover, the first enemy parties arrived mixed with the last of the retreating French troops.'

IX Corps

50th Division, Californie Plateau and Chevreux

Major General Henry Jackson's men held the 5½-mile-wide sector across the narrow, flat-topped Californie Plateau. The division had been engaged on two occasions in the Somme battle and then during the Lys battle

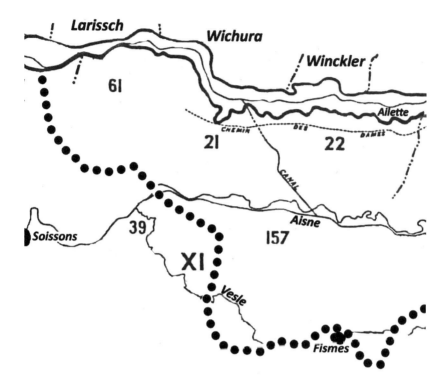

The French Sixth Army was driven from the Chemin des Dames, across the Aisne and as far as the Vesle.

only two weeks later. Many of the officers and men were inexperienced replacements, making the most basic of tasks difficult to carry out.

Brigadier General Rees's 150 Brigade was holding the summit of the Californie Plateau, north of Craonne. The 4th East Yorkshires were holding a thin line and many of the NCOs were away on leave or on courses, leaving the young soldiers short of leaders. Only a few men in the Forward Zone dugouts survived the bombardment while the rest had to use French grenades after the battalion's ammunition dump blew up.

The front companies were attacked from the flanks and the survivors were soon taken prisoner. The first Major Haslett knew what was happening was when German troops reached his dugout; he was just one of twenty officers taken prisoner. The East Yorkshires soon 'ceased to act as a battalion' and only a few escaped down the slopes to the Aisne, where Company Sergeant Major Jackson of the 4th Green Howards rallied them at Maizy. Lieutenant Colonel Stead, the only battalion commander of the brigade who was still fighting, gathered together the brigade details to hold the bridges. Only one hundred East Yorkshires answered the roll call the following morning.

The bombardment cut all but one communications cable on the 5th Green Howards' front but Lieutenant Colonel Thomson was able to report that he was being attacked from both flanks. Brigadier General Rees ordered Captain Goring to counter-attack with his company of the 4th Green Howards but they were scattered by shell fire as they clambered up the steep slope. Thomson's final message was, 'I'll say goodbye, General. I'm afraid I shall not see you again.' Rees replied, 'Try to escape, the British army cannot afford to lose you,' but Thomson was killed shortly afterwards. With the Californie Plateau lost, Rees told the 5th Green Howards to make their escape, but it was too late for most of them. Over 650 Green Howards were either killed or captured, including twenty-five officers; the Green Howards would be disbanded after the battle.

Lieutenant Colonel Kent led two companies of the 4th Green Howards to the Battle Zone around Mount Hermel when the barrage started but he had to rely on runners to stay in contact with Major Newcombe and the rest of the battalion. Stragglers were soon seen running from Craonne with storm troops in hot pursuit. Some were bombing along the French trenches and machine-gun fire hit the rest of the 4th Green Howards as the deployed around Mount Hermel. Both Lieutenant Colonel Kent and Captain Wiggins were killed fighting off the onslaught while Major Newcombe found German troops around his battalion headquarters when he returned from the brigade headquarters.

Brigadier General Rees was shocked to see 150 Brigade in its death throes when he visited Mount Hermel to find out what was happening. He then found his brigade headquarters had been surrounded when he returned. Rees was taken prisoner as he tried to escape across the River Aisne; he would be taken to meet the Kaiser on the summit of the Chemin des Dames the following day.

The bombardment levelled 151 Brigade's trenches across the slope east of Californie Plateau, causing many casualties around Chevreux. It knocked out all the communications and Brigadier General Martin lost contact with everyone early on. Storm troops then surged forward and only a few Durham men escaped.

Gas shells rained down on the 8th Durhams' headquarters and it was several hours before runners reached the acting battalion commander, Major Gould, with news of the disaster. Captain Wharrier's position was soon overrun while Captain Williams made a stand along the railway

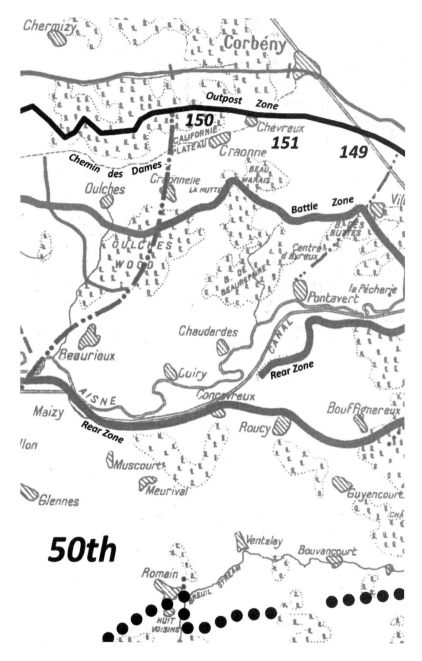

50th Division was driven from the Californie Plateau, back across the Aisne.

embankment, near the Ouvrage du Chemin de Fer, with the help of the 7th Durhams. But few escaped to help the battalion reserve company hold the Battle Zone strongpoints on the north edge of Bois de Beaumarais.

Major Gould was joined by Lieutenant Colonel Arthur Birchall, with more of the 7th Durhams along the Aisne, but they could not hold the river crossings and fell back across the river at Maizy, Cuiry and Chaudardes. Major Dickson, of the 7th Durhams, was killed fighting for Maizy while the ill commander of the 8th Durhams, Lieutenant Colonel Kirkup, organised a spirited defence of Concevreux, having checked out of a field ambulance where he was being treated when he heard of the attack.

The storm troops overran Captain Lyon's line of outposts and then captured the majority of the 6th Durhams in the support line. Captain Green made a stand around the battalion headquarters until the Germans outflanked his position, forcing him to withdraw. Lieutenant Colonel Walton left Captain Lyon in charge of the few men he could find while he went to his brigade headquarters. He found it had moved and Brigadier General Martin was dead; he returned to find all Lyon's men had been killed or captured. All Walton could do was rally every straggler he could find and guard the Aisne crossing at Concevreux until everyone was across.

Lieutenant Colonel Robinson had moved his 5th Durhams to the brigade headquarters at Centre d'Evreux during the night. The Germans had already taken 151 Brigade's Battle Zone by the time Brigadier General Martin issued orders to man it. Major Raimes led two companies along communications trenches through the woods with their gas masks on and they were taken prisoner en masse. The rest of the battalion waited for instructions which never came, even though the brigade headquarters was only a short distance away. They were 'surrounded and captured before they could leave their shelters. No news of them is to hand.'

Officers led everyone they could find down to the Aisne only to come under fire from the far bank of the river because they were mistaken for enemy troops. Captain Moscrop was killed defending Maizy bridge while Captain Hessler was killed fighting for Pontavert. Brigadier General Martin was dead so he could not answer why he had not deployed the Durhams earlier but the failure to do so meant that twenty-four officers and 650 men had been killed or captured.

Brigadier General Riddell had many concerns about 149 Brigade's sector around Chevreux. The 4th Northumberland Fusiliers' outposts withdrew as soon as they were warned about an attack but many were hit during the bombardment. The Forward Zone was soon overrun and four tanks supported the advance towards the Battle Zone, where the storm troops broke through the right company and took the left company in the rear.

Lieutenant Colonel Gibson withdrew his headquarters to the Centre Marceau but the Germans kept advancing and both the 4th and 6th Northumberland Fusiliers were soon fighting for the Battle Zone. Riddell promised reinforcements as he encouraged Gibson to hold on and he ended with the words 'very good sir, goodbye'. Gibson was killed soon afterwards 'and the 4th Northumberland Fusiliers ceased to exist as a fighting unit'.

The storm troops infiltrated between the redoubts held by two companies of the 6th Northumberland Fusiliers while the Lewis gun teams wasted their ammunition firing blindly into the mist. The support waves tackled them with grenades, flamethrowers and tanks and Bastion de Rotterdam, Centre de Quimper, Poste de Blois and Centre Marceau fell, one-by-one. Many were captured including Lieutenant Colonel Temperley and his staff.

Major Tweedy was ordered to move the 5th Northumberland Fusiliers along the Aisne from Concevreux to Pontavert. Brigadier General Riddell wanted him to cross the river and counter-attack but the Germans were moving too fast. Major Tweedy was heading towards Centre d'Evreux with the rest of the 5th Northumberland Fusiliers when they ran into the Germans in the nearby woods.

Lieutenant Colonel Temperley of the 6th Northumberland Fusiliers led two companies forward but they were soon pinned down by the Germans holding Butte de l'Edmond. The storm troops got behind the 5th Northumberland Fusiliers after clearing the Bois des Buttes and only a few escaped to the Aisne where they were rallied by Major Leathart of the 6th Northumberland Fusiliers.

Brigadier General Riddell visited Brigadier General Martin to see if they could organise a bridgehead at Centre d'Evreux, using the rest of the 5th Northumberland Fusiliers. But Martin said it was too late; he was killed soon afterwards. So Riddell formed a defensive position around Centre d'Evreux and it was 'all hands to the pumps!' He was wounded soon afterwards but he made sure the river bridges were secure before he was evacuated. Tweedy took over 149 Brigade and his staff joined the 5th Northumberland Fusiliers survivors as they retired to the Aisne at Chaudardes.

Brigade Major Jackson and Major Robb, of 4th Northumberland Fusiliers, collected around 200 stragglers from the three Northumberland battalions along the Aisne canal. They managed to cover the bridges near Chaudardes and Concevreux but the Germans had soon crossed at Pontavert, one of the bridges still standing along IX Corps' front. General Duchêne had been 'so anxious not to lose the forward position' that he had not authorised their demolition. Usually it was left to the man on the spot to decide when to blow them up and Major Hillman's men ended up destroying ten bridges, often while under fire, but around eight were still standing.

Jackson was looking for the 5th Northumberland Fusiliers and Major Tweedy while Major Robb fought off an attack against his right flank. Just then, a major arrived with news that they had to hold on because the 3rd Worcesters of 25th Division were approaching. A plan to recapture Pontavert, blow up the bridge and re-establish contact with 8th Division had to be abandoned because the Germans were too strong. So Robb abandoned Chaudardes bridge and rallied behind the Worcesters during the afternoon.

The batteries of 250 and 251 Brigades had been hidden in the woods on the slopes below the Californie plateau. They were well dug in and the gunners lived in deep dugouts while the observers used tunnels to access their lookout posts on the summit. Major General Jackson warned his artillery officer, Brigadier General Stirling, about the impending attack during the evening and he in turn gave the battery commanders their instructions. They were to bombard the roads until midnight and then start counter-battery fire as soon as the German guns opened fire. The gunners did not have long to wait.

The bombardment started only an hour later and high explosive blasted the emplacements apart while gas incapacitated the crews. The barrage knocked out all the communications so the surviving gunners had to continue firing at predetermined targets, unaware the Germans were heading their way. In some cases the first the crews knew there had been a disaster was when the storm troops approached their position. All they could do was disable their guns and escape while the few limbers ordered forward were hit by machine-gun fire before they reached their guns.

All forty-eighty of 50th Division's field guns and howitzers were lost. The two brigades suffered 270 casualties, many of them captured, including 251 Brigade's commander, Lieutenant Colonel Moss-Blundell. Lieutenant Colonel Johnston, commander of 250 Brigade, was lucky to escape Bois de Beaumarais.

General Duchêne's insistence on holding the Californie Plateau and the Forward Zone had cost 50th Division dearly. Around 1,000 men had been killed and another 4,000 had been taken prisoner in just a few hours; 'the majority were surrounded and forced to surrender before they could come into action.' The brigadiers had also paid the price for sticking with their men: Martin was dead, Riddell was severely injured and Rees was in captivity.

It was down to Lieutenant Colonels Walton and Kirkup to organise around 700 stragglers into a composite brigade. The shattered division would eventually return to the British zone at the beginning of July and it would be rebuilt, using battalions returned from Macedonia.

8th Division, Juvincourt and Berry-au-Bac
Major General William Heneker's men held a 4-mile-wide salient between Juvincourt and Berry-au-Bac on the River Aisne. The area had been fought over for three years and was covered in shell holes and entanglements while a maze of trenches connected the pillboxes and dugouts. The Miette stream ran through the centre of the sector, making lateral communications difficult.

Brigadier General Grogan's 23 Brigade was south-west of Juvincourt, with the 2nd West Yorkshires in the front line. Lieutenant Colonel Lowry was only 25 and the BEF's youngest battalion commander. He evacuated the forward line as soon as the barrage started but there were still many casualties by the time the Germans advanced.

The West Yorkshires stood to as 'the enemy came over in very large numbers and, though at a disadvantage owing to having to wear box respirators, we promptly replied with machine-guns and rifle fire.' They held on until the units either side had fallen back, by which time the majority of the Yorkshire men had been killed or captured; only twenty escaped, including an injured Lowry.

Lieutenant Colonel Page had made sure the 2nd Middlesex improved the Battle Zone around Ville-aux-Bois and they were waiting for the storm troops as the bombardment passed over. They stopped the frontal attack but were soon under attack from the left flank where the Germans had broken through 149 Brigade.

Page eventually went forward saying, 'I must go and see what all this bloody row is about!' He was wounded and then taken prisoner before he reached his destination but he was able to send a messenger back to find Captain Worstall and tell him to counter-attack with his company. The runner found Worstall with Lieutenant Colonel Anderson-Morshead and the 2nd Devons' dugouts under the Bois des Buttes. Worstall led two companies forward but they were pinned down by machine-gun fire; he was wounded and captured along with many of his men.

Brigadier General Grogan received two messages, warning that the Germans had broken through 149 Brigade on his left and 24 Brigade on his right. La Ville-aux-Bois was soon to be cut off and 'this created a degree of panic and confusion in brigade headquarters: Our position was no longer a stronghold but a death trap.' Grogan gave instructions to evacuate the line but he forgot to tell Lieutenant Colonel Anderson-Morshead because he had moved half the 2nd Devons into the trenches north of the village

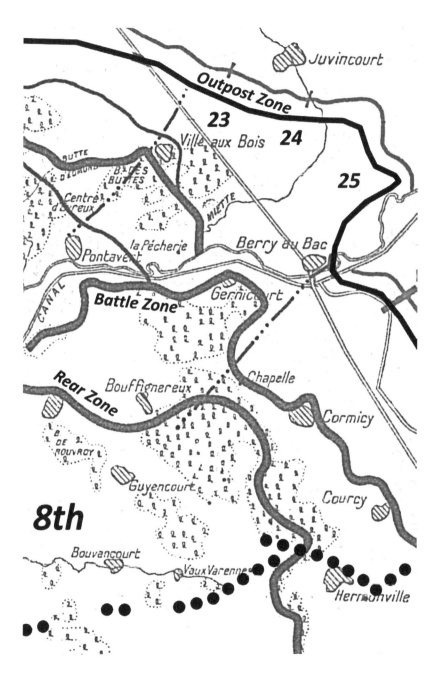

8th Division was forced across the Aisne and beyond its Rear Zone.

during the bombardment. The Devons kept 'an unbroken front up to a late hour in the morning. Although surrounded and repeatedly attacked, it successfully defeated all attempts of the enemy to advance on its front.' Three companies were eventually outflanked, and captured three companies while Anderson-Morshead used his final company to form a rearguard, so what remained of 23 Brigade could reach the Aisne. They escaped across the river at Pontavert and deployed on the south bank under Captain Saunders of the West Yorkshires.

Major Ellis of 57th Battery RFA joined the Devons and he was impressed by the way Anderson-Morshead kept his calm giving out orders while under fire. The Devons' colonel was killed leading fifty men in a charge against a battery of German artillery heading for Pontavert; his death marked the end of the Devons as a fighting unit.

In December 1918, General Pierre de Laguiche, head of the French Military Mission to the BEF, awarded the Croix de Guerre to the 2nd Devons and the citation read:

> *The 2nd Battalion Devonshire Regiment repelled successive enemy assaults with gallantry and determination, and maintained an unbroken front till a late hour. Inspired by the sangfroid of their gallant commander, Lieutenant Colonel Anderson-Morshead, in the face of an intense bombardment, the few survivors of the battalion, though isolated and without hope of assistance, held on to their trenches North of the River and fought to the last with an unhesitating obedience to orders. The staunchness of this battalion permitted the defences south of the Aisne to be organised and their occupation by reinforcements to be completed.*

Hardly any of the Devons answered the morning roll call and the popular view at the time was that 'this Battalion perished en masse. It refused to surrender and fought to the last.' However, it later transpired that twenty of the battalion officers had been captured. Only seventy-five men were later discovered to have died as a result of the fighting on 27 May. So it is logical to assume that the forward three companies were surrounded and captured en masse while Anderson-Morshead's company fought to the last.

The 2nd Northants held 24 Brigade's front line facing Juvincourt. Lieutenant Colonel Buckle issued an uncompromising message to his platoon commanders at the start of the German bombardment. They had to 'remain with their platoons and ensure that the trenches are manned immediately the bombardment lifts… No short bombardment can possibly cut our wire and if the sentries are alert it cannot be cut by hand. If they try it, shoot the devils.'

Storm troops penetrated the Northants' right flank but the five captured British tanks were either knocked out or broke down early on. So the infantry pushed on alone through the mist down the Miette valley. Buckle's men were forced to abandon their position and they fell back on the 2nd Worcesters, who were under attack from the Germans who had overrun 25 Brigade on their right flank.

Captain Marshall had been expecting to be relieved when the bombardment began and had left few men in the Worcesters' forward trench. The shelling had scattered the 1st Sherwoods as they marched forward, so Marshall went to the brigade headquarters to find reinforcements. En route he heard that Major Cartland had been killed and that he had to organise the defence along the Aisne.

Captain Pratt, the adjutant of the 1st Worcesters, made sure many stragglers crossed the river before he was cut off but only a few dozen men rallied in the Green Line, north of Roucy. Brigadier General Haig had ordered the rest of the 1st Sherwoods north of the river but German troops reached it first and they could not cross. Instead they lined out along the river bank, covering the last bridge still standing at Gernicourt. They deployed alongside the 22nd Durhams (Pioneers) who were holding a wooded ridge with the help of French troops.

Brigadier General Husey's 25 Brigade was holding a salient between the Miette stream and the River Aisne, on 8th Division's right. Captured British tanks crushed the wire but the storm troops moved past them, advancing through the mist. There was no one to stop them after overrunning the two companies of Lieutenant Colonel Richardson's 2nd Rifle Brigade, north-east of Berry-au-Bac. The two support companies of the 1st Worcesters had been ordered back, so they were able to get behind the rest of the 2nd Rifle Brigade and the 2nd Berkshires. Lieutenant Colonel Griffin and Captain Clare of the Berkshires were just two of the many men captured; the battalion suffered 730 casualties including nineteen officers and over 650 men reported missing.

That left only two companies of 1st Worcesters holding isolated strongpoints in the Battle Zone. Some of the abandoned trenches had been blocked but the German bombers soon found their way to Brigadier General Husey's headquarters.

Lieutenant Colonel Hill had sent two companies of the 2nd East Lancashires to the Battle Zone during the hours of darkness but one of the Worcesters' guides lost his way. The Lancashire men endured the bombardment as they looked for the trenches covering Berry-au-Bac they were supposed to occupy. They found that they had been abandoned and were taken by surprise in the mist and captured. It left only one company to defend 25 Brigade headquarters.

Major General Heneker instructed the rest of 2nd East Lancashires to report to Brigadier General Coffin's headquarters but their advance nearly ended in disaster as well. Lieutenant Colonel Hill and his adjutant crossed the Aisne near Gernicourt to reconnoitre the way forward. They followed a communications trench towards the brigade headquarters only to find themselves surrounded by Germans. Fortunately, a messenger told the two companies to stop on the south bank and they were able to stop the Germans crossing the river.

Brigade Major Basil Pascoe was killed organising the withdrawal to Gernicourt but his last stand allowed Brigadier General Husey's men to cross the Aisne. He formed a defensive line on the south bank of the river with 25 Brigade's survivors, next to the East Lancashires. A seriously wounded Husey was captured and died three days later.

Many of 8th Division's guns had been deployed in long established battery positions and Major General Heneker had not had time to build new ones. It meant the German gunners knew exactly where to shoot at and many guns had been knocked out before zero hour. The collapse of the Forward and Battle Zones happened so fast that the German infantry were on top of the field guns and howitzers of 33 and 45 Brigades before their limbers arrived.

Some crews disabled their guns and made a run for it but others fought on, firing at point blank range before trying to escape. Major Ramsden saw to it that 'all maps, records and kit, which could not be moved had been burnt' while his crews made sure their guns 'had been rendered useless by the removal of breech blocks and sights.' In 8th Division's sector, 'all the field guns in action, both British and French, were lost' and the only guns Heneker had left were a couple being mended in the workshops.

21st Division, Along the Aisne Canal

Major General David Campbell's men held a 5-mile-long sector between Berry-au-Bac and Loivre. The Front Zone was on the east bank of the Aisne–Marne canal where it was overlooked by the German trenches. The canal had been drained until it was no more than a wide marshy area crossed by duckboard paths hidden under camouflage. The Battle Zone strongpoints, on the west bank, were surrounded by too many abandoned trenches.

Major General Campbell had asked Lieutenant General Hamilton-Gordon if he could abandon the vulnerable trenches on the east bank of the canal but General Duchêne had refused. Instead, all he could do was to reduce the number of men deployed in the Forward Zone, remove many of the tracks across the marsh and prepare the rest for demolition. Meanwhile, the engineers tried to improve the Battle Zone strongpoints while the pioneers blocked the spare trenches.

Shrapnel and high-explosive shells hammered 21st Division's positions along the Aisne–Marne canal, cutting all communications with the Forward Zone. Gas shells thickened up the mist and it was impossible to see anything along the waterway until several hours after sunrise.

On 62 Brigade's front, the 12/13th Northumberland Fusiliers held on for some time but the 2nd Lincolns were quickly overrun and only thirty men escaped across the marsh. Brigadier General Gator ordered the 1st Lincolns forward but they were met by the fleeing Northumberland Fusiliers in the woods around Cormicy.

French territorial units deployed to stop the Germans infiltrating the woods on 62 Brigade's left flank but the 1st Lincolns were driven from Cormicy. They fell back towards Châlons le Vergeur, where they were reinforced by the 4th South Staffords. The Staffords were a welcome sight because they were from 25th Division, which was marching up from corps' reserve.

Brigadier General Cumming was worried because he had two weak battalions holding 110 Brigade's Forward Zone canal and they had just received many young replacements. The flank companies had the waterway close to their backs while the centre ones had some distance to travel before they could cross. Keeping so many men forward meant Cumming did not have enough men to hold the Battle Zone, a strong position between Cormicy and Cauroy-lès-Hermonville.

The company of the 6th Leicesters which had reinforced the 7th Leicesters just before the attack was overrun around La Neuville on the east bank of the canal. Meanwhile, the 8th Leicesters' Forward Zone was cut off by storm troops coming from the French held sector around Loire. All communications had been cut and the first news Brigadier General Cumming heard was when runners reported enemy patrols on the west bank of the canal.

The attacks from the flank had isolated the entire Forward Zone, taking many of the Leicesters prisoner. Those trying to escape to Cormicy and Cauroy soon discovered that German machine gun teams had crossed the canal and the clearing mist gave them targets along the Berry–Reims road. 'There were hundreds of our fellows running along it, like a football crowd running for the trams. Jerry's machine guns were going and they were dropping, a score at a time and lying in heaps, khaki heaps.'

The storm troops used the abandoned trenches to get past the strongpoints manned by the Leicesters east of the road. They pushed on towards the

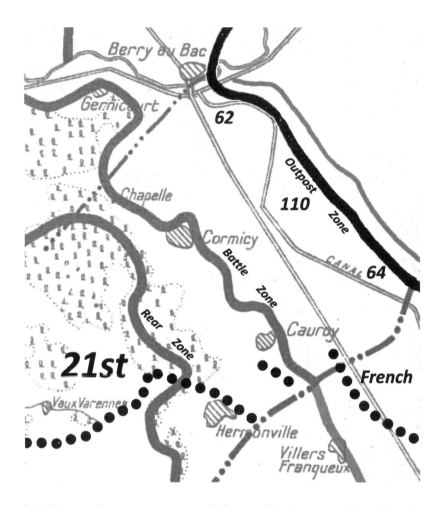

21st Division lost many men around the canal before it was driven from the Battle Zone and Rear Zone.

Battle Zone while the support waves tackled them, overrunning the 8th Leicesters' headquarters. One by one the strongpoints fell as the surviving Leicesters fell back through the woods around St Auboeuf.

Brigadier General Headlam's 64 Brigade held IX Corps' right flank, north-west of Loivre. Headlam thought the decision to keep so many men east of the Aisne–Marne canal was 'ludicrous' and he was worried they would be 'marooned' if the Germans attacked. General Duchêne's refusal to abandon the ground meant that three companies of the 9th KOYLIs and 1st East Yorkshires were indeed overrun. The Lewis gunners fought on, keeping the storm troops at bay for a time, but only a few men escaped. The late warning of the attack meant there was only time to destroy the bridges but no time to get rid of the spare material stacked around the crossing sites. It meant the German infantry had soon bridged the canal and were heading for the Battle Zone.

The rest of the 9th KOYLIs and the 1st East Yorkshires had been hammered with gas and high-explosive shells since the early hours. They knew nothing of the disaster on the east bank until two officers staggered into their lines. Both Lieutenant Shaw and Lieutenant Holmes had been taken prisoner and had then escaped to report the bad news.

Once across the marshes, the German infantry bombed down the British trenches between the strongpoints, leaving them for the support waves to deal with. The KOYLIs were soon under fire from behind their left flank, where 110 Brigade had fallen back, so Lieutenant Colonel McCulloch asked for reinforcements, and two platoons of the 15th Durhams formed a defensive flank. Other storm troops infiltrated between the KOYLIs and the East Yorkshires, so McCulloch asked Lieutenant Colonel Alexander to make a defensive flank. Second Lieutenant Middlebrook's trench mortars helped Captain Watson's company cover the gap with fire.

The rest of McCulloch's message said he was withdrawing the KOYLI headquarters to Cauroy and a confused Alexander decided to retire to Hermonville, abandoning the East Yorkshires' part of Battle Zone. Only the left company received the order and the right company was left behind, leaving a gap in the line which the Germans exploited. Brigadier General Headlam sent his brigade major, Captain Spicer, forward to tell Alexander to reoccupy the Battle Zone, but it was too late, the Germans had beaten them too it. An infuriated Headlam would sack Alexander at the first opportunity for withdrawing without the brigade's permission.

By the early evening the remnants of 21st Division were being driven from the Battle Zone with 62 and 110 Brigades falling back either side of Cormicy. On the right, the KOYLIs and East Yorkshires lost the rest of the Battle Zone and 62 Brigade's stragglers fell back onto the 15th Durhams around Cauroy and Hermonville, where they held on throughout the night.

After the battle the infantry complained about the lack of support from the artillery, stating that the SOS barrage gave 'no help to the morale of our infantry'. Meanwhile, the gunners criticised the infantry for abandoning them, unaware that most had been killed or captured on the east bank of the canal. Both 94 and 95 Artillery Brigades managed to withdraw most of their guns to the St Auboeuf Ridge before the Germans reached the gun lines. Only five guns had to be abandoned around Chapelle, on the left flank, where the Germans had overrun 8th Division's Battle Zone.

Chapter 14

Nothing to Oppose
Them but Mere Dust

27 May to 6 June
The Aisne Continued

Afternoon of 27 May

There was a lull in the fighting as the Germans regrouped and prepared to cross the River Aisne and canal. The survivors of the three front line divisions had escaped across the river but General Duchêne's order not to move 25th Division across the river meant there was a vacuum into which columns of German infantry were marching. They crossed the bridges the engineers had been unable to destroy, including those at Pontavert, Concevreux, and Maizy.

The bottlenecks of troops along the river would have been lucrative targets for the gunners but few batteries had crossed the river. Both 50th and 8th Divisions had lost all their guns on the north bank while 21st Division had lost most of its, including those sent to it from 25th Division. The batteries that had escaped could do little because they had been forced to abandon their dumps. They had to conserve the stock of shells they had with the limbers until they found new ones. So it was down to the infantry to stop a breakthrough. All afternoon 'the Germans were dribbling men forward, utilising folds of the ground to get cover from the Lewis guns and rifles which were all the defence could bring to bear.'

25th Division, South Bank of the Aisne

Not long after dawn, General Duchêne released 25th Division so Lieutenant General Hamilton-Gordon could deploy it. The first two battalions to march to the sound of guns were the 8th Border Regiment and 3rd Worcesters. They were supposed to guard the bridges around Chaudardes and Pontavert but the Germans beat them to it.

Major General Guy Bainbridge had instructions to support the three shattered divisions by forming a line on the south bank of the Aisne, and he sent one brigade to each. By late morning the 9th Loyals and 11th Lancashire Fusiliers, of 74 Brigade, had deployed along the Aisne between Maizy and Concevreux, in support of 50th Division's stragglers. But Brigadier General Craigie-Halkett soon discovered there was a large gap on his left, so he needed to throw back a defensive flank around Muscourt. All he had were some engineers supported by trench mortar teams and the trainers from a Lewis gun school.

A mid-afternoon attack penetrated 74 Brigade's line at several points but the Loyals and Lancashire Fusiliers held on around Muscourt. Lance Corporal Joel Halliwell rode a stray German-owned horse under heavy fire around the area as he rescued ten wounded Fusiliers; he would be awarded the Victoria Cross. However, the Germans were soon around the brigade's right flank, pushing the 3rd Worcesters away from the Aisne around Concevreux.

They fell back onto the high ground to the south Roucy and then waited for the Germans to attack them. Low flying planes strafed the British positions and dropped flares, to mark their line of shell scrapes for the artillery. Then the infantry charged:

> *Emerging from the wood cheering and shouting, they were quickly mown down by machine gun fire and driven back with heavy casualties. Foiled in this attempt to drive in the line by a frontal attack, the enemy now commenced an encircling movement round the right flank, at the same time bringing up trench mortars with which to bombard the front.*

The 11th Cheshires and 2nd South Lancashires, of 75 Brigade, deployed between Concevreux and Roucy alongside the men of 8th Division. Brigadier General Kennedy's men were holding their own until 74 Brigade fell back on their left. The two brigades were soon across the stream around Ventelay while the 8th Border Regiment acted as a rearguard. By midnight they were on the high ground north of Montigny with the men of 50th and 8th Divisions. But it had been a costly withdrawal as the two brigades had been reduced to around 350 men in just a few hours fighting.

Brigadier General Griffin had marched his men to IX Corps' right flank, where he found 21st Division between Cormicy and Bouffignereux. The attack which drove 75 Brigade out of Roucy also forced 7 Brigade to withdraw, and the 1st Wiltshires, 10th Cheshires and 4th South Staffords fell back across the Breuil stream around Bouvancourt.

It had been a traumatic day in which all three of IX Corps' divisions had suffered huge losses, both amongst the infantry and the artillery. They had been driven back 8 miles in places, crossing a major river, a canal and a stream on route. The reserve division had been badly mauled during the retreat too, as it tried to rally the stragglers and slow up the German advance. IX Corps now held a thin, ragged line, with several gaps in it. But this was just part of the overall story because the German Seventh Army's attack had also torn a 25-mile wide hole in the French Sixth Army's line.

28 May

Little information about the scale of the German attack had been collected by dawn on 28 May. The Allies knew that Sixth Army's front had been broken along a 40-mile front between Soissons and Reims. The break-in had been absolute and there was a breakthrough in the making because troops had already crossed the Aisne and Vesle rivers, penetrating over 12 miles into the Allied position in places.

There was little news from the front because battalion and brigade headquarters had usually been overrun. Thousands of British and French soldiers were heading into captivity but few German prisoners had been taken, leaving General Duchêne in the dark. Estimates put the size of the attack at twenty divisions and there were likely to be an equal number following up.

The situation in Sixth Army's centre was worrying because there were few troops and even fewer guns to stop Seventh Army's onslaught. Haig had sent an aide by aeroplane to see Lieutenant General Gordon-Hamilton and he heard that nine out of the seventeen Allied divisions engaged so far had been decimated. Sixth Army only had a handful of divisions close by and it would be several days before others reached the area. The shocking report was confirmed by Brigadier General Clive, the head of the British Mission with the French.

The only good news to the west of IX Corps was that XXX Corps' line north of Soissons was only being pushed back slowly. But General de Maud'huy's XI Corps had lost the city and had been forced back 5 miles over the River Vesle. General Degoutte's XXI Corps had insufficient troops to hold his long sector and they were pushed back over 5 miles across a 15-mile front. This retirement endangered Lieutenant General Hamilton-Gordon's position but he was relieved to hear that the I Colonial Corps was holding on around Reims, on his right flank.

All along IX Corps' line, men had spent the night digging shallow trenches which would give little protection from the German guns. As the morning mist cleared, they could see horse teams hauling the gunners to better positions while long columns of infantry snaked towards them. They deployed into 'a swarm of grey-clad skirmishers' as soon as the Lewis guns and rifles opened fire.

IX Corps
Lieutenant General Hamilton-Gordon's new line was on the south side of the Breuil stream, between Romain and Hermonville. The River Vesle was to his rear. He wanted his men to hold on but it was unlikely they would be able to because they were outnumbered three to one. Both 50th and 8th Divisions would have to fall back over the River Vesle if they were driven back while 21st Division would retire to the high ground between Trigny and Prouilly. There were hardly any British guns left (8th Division only had seven) but the Germans had been hauling theirs forward all night and there was a short bombardment at dawn before the infantry attacked.

<u>50th and 8th Division, Jonchery on the Vesle</u>
Major-General Heneker had taken command of the groups of men fighting alongside 25th Division but they had few officers, no orders and were supported by only seven 18-pounder field guns. The 11th Lancashire Fusiliers made a stand with the French on the north bank of the Vesle at Breuil until midday. The rest of 74 and 75 Brigades retired behind the Vesle as 'they were almost surrounded and heavily engaged... There is little doubt that the commanding officer carried out his orders to the letter in maintaining his position to the last. Nothing further has been heard of the battalion.' A wounded Lieutenant Colonel Pollitt had been taken prisoner with over 300 Fusiliers. (The battalion had lost four commanding officers, 84 officers and 1,250 men in just ten weeks.)

Brigadier General Grogan was ordered to take command of all troops along the Vesle around Jonchery but he found men from many battalions escaping across the bridge with the Germans close behind. Grogan played a big part in rallying stragglers: '[I] met a solid mob of men, marching away from the fight quite steadily. As I had no time to deal with them, I gave orders to a junior officer to get them headed and stopped and brought up again.' He then found another group and 'took steps to arrest this stream of stragglers and, having collected all available men, he formed a firing line along the Vesle, aligning the men on the railway embankment.'

As Grogan organised a new line on the south bank of the Vesle, 'they could see enemy artillery and transport pouring in continuous streams down the two roads converging on Jonchery, while infantry swarmed busily

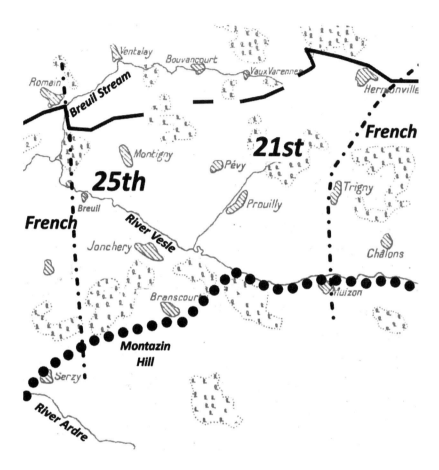

IX Corps was driven back across the River Vesle to Montazin Hill on 28 May.

across the open country. It was a sight given to gunners only in dreams, but not a gun was available.' The division's senior engineer, Lieutenant Colonel Browne, had tried in vain to blow up Jonchery bridge and the Germans had crossed the river between Breuil and Jonchery before midday.

Grogan's flank was now exposed so his command fell back onto French troops holding the high ground between Vandeuil and Branscourt. The enemy then pushed past Hourges on his left flank, forcing him to withdraw beyond Montazin Hill. Major Cope retook the summit with the 2nd Devons while French troops stopped the Germans crossing the River Ardre at Serzy behind their left flank.

21st Division, Hermonville back to the Vesle

Officers rode back and forth along the line, assessing the situation, while their staff delivered their orders. But the Germans pushed on, getting past their left flank, forcing a retirement to the high ground behind them. The men of 7, 62 and 110 Brigades had to cross the Prouilly stream under machine-gun fire from the Pévy area, finding a shallow trench waiting for them on the wooded slope.

Brigadier General Headlam did not get the order to fall back, so 64 Brigade fought on around Hermonville until he had his horse shot from under him. Most of the 1st East Yorkshires were captured or killed when the Germans got around their flank; only forty made it back to Muizon. The 6th SWBs (Pioneers) and 9th KOYLIs pulled back alongside the French, finding the 6th Leicesters and 15th Durhams waiting for them around Trigny.

Again the Germans concentrated their efforts on 21st Division's left flank, driving 110 Brigade off the high ground around Prouilly. Brigadier General Cumming withdrew the Leicesters to the Vesle at Jonchery and the 1st Lincolns kept the Germans at bay while 7 and 62 Brigades crossed. Brigadier General Headlam eventually heard about the retirement and withdrew across the river at Muizon during the early hours.

Summary, 28 May

By the time Pétain's order to stop the Germans reached Sixth Army's headquarters, they were out of date. Seventh Army had advanced before dawn, often finding no organised resistance to stop them. Pétain had also wanted General Duchêne to counter-attack but the line was falling back by the time they arrived, so they were used to shore it up.

After hearing the bad news from Sixth Army, Pétain toured the front to hear what his generals had to say. He then decided to assemble four divisions around Soissons and four around Reims. The Germans would have advanced further by the time the French reserves were ready and the divisions would be able to attack their vulnerable flanks.

As Pétain formulated his plans, Prime Minister Clemenceau visited Foch to hear how the battle was progressing; it did not sound good. The BEF's situation was still precarious so he dared not divert many French divisions south to help; not that they would arrive for several days. Pétain was away from his headquarters, so he continued to Sixth Army's headquarters where he learnt that Duchêne had not seen the Chief of the General Staff either. He told the Prime Minister that his line was falling back in front of around twenty divisions and that 'he had nothing to oppose them but mere dust'.

29 May

General Pétain's plan was to counter-attack the flanks of the German salient. There was little progress around either Soissons or Reims but it did stop the Germans pushing west or east. Instead they advanced south, driving Sixth Army's centre back around 7 miles towards the Marne. It also exposed the flank of the French troops on IX Corps' left. Lieutenant General Gordon-Hamilton had spread 25th Division across his front, to support his three decimated divisions. French troops held two sections in the middle of his line but he was expecting to receive 19th Division.

The 29th of May was another difficult day for General Duchêne and the only good news was the arrival of General Lacapelle's I Corps. On the left, General Chrétien's XXX Corps was pushed back 3 miles north of Soissons while XI Corps' left flank held on south of the city, where the Germans struggled to get across the Aisne. However, General de Maud'huy's centre and right again fell back around 7 miles, crossing the La Crise stream between Buzancy and Nampteuil. The German troops were told to leave their heavy equipment behind and push to the Marne and some were in sight of the River Marne by the end of the day. General Degoutte's left fell back a similar distance, abandoning Fère-en-Tardenois, while the rest of XXI Corps retired 4 miles, opening a gap on IX Corps' left flank.

IX Corps

<u>8th and 50th Divisions, Montazin Hill across the Treslon Valley</u>

An early German attack aimed at taking the high ground east of Lhéry was disjointed but the advance along the Ardre valley was a success. It drove the French troops out of Serzy, compromising Montazin hill, so Heneker had to tell the men of 8th and 50th Divisions to fall back to the next ridge, between Lhéry and Tamery. Brigadier General Grogan and Major Wass rode back and forth along the line, making sure their men held on until dusk. Grogan would be awarded the Victoria Cross for again saving the day. They were then able to withdraw across the Treslon valley to find the 2nd Wiltshires of 19th Division waiting for them on the last ridge north of the Ardre. Major Rapson's men gave covering fire, pinning the Germans down while Heneker's men dug in.

<u>19th Division, The Ardre Valley</u>

Buses began delivering the infantry battalions to Chaumuzy and Chambrecy some 7 miles behind the line early in the morning. Major General Jeffreys visited Lieutenant General Gordon-Hamilton's headquarters at Romigny, west of Fère-en Tardenois, to learn that there was a gap in IX Corps' line in the Ardre valley. IX Corps cyclists had been sent ahead to scout the area

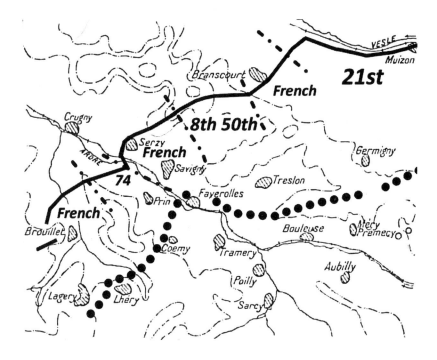

IX Corps was forced to retire astride the River Ardre.

and he wanted 19th Division to cover it. He sent 57 Brigade to investigate Brouillet, and Brigadier General Eden reported the Germans held it. Meanwhile, 58 Brigade was sent to check who held Serzy; Brigadier General Glasgow found that it had been lost, as had Savigny a mile to the south-east.

The two brigades deployed between Lhéry and Faverolles, and while Jeffreys welcomed his artillery later that night, his situation was still precarious. But the Germans were pushing through the large gap between the British and the French to the west. The 74 Brigade sent the 1/6th Cheshires and the 8th Border Regiment to the flank and they managed to fill the gap. Jeffreys was also worried about his right flank, where the 8th Division Battalion (the survivors of 8th Division) had fallen back east of Faverolles.

During the night the 8th North Staffords and the 1/4th Shropshires extended Major General Heneker's position on the ridge north of Bouleuse, making contact with the French. Brigadier General Heath would take over from an exhausted Grogan.

21st Division, The River Vesle Around Vesle

Most of Major General Campbell's line was behind the River Vesle and an attack from Branscourt in the afternoon was stopped. However, his position was compromised when the French were driven off the high ground on his left flank. A final position was taken up at dusk, south of Germigny.

IX Corps Summary, 29 May

By nightfall, the three divisions which had been attacked two days earlier could do no more. Lieutenant General Gordon-Hamilton asked for help and French troops took over from 21st Division on the ridge north of Bouleuse during the night. He placed Major General Heneker in command of the troops south of the Ardre and Major General Jeffreys responsible for the north bank. The weak point in the line was where Senegalese Tirailleurs held the valley between them.

General Summary, 29 May

General Micheler and Fifth Army staff arrived on the Aisne during 29 May, to take over the east side of the salient, including IX Corps. So far all attempts to push the German flanks back had ended in failure, so Pétain intended to change tactics. He would use the reserves rushing to the area to take the enemy head on and drive him back across the Vesle and the Aisne, starting on 31 May. General Pershing had handed over the 3rd American Division (which was twice the size of a French and British division) and the infantry battalions were en route to Château-Thierry.

During the day there was worrying news from the French military attaché in Copenhagen, Denmark, who had picked up on a rumour doing the rounds in Germany. He had heard that the attack on the Aisne was just a huge diversion and that the Germans were still planning to capture Amiens. Haig warned his army commanders that the French could move their reserves from the BEF. But for now, all Foch did was to instruct the divisions of the General Reserve to march closer to their nearest railway station.

Meanwhile, Clemenceau had gone to the French Sixth Army to see General Duchêne. He could not find him in Fère-en-Tardenois and instead found General Degoutte, who complained that his commander had lost control. He also learnt the Germans were on the outskirts of the town, so he made a hasty departure. Clemenceau eventually found Duchêne only to find that he knew little about Sixth Army's situation; the corps commanders were not much better informed. Clemenceau decided he had to speak Foch, only it would be two days before they would finally meet.

30 May
General Pétain's plan to counter-attack was disrupted because the Germans struck faster and harder. On Sixth Army's left, XXX Corps was driven back 5 miles in places but it held on around Soissons. In the centre, XI Corps lost around 5 miles, and General Lacapelle's I Corps' headquarters took command of XI Corps' left during the evening. Meanwhile, on the right, XXI Corps was pushed back to the River Marne between Chartèves and Dormans. The French engineers did not always have time to demolish the bridges, so the Germans were to secure a bridgehead at Jaulgonne.

IX Corps
74 Brigade, Lagery
The withdrawal of the French meant Brigadier General Craigie-Halkett's left was exposed, while a dawn attack pushed past 74 Brigade's right flank near Lagery. It had to fall back 3 miles, towards Romigny, where it was reinforced by the 5th SWBs (Pioneers) and a composite battalion of the 50th Division. The Germans kept up the pressure and Craigie-Halkett's men were pushed back onto the high ground south of Romigny.

19th Division, Lhéry, Faverolles and Bouleuse
The early morning attack bypassed 57 Brigade's left flank around Romigny, allowing the Germans to enfilade Brigadier General Eden's position. A company of the 10th Worcesters sent to cover the flank was shot to pieces, so the rest of the 10th Worcesters and the 3rd Worcesters had to retire while the 5th SWB were driven from Romigny. They struggled to keep in touch with 74 Brigade, but they managed to protect the supply dumps around Ville-en-Tardenois. The Germans then turned their attentions on the 8th Gloucesters, forcing the entire brigade to fall back even further, so the 10th Warwicks had to move up to reinforce the line.

In 58 Brigade's sector the position around Faverolles was compromised early on because 57 Brigade withdrew on its left while the Senegalese troops to the right disappeared. Companies from both the 9th Welsh and the 9th Welsh Fusiliers were cut off and captured. Brigadier General Glasgow was wounded but he managed to deploy the 9th Cheshires on the high ground north-west of Sarcy, providing a line for the Welshmen to rally on.

On 19th Division's right flank, both 56 Brigade and the 8th Division Battalion were holding on until the French withdrew. The 2nd Wiltshires had a tough battle for Bouleuse and Brigadier General Heath's command suffered many casualties as they were made 'to run the gauntlet of heavy machine gun-fire which was directed at them from all sorts of unexpected

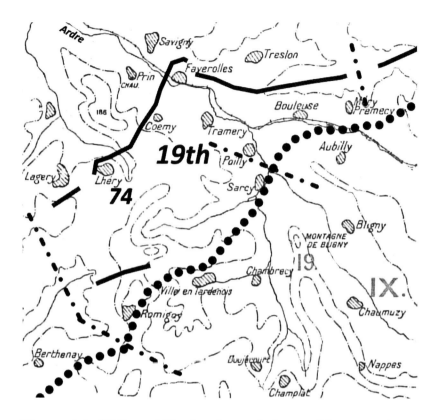

What was left of IX Corps fell back on the supply dumps of Fère-en-Tardenois.

points' across the Ardre valley. The Germans then used a smoke screen to cover their machine gun teams, as they hauled their weapons forward. The 8th North Staffords and 1/4th Shropshires were then forced back and the 2nd Wiltshires had to withdraw to the Ardre next to Bligny. Heath would take command of 58 Brigade from the wounded Glasgow while French troops relieved his own brigade around Aubilly.

Many small groups were cut off and while some fought on behind enemy lines until they ran out of ammunition, others made a break for it or joined French units. Captain Boughton-Leigh's group of the 2nd Rifle Brigade spent three days living off the land and drinking champagne they found in cellars. They stayed one step ahead of their enemy but one group escaped because the Germans were too drunk to catch them.

Summary, 30 May

Lieutenant General Gordon-Hamilton felt his troops could not hold on any longer, so he asked General Joseph Micheler and General Louis Franchet d'Espèrey if either the Fifth Army or the Groupe d'Armées du Nord could help. General Pellé's V Corps would take over IX Corps' sector during the afternoon but it would take time to relieve all the British troops.

Clemenceau visited General Duchêne only to hear that he doubted if he could stop the Germans crossing the River Marne. That would leave them only 40 miles from Paris and they had advanced 20 miles in the past three days. General Foch had directed the four divisions of the General Reserve to help while General Pershing had already sent one American division. The situation was looking desperate and the politicians in Paris were looking for scapegoats; they chose Pétain and Duchêne.

31 May to 6 June

The battle was coming to a close by 31 May because the German OHL were having to reconsider their situation. It wanted to hold a solid line along the Marne and make the salient safe, so attention could be turned once more to the British, now the French reserves had moved south. Haig thought the Germans would attack the BEF again but Pétain thought Paris was still the target.

Sixth Army's counter-attack around Soissons gained nothing but it stopped the Germans improving its situation on the west flank of the salient. Fifth Army was supposed to counter-attack around Reims but the troops were too tired. Again the Germans made the most progress in the centre. They pushed XI Corps back around 4 miles around Oulchy-le-Château and forced XXI Corps back 6 miles to the Marne, east of Château-Thierry.

IX Corps

19th Division, Montagne de Bligny, 31 May and 1 June

The French were driven out of Bois de Bonval, so 57 Brigade had to fall back through Chambrecy, onto the ridge south of Montagne de Bligny. French troops helped the 8th Gloucesters hold the high ground west of the hill. A morning attack drove 56 Brigade off the ridge north of Chambrecy but Lieutenant Colonel Cunninghame rode forward leading the 9th Cheshires and they rallied the retiring troops. Cunninghame had his horse shot from beneath him and was wounded but he led the counter-attack on foot to recapture the high ground.

Major General Jeffreys was at Brigadier General Heath's headquarters when he heard that Montagne de Bligny, the highest peak in the area, was in danger of being lost. So he ordered the 2nd Wiltshires to retake Chambrecy at dusk but they found the Cheshires already on the objective, so Major Rapson helped them secure it.

The French were driven from Aubilly on 56 Brigade's north flank during the afternoon and Second Lieutenant Owen was mortally wounded leading the 1/4th Shropshires' counter-attack which restored the situation. A new position was taken up around Montagne de Bligny during the night.

Battle of the Aisne Summary
Haig and Foch spent the morning discussing whether to send more tired British divisions to the French sector. However, the Germans had not

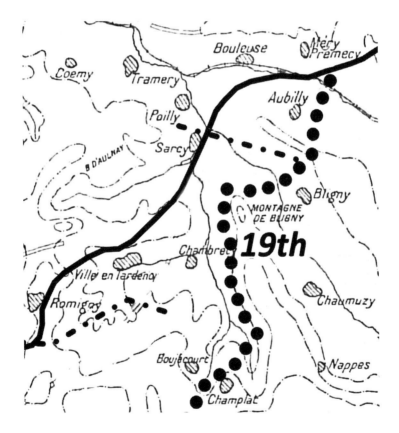

19th Division held onto Montagne de Bligny but it lost Fère-en-Tardenois.

shifted any of their divisions south, so there was still the possibility they could renew the attack in Flanders. Haig went on to meet Lloyd George, First Lord of the Admiralty Sir Eric Geddes, and First Sea Lord Admiral Sir Rosslyn Wemyss in Paris. Meanwhile, Foch met Clemenceau, Pétain and Duchêne at Sixth Army's headquarters. Although the danger along the Marne appeared to be receding, Pétain's plea for extra reserves was delayed until after the Supreme War Council had met.

By now it was obvious the Germans were slowing down, and while fifteen of the assault divisions were still engaged, most of the reserve divisions were thrown into the fray. The Germans were again unable to advance around Soissons or cut off Reims on the flanks on 1 June. However, the centre had advanced another 5 miles between Vierzy and Château-Thierry. The French had relieved 74 Brigade around Ville-en-Tardenois and they held on until the commander gave notice that he had to withdraw during the afternoon. It exposed the 2nd Wiltshires' flank to attack and 'in the absence of any other orders the battalion hung on and prepared to make a stand against the odds, knowing they were in danger of being annihilated.' Major Rapson received the order to withdraw to Bois d'Eclise just in time.

The Germans were able to penetrate between 57 and 56 Brigades and they rolled up part of the 8th Gloucesters, taking the summit of Montagne de Bligny. The loss of the observation point compromised the whole of 19th Division's line, so Captain Pope led a counter-attack and the Gloucesters recaptured the hilltop position with French help. The line had been saved but Major General Jeffreys had to pull back his left flank south of the hill where the French had fallen back to Champlat-le-Boujacourt. Although 19th Division had saved the line, it had cost it dearly; 57 Brigade was down to 750 men while 58 Brigade had only 350.

6 June

There were further attacks on 2 and 3 June but all they did was make the salient deeper and more vulnerable. Indeed, the French even drove them back across the Marne at Jaulgonne.

19th Division, Montagne de Bligny

Major General Jeffrey's men had been digging in for four days when the final attack of the campaign was made to capture Montagne de Bligny from 19th Division. An early morning bombardment on 6 June hit the artillery with Green Cross shells, smothering the battery positions with phosgene and chlorine gas. High explosive shells followed but the German observers could not see the shallow British and French trenches 'as the standing corn masked the position considerably'.

Even so, they drove Lieutenant Colonel Cunninghame's 9th Cheshires and Lieutenant Colonel Koebel's 8th North Staffords from the summit of Montagne de Bligny while the French lost Bligny village. The hill overlooked the whole area, so Brigadier General Heath ordered a counter-attack by the 1/4th Shropshires. The senior officer, Lieutenant Bright, led the 200 survivors of the 1/4th Shropshires 'in four waves at 100 paces distance' under fire for one mile up the hillside. They found the survivors of the Cheshires and North Staffords and then all three battalions drove the Germans from Montagne de Bligny 'at the point of the bayonet'. The supporting barrage started after the hill had been taken 'owing to an error in timing and the rapidity with which the attack went forward'. The French cleared the nearby village later in the day.

The attack on Montagne de Bligny was the final attack on the Aisne. The British troops sent to the 'quiet sector' were finally withdrawn on 19 June and they headed north to re-join the BEF. The battalions of the 50th and 25th Divisions would be reduced to cadres and reformed in time for the final campaigns. The 8th and 21st Divisions were rebuilt with more replacements and sent back into the line.

The Supreme War Council
Another session of the Supreme War Council was due as the Battle of the Aisne came to an end. But Haig received bad news from Secretary of State for War Lord Milner, General Sir Henry Wilson (CIGS), and Lieutenant General Sir John DuCane who was based at Foch's headquarters, before it started. The BEF had to hand over all the American troops in training to the French, so they could take over quiet parts of the line. Haig was against the idea but he was overruled.

Next came a conference between the French and the British during which Lloyd George and Foch argued over the number of British replacements being sent to France and Flanders. Foch proved his point by pointing out that the BEF had already stripped nine divisions of all their troops while another two were about to be reduced to cadre. The only way to appease the French was for them to be allowed to send an officer to assess the BEF's manpower situation.

After all the anticipation, the Supreme War Council achieved little. There was discussion over naval command in the Mediterranean and it agreed the programme for transferring American troops to France would continue. There was some discussion about the dangerous situation on the Western Front and the chances of a new German attack between Montdidier and Noyon. Otherwise there was just gloomy talk about the Allies' chances after two months on the defensive.

Conclusions

Planning the Attack

The Germans had been considering an attack in the Lys area for over two years by the time Operation Georgette was launched on 9 April 1918. A relatively short advance would bring the railway junction of Hazebrouck in range of their heavy artillery, interfering with the supply route to Ypres. That would force the British to abandon the Salient and the Belgians would have to withdraw from the flooded area next to the coast. It meant a relatively small attack could threaten the BEF's bases along the coast.

The problem was that OHL never had enough troops to carry out such an attack as long as Germany was fighting a two-front war, as had been the case at the battle of Verdun in 1916. They also saw the Allies try time and again to break their own defences with too few divisions and too little ammunition. The opportunity came with an armistice with the Russians in December 1917 and the Lys was one of several areas considered by OHL.

An extra thirty-five divisions on the Western Front (nearly 250,000 rifles) meant Ludendorff was able to plan two large attacks, in close succession. The first attack by three armies on the Somme would drive a wedge between the British and the French and capture the important rail junction of Amiens. That would restrict the movement of reserves from north to south while the British flank was pushed north of Arras and the French were kept south of the Somme.

Operation Michael was launched on 21 March and it nearly succeeded in its first two aims. Fifth Army's collapse made it difficult for the French divisions to deploy behind the British line. However, the soldiers of the two nations fought together to maintain contact south of the Somme, despite being driven back over 40 miles in places. The Germans had also failed to roll up the British line south of Arras and the attempt to widen the breach, called Operation Mars, failed completely on 28 March.

The planning for the attack across the Lys took a number of twists and turns as Operation Michael developed. The failures on the Somme meant the number of divisions available for Flanders was considerably reduced. The date was also delayed until the heavy artillery train could be moved north from the Somme. Several smaller attacks were planned, and while some were abandoned, the rest merged into a two-stage attack. Sixth Army hit south-west of Armentières first, taking advantage of the anticipated poor performance of the Portuguese. Twenty-four hours later Fourth Army would seize the Messines Ridge, north of the town, threatening the supply line to the Ypres Salient. The combination of the two attacks would force the town to be abandoned, extending the breach in the BEF's line to over 20 miles.

OHL's planning had been flexible, to accommodate the progress of Operation Michael. However, the number of divisions and guns diminished over time until there were too few to achieve the initial objective. OHL also correctly anticipated that the ground would be dry enough to cross early in April. It seems that they also made enough bridging units available to cross the Lys and they reached the river at some points, close behind the infantry. However, the German high command did not seem to appreciate that the many ditches would restrict movement of the artillery limbers and supply wagons to the few roads. The early success by the infantry would be tempered by the difficulties experienced by the support arms.

British Manpower Situation
The BEF had been understrength before Operation Michael and over 175,000 casualties during the retreat weakened it even more. Four of the divisions involved in the opening days of Operation Georgette, 34th, 40th, 50th and 51st Divisions, had all suffered terrible losses. They had been sent to the Lys because it was a quiet area, where hardly anything of consequence had happened for three years. As it turned out they had been deployed right in front of the new attack. Nothing was done to replace them or reinforce them, despite all the signs that an attack was due.

The BEF's manpower situation meant it had to rely on the *Corpo Expedicionário Português* to hold a sector of the front line. The Portuguese soldiers were not interested in the war, their morale was low and there were language problems. All this became known to the Germans and it encouraged Ludendorff to plan an operation to attack them. All General Horne could do was to make sure First Army's limited reserves were ready to deploy to the Battle Zone to limit the inevitable breakthrough. First Army had put a plan into place to relieve the Portuguese but it came too late. The preliminary bombardment caused many to desert before zero hour and few faced up to the attack. General Horne had been expecting the Portuguese to fall back after putting up a token resistance. However, their line collapsed far quicker than expected, leaving the British divisions no time to man the Battle Zone. The shortage of manpower meant that little work had been done on the Rear Zone and it was lucky for First Army that the River Lys and the Lawe canal could be used as a natural line of defence.

The British troops on the Portuguese flanks put up a good fight, despite the fact they were recovering from their trials on the Somme only two weeks earlier. But it had not been easy because the machine gunners had to fire blindly into the morning fog until it cleared. The artillery rarely saw the flares calling for SOS barrages and they were unable to provide much assistance. But the mist had also slowed down some of the storm troops and they could not keep up with the barrage as it crept forward. The disorientated groups of infantry came under fire as soon as the mist cleared.

The main British success on 9 April was 55th Division's fight for Festubert and Givenchy. The Lancashire men had spent two months preparing their defences and they held them admirably. The Forward Zone broke up and delayed the storm troops long enough for the support companies to man their defences. A maze of wire entanglements and ditches then funnelled the attacking soldiers into the path of strongpoints and machine-gun posts. The Germans may not have had a high opinion of 55th Division before the attack but they certainly did afterwards. It was a case of, as their memorial at Givenchy states, 'they win or die, who wear the rose of Lancashire.'

The Battle Begins

German observers flew across the battlefield as soon as the weather allowed and the early reports were promising. So promising in fact, that Crown Prince Rupprecht instructed General Quast to push across the Lys during the night. However, later reports were less optimistic and the British spotter planes noted that the advance was slowing down because the Germans were victims of their own success. Hedges and ditches delayed the infantry, while the gun limbers and supply wagons had to queue up to cross the bridges and culverts.

The river and canal line would add to the undoing of Sixth Army's attack. Once across the watercourses, bridges had to be repaired or built so everything could be carried across them. The British gunners knew where the crossings were and they targeted the inevitable bottlenecks which built up around them. It was the same for the RAF's pilots, who were able to find lucrative targets around the bridge sites when the weather allowed them to take off. Eventually it was a breakdown in logistics beyond the Lys and the Lawe that stalled the advance rather than enemy action.

The British reserves sometimes fared no better. For example, Bailleul was 'crowded with fugitive civilians and in a general state of turmoil and confusion'. The infantry often had to move across country to avoid the traffic jams. They would then march to the sound of guns and deploy open order when they came close to the front line because the front line was so fluid.

Orders were often out of date by the time they reached the front line during the fast moving actions and it was down to the local commanders to decide what to do. Sometimes the message never got through, because runners were killed or wires were cut, and it was again down to the company and platoon officers to decide what was best. Occasionally, orders from above confused the situation at the front line, resulting in disaster, like the loss of Hill 63, where the front line companies thought they had to hold on until dusk.

The Army Service Corps struggled to deliver ammunition to the batteries for the same reason as their German counterparts. Their limbers also had to stick to the congested roads and they rarely found their units because they were moving so fast. It meant men were often left short of ammunition and rations while officers looked to the scroungers in their units to find abandoned dumps.

Backs to the Wall

There was insufficient time to send enough replacements for the Somme casualties over to France before the attack on the Lys. Those who did reach their units in time had no battle experience and were often young men. There were too few veteran officers and NCOs to train them in trench warfare and some barely knew their officers' names before they were thrown into the battle. Despite this, they fought a determined enemy, often from ditches and hedges, to a standstill. In doing so they had fulfilled Haig's order 'to fight it out. Every position must be held to the last man: there must be no retirement. With our backs to the wall and believing in the justice of our cause each one of us must fight on to the end.'

Haig's despatch dated 20 July 1918 outlined his admiration for the fight the British conscripts had put up:

> *All these divisions, without adequate rest and filled with young reinforcements which they had no time to assimilate, were again hurriedly thrown into the fight and in spite of the great disadvantages under which they laboured, succeeded in holding up the advance of greatly superior forces of fresh troops. Such an accomplishment reflects the greatest credit on the youth of Great Britain as well as on those responsible for the training of the young soldiers sent from home at this time.*

Artillery and Tanks

The fast moving front line made it difficult for the artillery of both sides to fire accurate barrages. It was especially difficult for the British batteries because they were often supporting divisions other than their own. Special measures were taken in some areas; for example Brigadier General Metcalfe organised all the artillery behind IX Corps' long front into four artillery groups. Each one contained a mixture of field guns and heavy howitzers and supported a division.

Locating the front line in the flat fields was difficult. Soldiers usually had nothing more than ditches and hedges for cover, while the guns were deployed behind buildings. The variable weather meant the RAF's pilots were often unable to spot targets for the gunners. Meanwhile, ground observers did the best they could from the roofs of buildings and tree tops. In one case British gunners established a crude flash-spotting system using church spires to orientate themselves.

The German bombardment often reduced in intensity when the infantry advanced, at a time when they were needed the most. The field guns and trench mortars had to stay in range but the limbers had to stick to the congested roads, leaving them vulnerable to air attack, if the skies were clear. The heavy guns needed to conserve their ammunition stocks in case the French or British troops were seen gathering to counter-attack.

During the later stages of the campaign the Germans used a simple yet effective method to locate targets. The infantry began their advance from a long distance away, drawing fire from the British artillery and machine-guns, before going to ground. Observers would report the locations and angles of all the firing positions, so the artillery could locate them. The infantry moved closer to the British line in small groups during the lull in the firing. A second barrage, this time far more accurate, would herald the start of the real attack.

There is little to say about tanks because the Flanders clay was unsuitable for them and they dared not venture off the roads. The Germans deployed ten captured British Mark IVs on the first day but most broke down and stopped the traffic. The most notable thing about the Tank Corps was how readily the crews were deployed to trouble areas with their Lewis guns. They could quickly add an enormous amount of firepower to a weak sector of the line.

The Battle of the Aisne
All belligerents used similar defensive schemes, with troops deployed across three zones. Artillery bombardments were so effective by this stage of the war that it was unwise to put too many troops too far forward. Usual policy was to put a minimum number of troops in the Outpost Zone, where they could disrupt and delay the attack. The bulk of the troops were distributed across the Battle Zone, where strongpoints and machine gun

posts were used to stop the storm troops. The divisional reserves would be able to reinforce the Battle Zone and protect the artillery. The corps reserves would deploy to the Rear Zone, either ready to counter-attack or collect any stragglers.

The dilemma for the French Sixth Army on the Chemin des Dames was that the ridge was an important place. To give it up without a fight would have been bad for morale but it was impossible to hold it the conventional way. The outpost zone was situated along the summit of a narrow ridge while there was the River Aisne just behind the Battle Zone. Elsewhere there was a reluctance to give up any ground, and it resulted in troops being deployed in vulnerable positions. While General Duchêne's concerns are understandable, it should be noted that the BEF had recently abandoned the Ypres Salient, as soon as reserves were needed to stop the Lys offensive. The area could be considered to be as iconic to the British because so much blood had been shed there the previous autumn.

General Duchêne convinced General Pétain to hold the Outpost Line in strength and it ended in a disaster for the British and French alike. The front line battalions were overrun in the mist and while the casualty figures are high, the low number of deaths indicate that some did not put up a fight. It seems that many front line companies surrendered en masse, probably while sheltering from the barrage. It is clear that the storm troops used infiltration tactics where possible, leaving any difficult areas for the support waves to mop up later. They also got around the flanks of the front line troops when possible before driving deep into Allied territory. The number of guns lost is testament to the rapid advance; virtually all of 8th Division's artillery was lost.

The German order during the advance beyond the Aisne had been simple: 'Pursuit to be continued at once. Forward to the Marne!' But their eagerness to keep advancing was just funnelling them into a narrowing salient. The further the divisions moved south, the harder it was to keep them supplied and the more their flanks were threatened.

The rapid advance also meant that the German assault troops again stumbled on Allied dumps before they could be emptied. Time and again they found huge stacks of ammunition, food, clothing and, the most dangerous thing, alcohol. They filled their knapsacks and then ate and drank what they could as a welcome change from the dull rations they were used to. They had been told the submarine blockade had caused shortages which had brought the Allies to their knees. But the evidence was, it was Germany that was suffering from shortages. Officers often had to resort to guarding stores to maintain discipline and limit drunkenness so the troops would keep advancing.

The Germans advanced 28 miles in just five days between 27 May and 1 June and they were only 35 miles from Paris. Altogether, IX Corps had suffered nearly 30,000 casualties, the majority taken prisoner on the first day. Ironically the British soldier fought better than the Germans when moving in the open. Again many of the soldiers were young and inexperienced but they were rarely beaten during the retreat from the Aisne. The rapid advance against the French left the Germans in a vulnerable position, with their flanks exposed to counter-attack. They found themselves needing to wait for the artillery and supply chain to catch up.

For the third time in ten weeks, the German storm troops had broken through the Allied defensive systems in just a couple of days, causing many casualties and taking many prisoners. They had mastered the art of breaking into the Allied positions, taking advantage of weaknesses such as the Portuguese and the vulnerable Aisne position.

Although they could break in, they were unable to break through due to problems with logistics. The problem was, the German Army was still relying heavily on horse-drawn transport to move everything. The BEF was using huge numbers of lorries by 1918 and the combustion engine was far more efficient at moving supplies than the poor horse. General von Unruh commented, 'ammunition was running short and the problem of supply, in view of the large demands, became more and more difficult. It became all too clear that actions so stubbornly contested and involving us in such formidable losses would never enable us to capture Paris.'

Later Offensives

The battle was coming to a close by 31 May because the German OHL were having to reconsider their situation. It wanted to hold a solid line along the Marne and make the salient safe. Ludendorff's original intention had been for the attack on the Aisne to worry the French, so they would remove their reserves from behind the British sector. He could then launch Operation Hagen in Flanders and complete what Operation Georgette had started, by driving the British back to the English Channel. However, Ludendorff made two mistakes. He moved too many divisions from Flanders to the Aisne – far more than the French did; he also launched Operation Gneisenau.

The intention of Gneisenau was to advance west of the Marne salient, and strip the BEF of French support. But prisoners and deserters warned the attack was in preparation and the French deployed in depth, reducing the casualties from the preliminary bombardment. The Germans still advanced up to 9 miles across a 23-mile-wide front along the Matz River but again they could not break through. The attack was abandoned after the French made a surprise counter-attack seven days later.

Ludendorff planned a final attack east of Reims, to draw yet more French support south. Operation *Friedensturm* or Peace Storm began on 15 July but it had little success. The German Air Force was short of fuel, so the French maintained air superiority and their aerial observers guided accurate artillery bombardments onto the storm troops. Few got past the Forward Zone and none breached the Battle Zone. Three days later a combined French and British offensive hit the Marne salient, throwing the Germans back in what became known as the battle of Fère-en-Tardenois. It was the first of many Allied offensives which would continue until the end of the war.

Index